100

PLACES THAT MADE

BRITAIN

100

PLACES THAT MADE

BRITAIN

DAVID MUSGROVE

1 3 5 7 9 10 8 6 4 2

Published in 2011 by BBC Books, an imprint of Ebury Publishing.
A Random House Group Company

The Random House Group Limited Reg. No. 954009

Addresses for companies within the Random House Group can be found at
www.randomhouse.co.uk

A CIP catalogue record for this book is available from the British Library.

ISBN 978 1 84 990049 2

Commissioning editor:
Editor: Caroline McArthur
Copy editor: Trish Burgess
Designer: seagulls.net
Maps: Encompass Graphics
Production: Phil Spencer

Printed and bound in Great Britain by CPI Mackays, Chatham ME5 8TD

CONTENTS

INTRODUCTION

This book has a simple premise. I asked 99 historians each to nominate one place that is particularly significant in Britain's history. I left them to decide what was meant by that, but the only point I insisted on was that the places must be open to the public and interesting to visit. However, I did set some limits in terms of location and date: the places had to fall within the current boundaries of the United Kingdom of Great Britain and Northern Ireland, and they had to date from the arrival of the Romans to the 1960s.

Once I'd received each historian's nomination, I had a chat with them to find out why they felt the place was significant and what they would suggest a visitor look out for. I then took myself off around the country to investigate each site. I also decided to make one nomination myself, and chose the site of the battle of Bosworth Field, which has become even more interesting in recent times as archaeologists have demonstrated that the fighting took place some distance from where previously thought. (You might think that battlefields are rather under-represented in the list, given their propensity for dramatic outcomes, but that probably reflects the fact that battlefields are often now just fields, where it's rather hard to visualise the action.) The result is, I hope, a slightly different sort of guide to Britain's history – one where the underlying threads of the national story can be teased out.

The entries are arranged chronologically, according to the date of the key reason for the nomination. This means that the book can be read from start to finish as a narrative of some of the key moments of British history told through 100 places. Equally, it can be dipped into at any point and provide an interesting read, hopefully one that might also encourage you to get out and see these fascinating places.

I realise, of course, that there are many omissions among the places included. Britain is blessed with a wealth of historic sites, and 100 is a small number to do justice to our rich heritage. There are many aspects of Britain's past that are not touched upon here, the broad span of prehistory prior to the Roman period being the most obvious gap. In the centuries that are covered, some of the places are conspicuous choices, while others are more surprising and eclectic. Whether 100 different historians would choose 100 completely different places I do not know (though I'd be interested to find out), but I'm sure at least some of the choices would crop up again.

The criteria on which the historians based their choices vary. Some have gone for pivotal events that we know happened in a given place (the site of the Battle of Hastings, for example), while others have chosen sites that are indicative of a broader theme (Wharram Percy, and the desertion of medieval villages, for instance). Personally, I think that makes for an interesting blend.

Are there some periods and themes that are getting more coverage than others? Perhaps, and in part that reflects the particular historians I invited to get involved in the project (most, though not all, have kept within their area of specialist knowledge), but it also reflects the survival of upstanding remains and the ease with which certain aspects of the past can still be visited.

It's notable that the role of Christianity in the story of Britain is one of the strongest themes to have emerged from the nominations. That's not surprising, of course, because we have many beautiful and beautifully located historic churches, abbeys and monasteries to visit across Britain. But in our more secular age, it's interesting to note how much of a hold religion had on the people of Britain in times past, and how you can see that in buildings today.

As I've said, all the places in the book are open to the public, but some are more open than others, so do please check opening hours before you go. If you're making a special trip, it's worth double-checking with the property that the stated opening hours apply on the day you want to go: I was nearly thwarted in my ambition to explore Canterbury Cathedral because a lecture was being given by the archbishop, while a St George's Day parade almost stopped me from getting into Lincoln Castle. The cost of visiting the sites varies: some are in the care of national heritage bodies, so if you are a member, you might get free entry or a reduction; others are privately owned and may be free or cost quite a bit to get in. Some places are very busy, particularly in summer, while others you might well have to yourself.

I hope you enjoy the book and are inspired to get out and about visiting Britain's history, whether to the places chosen here, or to others you think should have been included. Finally, let me remind you that if you enjoy reading about and visiting Britain's history, you will certainly enjoy *BBC History Magazine*, Britain's bestselling periodical on all things historic.

MAP OF PLACES

1 Albert Dock
2 Apsley House
3 Arbroath Abbey
4 Athelney Island
5 Badbea Clearance Village
6 Bank of England
7 Banqueting House
8 Bath – Queen Square, the Circus and Royal Crescent
9 Battle Abbey and the Battlefield of Hastings
10 Battle of Britain Memorial
11 Bevis Marks Synagogue
12 Blackfriars' Hall
13 Blaenavon
14 Blenheim Palace
15 Bletchley Park
16 Bosworth Battlefield
17 British Museum Round Reading Room
18 Brixham Harbour
19 Canterbury Cathedral
20 Captain Cook Memorial Museum
21 Cartmel Priory Church
22 Cavern Club
23 The Cenotaph
24 Conwy Castle
25 Covent Garden
26 Derby Arboretum
27 Derry/Londonderry City Walls
28 Museum of Free Derry
29 Dolbadarn Castle
30 Dr Johnson's House
31 Dover War Tunnels
32 Down House

33 Dunfermline Abbey
34 Dunluce Castle
35 Edward Jenner Museum
36 Exeter Castle
37 Fishbourne Roman Palace
38 Fort George
39 Framlingham Castle
40 Free Trade Hall
41 Hampton Court Palace
42 Hardwick Hall
43 Harewood House
44 Harlech Castle
45 Hatfield House
46 Hever Castle
47 HMS *Warrior*
48 Houses of Parliament
49 Iona Abbey
50 Ironbridge Gorge
51 Kingston Coronation Stone
52 Lincoln Castle
53 Lincoln's Inn
54 Lindisfarne Priory
55 Longthorpe Tower
56 Ludlow Castle
57 Old Course
58 Old Parliament Hall
59 Old Royal Naval College
60 Pankhurst Centre
61 Penydarren Tramway
62 People's Palace
63 Piece Hall
64 Plymouth Hoe
65 Porthcurno Telegraph Station
66 Rochdale Pioneers Museum
67 Royal Festival Hall
68 Runnymede

69 Rushton Triangular Lodge
70 St Davids Cathedral and Bishops' Palace
71 St George's Hall
72 St Giles' Cathedral
73 St John's College
74 St Mary's Church
75 Saltaire
76 Scutchamer Knob
77 Soho House
78 Spean Bridge Commando Memorial
79 SS *Great Britain*
80 Stirling Castle
81 Stockton and Darlington Railway
82 Sutton Hoo
83 Tintagel Castle
84 *Titanic*'s Dock and Pump-house
85 Tolpuddle
86 Tower of London
87 University Church
88 Verdant Works
89 Verulamium
90 Vindolanda
91 Westminster Abbey
92 West Stow
93 Wharram Percy
94 Whitby Abbey
95 White Rock Copper Works
96 Wilberforce House
97 Winchester Cathedral
98 Windsor Castle
99 York Minster
100 York Watergate

SCOTLAND
NORTHERN IRELAND
WALES
ENGLAND
ATLANTIC OCEAN
NORTH SEA
Aberdeen
Dundee
Edinburgh
Glasgow
Newcastle upon Tyne
Middlesbrough
Belfast
Bradford
Leeds
Kingston upon Hull
Manchester
Sheffield
Liverpool
Nottingham
Leicester
Norwich
Birmingham
Oxford
Swansea
Cardiff
Bristol
Southampton
Portsmouth
Exeter
Plymouth
Central London Inset map
see Central London inset map

PICTURE CREDITS

PART 1

THRONES, CATHEDRALS AND CASTLES

The first half of this book takes us from the arrival of the Romans in Britain in the first century AD, represented by the once-glorious palace of Fishbourne in West Sussex, through to the revolution of 1688, when King James VII of Scotland/II of England was obliged to flee his throne on account of the invasion by his daughter Mary and her Dutch husband, William. Brixham harbour in Devon is the place to go to dwell on this revolutionary moment.

Why use 1688 as the dividing line? Well, the revolution that brought William and Mary to the throne also ushered in a system of mixed constitutional monarchy that meant the Crown was no longer seen as the superior power to parliament. The replacement of the Catholic King James with the Protestant William and Mary also meant that a line (albeit a shaky one) was starting to be drawn under the religious disputes that had underpinned much of the story of the 16th and 17th centuries.

Many of the places featured that precede the 1688 revolution are related either to kings and queens in Britain endeavouring to do pretty much what they want (as at Battle Abbey, Runnymede and Windsor Castle, for example), or to the rise of Christianity (at York Minster, Iona and Whitby Abbey, for instance), and the clash that eventually unfolded between Catholics and Protestants in the 16th century (Canterbury Cathedral, Oxford's University Church and Cartmel Priory provide examples of this). As these are dominant themes of the first half of British history, 1688 feels like a good point to draw an interval curtain.

Of course, there's much more that happened in the first millennium-and-a-half AD, not least the establishment of the constituent nations of the British Isles. You have the early stirrings of national consciousness at places such as Kingston, St Davids and Dunfermline Abbey, and then you can see the clashes that occurred between the blossoming national powers at such stirring sites as Dunluce, Stirling and Conwy castles.

Those are the bigger stories, but there are many places in this section that give you a glimpse into some of the other aspects of life over this long span of time, from the conditions on the Roman frontier (Vindolanda), through the cosmological view of the medieval peasant (Longthorpe Tower), to the battle for a new way of looking at the world (St John's College, Cambridge), and the gradual move away from the medieval and into the modern.

Fishbourne Roman Palace, West Sussex

Nominated by Barry Burnham, professor of archaeology,
University of Wales Trinity Saint David
'Where you can sense the start of the Roman presence
in Britain'

When the Romans, under their emperor Claudius invaded Britain in AD 43, they ushered in a 350-year occupation that brought an end to what we now call the Iron Age, the last phase of prehistory. Famously, Julius Caesar had attempted to drag the Celtic Iron Age peoples of Britain into the Roman Empire a century earlier, but his failure in 55 BC left the task to Claudius. At Fishbourne, on the edge of Chichester harbour on England's south coast, sit the remains of a sumptuous 1st-century AD palace, and this is a great place to visit to get an idea of how Roman Britain began.

In its day, Fishbourne Roman Palace was an immensely opulent place, designed to house someone of considerable importance. Most of the walls of that grand residence are long gone, but the floor does at least survive to give a glimpse of the grandeur of the site. Made up of a series of mosaics, the floor today is protected under a large covered frame, and visitors can view over 20 of the mosaics from above, via a series of elevated walkways. Granted, that means you don't have quite the same perspective on them as the Romans would have done when they were laid out – almost 2000 years ago in some cases – but given their age, that is a reasonable sacrifice.

What you're looking down on is the largest collection of *in situ* mosaics in Britain, and some of the earliest. A few of these intricate and beautiful arrangements of tiny tiles date back to *c.* AD 75–80. The mosaics are tremendous, and certainly merit a visit; the 2nd- or 3rd-century Cupid on a dolphin design is justly famous for the size and quality of its execution.

These beautiful floors were fit for a palace, and that's exactly what Fishbourne was. The building erected in the third quarter of the 1st century AD had something in the order of 100 rooms, with four wings enclosing a central garden. Excavations carried out since the site's discovery in the 1960s have established the floor plan of the original structure, which is helpfully demonstrated by a model in the visitor centre museum. The modern structure covering the mosaics stands over only the northern wing of the building.

That late 1st-century palace was not, however, the first structure on the site. Fishbourne's story takes us right back to the start of the Roman period in Britain, because excavations here have uncovered a timber fort dating to the mid 40s AD – in other words, just after the Claudian invasion of AD 43. Fishbourne must have been quickly established as a military outpost of some sort following the Roman landfall.

The Claudian timber fort was followed by a proto-palace before the great palace was built, and Barry Burnham is fascinated by the mystery of who this huge late-1st-century villa was built for: 'My reason for choosing Fishbourne is that it's a spectacular very early and very rich villa, which has all sorts of interesting implications for who was building it. Whether it was someone whom we can recognise historically, it clearly has to draw on inspiration from the Continent, and perhaps even from Italy, so there is no parallel for it in 1st-century AD Britain.'

One historical figure has long been linked with Fishbourne: Tiberius Claudius Togidubnus (or Cogidubnus – classicists differ on the first letter). The fact that we have a name has always excited attention because such individual references are not common in early Britain. Togidubnus is mentioned only once in Roman literature, by Tacitus, but his name also features on a dedication to a temple in Chichester, just a mile away from Fishbourne. The limited information we have suggests he was alive at the time of the invasion and still active into the 70s AD. He's often called a client king, an existing British ruler who in some way helped the Romans with their invasion and consolidation of power, and who was richly rewarded for his services. We know of other people in Roman Britain who fulfilled this role, so Fishbourne offers an insight into the way the Romans took control of Britain. They needed the support of the locals, some of whom at least were not unfamiliar with the Roman way of life, which we know because we have archaeological evidence of trade and exchange between Britain and Roman Gaul across the Channel.

However, we don't have a direct reference that says Togidubnus built Fishbourne, and the main palace of AD 75–80 would perhaps have been a little late for him. Whether it was his home, or his successor's, or some other senior official in the new government of the conquered Roman province, Fishbourne clearly demonstrates that there were people in Britain who bought into the Roman ideal. It shows, says Burnham, that 'there were individuals who already had a very strong perception of themselves as being Roman or having links with the Roman world, and were therefore very accustomed to the amenities of life'.

It also shows that someone had enough confidence in the new regime, only a few years after it had been installed, to expend a considerable amount of resources on this palace. The traditional view is that the Romans came ashore at Richborough in Kent, but Burnham points to the intriguing possibility that Fishbourne could have been a lot closer than that to the initial action: 'There was a supply depot that preceded the villa, relating to military activity. That links into a bigger debate about where precisely the Romans landed. Thirty years ago it was taught that they landed in Kent. Now there's a debate that the whole of the landing was actually in the Chichester area, and that Fishbourne may be an early indicator of where the army located itself as part of that early push forward. That's a huge debate and there's no way you can answer it unless you find another source that says "The Romans landed here in AD 43".'

Were that theory about the Chichester landing true, it would bring Togidubnus back into the Fishbourne frame. The place certainly did have a route in from the sea via one of the tendrils of water that snake into this part of the south coast from Chichester harbour, as you can see in the model in the museum. The early military structures aren't visible to the modern visitor, though, and what you can see at the palace today doesn't have much of an invasion feel to it. The mosaics and the recreated Roman gardens bring to mind not the clanking march of the advancing legions, rather the soft sandals and swishing togas of peace and civilisation. However, they do give a good idea of how rapidly Roman ideas infiltrated Britain, at least into the upper echelons of society.

Fishbourne Roman Palace
Salthill Road, Fishbourne, Chichester, West Sussex PO19 3QR
01243 789829
www.sussexpast.co.uk

Vindolanda, Northumberland

Nominated by David Mattingly, professor of Roman archaeology, University of Leicester
'Where you can feel what life was like on the Roman frontier'

Look down over the field that now holds the remains of Vindolanda and you see a swathe of grey, rocky debris spreading across a sloping grassy expanse, with the ground dropping away steeply into a wooded valley beyond. The stony heart of the site is a rectangular fort and the majority of the low walls inside it are outlines of the 3rd- and 4th-century structures that once stood within. This was an outpost on the far fringe of Roman Britain. Just a little way to the north lies Hadrian's Wall, the famous frontier boundary established in the 120s AD.

Vindolanda actually predates the wall by about 35 years. The first fort on the site was constructed around AD 85. At that point the Roman occupation of Britain was not yet half a century old (see Fishbourne, page 10), and the native Caledonians in what is now Scotland were far from reconciled to the imperial presence. Yet in 83 or 84, under the energetic Roman governor Agricola, the legions had pushed north, recording a notable victory somewhere in northeast Scotland at the battle of Mons Graupius. To consolidate their position, the Romans established a network of roads and garrisons. Vindolanda was one such garrison fort, its troops tasked with guarding the important east–west supply route known as the Stanegate.

Forty years later, the Romans had withdrawn from their position in Scotland and settled on a defensive barrier to delimit Roman territory to the south from non-Roman to the north. The emperor Hadrian ordered

Some of the low stone walls that remain at the frontier fort of Vindolanda: the wooden tablets found here have greatly enhanced our understanding of Roman Britain

the building of the wall that now bears his name along a line roughly parallel to the Stanegate. Vindolanda, set back from the wall, became a garrison settlement for the frontier troops, but by then it was already on its fifth fort because the Romans were building in timber not stone, so each fort lasted for less than a decade before rain and rot forced its replacement.

That, says David Mattingly, is one of the reasons why Vindolanda is so notable today: 'The most important forts at Vindolanda are the pre-Hadrianic ones – those dating from before the wall was built. They were built up on the hill slope and, because of later buildings on top of them, became sealed in and waterlogged. With these remarkable anaerobic conditions, we've got an incredible preservation of waterlogged material from the earlier phases of occupation of the site – textiles and leather and organic materials.'

Those particular oxygen-free conditions led to the survival of an amaz-ing cache of wooden writing tablets for archaeologists to discover in the 1970s. Since then, they have been turning up regularly on excavations at the site, their contents requiring us quite literally to rewrite the history books. These tablets are the everyday documentation and correspondence of the soldiers, officers and associated civilians at Vindolanda in the years immediately before the building of Hadrian's Wall, and they are a source of unparalleled richness for our understanding of what life was like in Roman Britain. There are party invites, personal letters, inventories, mili-tary reports and much more.

'The writing tablets open another window on the past, which, from a historian's point of view, brings it alive,' says Mattingly. 'Given the nature of the archives that we're dealing with, it's not surprising that Vindolanda has transformed our understanding of the day-to-day routine business of running a fort. It's all the more valuable because it is all about the social and daily life of a Roman military garrison. It illuminates our understanding not just of life in Britain, but across the empire. It shows that the Roman army lived by the book.'

The tablets themselves are mostly to be found in the British Museum in London, which holds the appropriate conservation facilities to preserve these thin and fragile slivers of wood. However, Vindolanda's museum, in the valley below the fort, does a great job of presenting the story of the tablets, and displaying some of the other outstanding organic finds as well; leather shoes, wooden combs and even a lady's wig have all been unearthed in and around the fort.

Back on site, you can see where these tablet treasures were discovered, under an area marked out by eight large posts that show the position of the original gates of the early wooden forts. Happily for visitors today, the Romans wised up to the need for a building material less susceptible to the Northumbrian weather, and left us the later stone remains that make this such a tremendous place to explore. It's a particularly interesting site to visit in summer when archaeologists are at work, excavating here as they have been doing for the last 40 years or so. It's because there has been such a long-running research project here that we know so much about Vindolanda and there is so much on view to the public today.

So, armed with an idea of what the tablets tell us about the daily concerns for Vindolanda's occupants and perhaps an insight into the latest findings from one of the excavation team, you could certainly spend a few happy hours wandering among the remains, trying to conjure up an image of what life was like back in the frontier days. The archaeologists have also found time to erect a reconstruction of a section of Hadrian's Wall, which gives further reason to dally here. Make sure you save a bit of daylight, though, to trek the mile or so north to the frontier proper, where you'll find some of the best and most dramatic remains of Hadrian's Wall itself. The section around Steel Rigg, Sycamore Gap and Crag Lough is particularly photogenic.

Eventually the Romans departed, leaving the Britons to look to their own defences early in the 5th century AD. Vindolanda's story doesn't come to a crashing end there and then. Right in the middle of the fort you'll find a semicircular collection of stones that has been interpreted as a Christian church, erected at some point soon after AD 400. This raises questions for the curious about who was using Vindolanda after the end of the Roman presence here, and to what ends. As Mattingly concludes,

'It's a site that illuminates both ends of the Roman period. It tells us about the formation of the frontier and the decline of that frontier, but also gives us the best evidence of the nature and quality of garrison life.'

Vindolanda

Chesterholm Museum, Bardon Mill, Hexham, Northumberland NE47 7JN

01434 344277

www.vindolanda.com

Verulamium (St Albans), Hertfordshire

Nominated by Stuart Laycock, classicist and author

'Where the story of the Roman occupation unfolds before you'

When you stand on the raised earthen bank around the Roman theatre of Verulamium, you're looking down on enough surviving remains to summon up a vision of what the place might have been like in the middle of the 2nd century AD. The horseshoe-shaped tiered seating area would have held several thousand spectators, and that would surely have made for a tightly packed audience to whatever entertainment or religious spectacle was on offer on the stage at the front.

A solitary replica column has been raised up on the stage area to hint at the colonnaded façade that once stood there. This makes for a useful prop to the imagination. Remember that the grassy banks that make up the theatre site today were only the base of a much larger wood and stone structure in Roman times.

The theatre is just one of several physical reminders of the fact that St Albans, under its Roman name Verulamium, was one of the key cities of Roman Britain, positioned 32 km (20 miles) north of London on Watling Street, the road running to the northwest. Just across from the theatre is the excellent Verulamium Museum, which brings together the story as we know it (and we know quite a lot because the place has been extensively excavated by archaeologists). Beyond that, in the lovely Verulamium park that hugs the river Ver below the modern town, are the other Roman remains that survive: sections of flinty city wall, and a tremendously well-preserved mosaic floor under a protective shell.

If you pick a clement day, you can spend a pleasant few hours wandering around the park over what was once the Roman town. For Stuart Laycock, 'It sums up the whole Roman period, including the pre-Roman and post-Roman. You have a pre-Roman site intimately linked with the rise of the Catuvellauni, probably the most powerful of the pre-Roman tribes. You have a city of Roman design, which is also the capital of the Catuvellauni during the Roman occupation, with walls, mosaics, a theatre and a great museum to visit.'

The museum does do a marvellous job of recreating the Roman St Albans experience. Particularly impressive are the pieces of painted plasterwork that were unearthed during excavation. They are displayed as they would have been originally, on walls. It's easy to forget as you wander around Romano-British sites today, which are invariably lines of low walls laid out on the ground, that above the foundations would have stood real houses with real people in them, and there's something about a painted wall that drives that home. The mosaics in the museum are also something to behold – clear evidence that the people who lived here had a bit of cash to splash around.

Verulamium appears to have been set up as a Roman settlement soon after the conquest in AD 43, on the site of the pre-Roman centre of the Catuvellauni. The paint was barely dry on the walls when the place was attacked and burnt in the revolt by Queen Boudicca against the Roman occupiers in 60–61. The townsfolk recovered from that early trauma to establish a major defended settlement over the following decades, with a forum, a basilica, baths, a hatful of temples to various pagan Roman deities, and, sagely enough, a wide ditch to protect it. By the mid 2nd century, the city also boasted the theatre, which was built around 140, just in time to see Verulamium's second major fire in about 155. This disaster doesn't appear to have been prompted by enemy action, but it did substantial damage and meant that many of the buildings had to be completely rebuilt. The town recovered once more and by the latter part of the 3rd century, it was a prosperous place protected by the stone walls that you can still see in part today.

Verulamium went on to become St Albans after the Romans had gone. St Alban was a Christian martyr who lived in the Roman city at some point in the 2nd or 3rd century. Christians were persecuted before the emperor Constantine converted to the religion (see York Minster, page 22), so when Alban, although a pagan at the time, took it upon himself to protect a Christian cleric who was a guest in his house, he faced severe consequences. After converting to Christianity, Alban was executed on a hill above the Roman town, but several miracles were said to have taken place as he was being put to death, most notably the eyes of his executioner falling out as Alban's decapitated head fell to the ground. A shrine grew up on the spot where he was thought to have been killed, and that has become the heart of the abbey in St Albans.

The importance of St Alban gave the place a reason for continuing after the end of the Roman period, and we have some rare and direct documentary evidence for the existence of a shrine here in AD 429, some years after the Romans had departed. What exactly happened here in the 5th and 6th centuries as Roman influence waned and Anglo-Saxon people from the Continent arrived is, as elsewhere, not entirely clear, but Laycock has an interesting view: 'In the post-Roman period Verulamium is at the heart of an area without signs of early Anglo-Saxon settlement and therefore may be the core of a post-Roman British kingdom. Visitors can take a short stroll from the ruins of Verulamium through parkland, past a lake and up the hill to the great Abbey of St Alban. So in a sense, in one visit, you can take in the story of the transition from pre-Roman Britain to Roman Britain to England.'

The abbey is a beautiful building, and its existence in part explains why there isn't more to see of the Roman town in the park beneath it. In the 11th century it was rebuilt, using bricks and stones removed from the ruins of Verulamium. It was also built in the Romanesque style, popular at the time, so when you're looking at the round arches in the central tower of the medieval abbey, you're viewing something that was built of Roman bricks in Roman style. The fact that those arches are painted in colours not dissimilar to those you'll have seen in the wall plasters in the museum might suggest to you that truly the Roman town lives on in the abbey.

Verulamium

Verulamium Museum, St Michael's Street, St Albans, Hertfordshire AL3 4SW

01727 751810

www.stalbansmuseums.org.uk

York Minster, North Yorkshire

Nominated by Stephen Marritt, lecturer in history,
University of Glasgow
'Where you can trace the early story of Christianity in Britain'

In the 1960s, the mighty medieval central tower of York Minster seemed in danger of collapse. Its foundations were looking decidedly shaky. That led to a huge programme of underpinning work beneath the church, in the course of which archaeologists found the remains of the Roman legionary headquarters dating back to the 1st century AD.

Once everything was back on a level footing above, the undercroft and crypt were opened up to visitors, and you can now head down there and walk through the Roman remains lying several metres below ground level under the minster. It's a tremendous experience, and one of singular historical significance because it was here, or somewhere nearby, that Constantine the Great was proclaimed Roman emperor by the legionaries in York in AD 306. This event was occasioned by the death of his father, Constantius, whom Constantine the Great had accompanied on a campaign against the northern Picts beyond Hadrian's Wall (see Vindolanda, page 14). It's assumed that the proclamation would have occurred in the legionary headquarters.

Before you go inside the minster, you'll note that there is a statue of Constantine the Great, seated and looking very Roman, just outside the entrance. It's a modern piece of work, so why all the fuss over this long-dead emperor? It's because he went on to become the first Christian Roman emperor, and thus laid the foundations for the adoption of Christianity as the state religion of the empire later on in the 4th century. For that act alone, the place where he was proclaimed emperor (though technically he was a usurper and had to spend a few years cementing his position) is of global importance, but it also had particular significance for the development of Christianity in Britain.

After the end of the Roman occupation of Britain in the early 5th century, Christianity lost the toehold it had established in England, until the later years of the 6th century, when the first Irish monks arrived from the west to bring back the word of God (see Iona, page 30). Then, in 597, Pope Gregory the Great sent Augustine from Rome on a mission to convert the pagan Angles (see Canterbury Cathedral, page 84). Stephen Marritt explains how Constantine's influence may have impacted on what happened next: 'Roman York was the chief city of the northern province of Britain. The minster is on the site of the *principia*, the headquarters, and the barracks of the legion based in the city. It is likely that it was this Roman legacy rather than any contemporary Christian that inspired Pope Gregory the Great to designate York as one of the two bishoprics from which he hoped Britain would be converted to Christianity.'

One of Augustine's followers, Paulinus, became the first Bishop of York and did much to convert the Northumbrian kings. After Augustine's mission, it wasn't too long before Christianity was back with interest, with the Anglo-Saxon rulers of the various kingdoms that made up what is now England converting to the religion one by one. Once the Synod of Whitby (see Whitby Abbey, page 38) in 664 had established that it was the Roman rather than the Irish model of the faith that would be followed, Christianity was firmly rooted again.

York had a succession of minster churches after the first wooden one of Paulinus, but it took quite some time for the current stone edifice to be constructed. 'Following the Viking conquest of York in 866, close relations were quickly established between the new kings and the archbishops and minster – coins survive with Thor on one face and St Peter on the other – but if the Vikings built a new minster, again, there are no remains,' says Marritt. 'York was burnt during the Norman Conquest, and it is with two Norman cathedrals that we first get structural remains. Like the Roman remains, these were exposed during the 1960s' excavations and, like them, the bases of the Norman columns can be seen in the undercroft. Also uncovered in the 1960s was the tomb of Archbishop Walter de Gray. His ring can be seen in the undercroft, and it was he who began the minster as we see it today. It would not be completed as it stands for another 250 years.'

Exploring the undercroft thus gives you a splendid view into the prehistory of this building, with the Roman and Norman innards on show. But obviously you would be foolish to gnomishly ignore the magnificent medieval building above. From 1220 to 1472, generations of masons laboured to transform the Norman minster into the Gothic masterpiece it is today. While you're taking in the airy majesty of it all (the windows are deemed to be a particular glory of the minster for the amount of light they let in), do have a look at the front of the choir screen, which includes statues of English kings from the Norman Conquest onwards. (Edward III must have got up the nose of his particular stonemason, as he boasts a curiously demonic visage.)

Inevitably, restoration and preservation are continuous at the minster, so there's always going to be some building work in progress. The West Front spent most of the 1990s under wraps, and now it's the turn of the Great Window in the East Front. Don't be put off, though; rather, remember that for most of the medieval period, it would have been a build-ing site in parts too. Whatever work has been going on, the minster has always remained a functioning place of worship, a point that Marritt stresses. 'It is this living, organic nature that makes it possible to imagine what the minster must have been like in the Middle Ages. The interiors of all our great churches changed fundamentally following the Reformation. We must try to imagine a building in which prayer and song hardly ever ceased because the fundamental role of all churches then was the work of God; paintings, tapestries, images would have covered the walls; side chapels would have been not havens of reflection, but would have had a constant presence. I would say that anyone who visits York Minster should go to choral evensong because that's the only time really you're going to see how the cathedral's supposed to work. You sit in the choir stalls, look up and hear the sound, and you experience the purpose of the cathedral.'

I would add that if you do want to get a sense of how different the place might have been before the Reformation, don't miss the 12th-century Doomstone in the crypt. This astonishing piece of carving shows the tortured souls on the Day of Judgement, complete with devils and evil toads. Before finding its way into the crypt, this stone would probably have been somewhere inside the minster, a warning to the flock of the fate that could befall them. A very different interior it must have been when that sort of image was on show.

York Minster
Church House, Ogleforth, York YO1 7JN
0844 9390011
www.yorkminster.org

West Stow, Suffolk

Nominated by Chris Callow, lecturer in early medieval history, University of Birmingham

'Where the everyday life of the early Anglo-Saxons is conjured up'

The problem with building homes in wood rather than stone, brick or tile is that not much is left upstanding to posterity. Of that particular crime the early Anglo-Saxon peoples of what was to become England can be found guilty.

The Romans who preceded them have left a fair few pieces of visible masonry around the country (and, in fairness to them, there would probably be a lot more today if succeeding generations hadn't coveted the building material for their own constructions). Meanwhile, the Normans, who followed the Anglo-Saxons, have endowed us with an impressive array of stone castles and churches to mark their presence.

The 350-year-long period of Roman occupation in Britain came to an end around AD 410, when the empire imploded across Europe. The Romanised Britons were told to look to their own defences, but there was no stopping the peoples of northwest Europe and Scandinavia who arrived on British shores. Whether they came as conquerors or friendly farmers has been much debated, but what's not in doubt is that they came, and they stayed, and they made England their own. When the first settlers stepped off their ships after crossing the North Sea, they didn't bring a tradition of towns and stone buildings, but rather one of villages built of timber. For that simple reason there are not that many early Anglo-Saxon 'sites' that you can visit today. That's not to say those settlers didn't leave their mark on the landscape: archaeologists have become adept at uncovering the ephemeral traces of their settlements. The excavations that these archaeologists have carried out have taught us much about the way the Anglo-Saxons lived.

West Stow is one such early Anglo-Saxon settlement, unique not in what it was in the 5th, 6th and 7th centuries AD, but in what it has become now. The place has seen a prolonged and detailed programme of archaeological excavation and investigation over several decades. Since the 1970s, researchers have been engaging in experimental archaeology to recreate buildings, the traces of which they had been uncovering in the sandy East Anglian soil. This means that there is actually something to see of the everyday existence of the Anglo-Saxons.

'We're usually seduced by the glitzy archaeology of the Anglo-Saxon period, like the Sutton Hoo ship burial [page 34], but West Stow is fascinating because it tells about the people whose work supported the warrior elite,' says Chris Callow. 'I think West Stow is so important because it gives us an insight into the lives of the peasantry in the distant past and in what must have been a dramatic time politically. When some people were fighting over objects like those found at Sutton Hoo or in the Staffordshire Hoard, the people at West Stow were just getting on with their lives, making the best of things.'

What you get when you visit the site today is a lovely, calm country park within which are set a group of ten or so reconstructed Anglo-Saxon buildings. Most of these buildings are on the sites of the original excavated houses. On a basic level, it's a pleasure to wander around between these timber and thatch constructions and to know that there would once have been the real thing in the same place.

You can pop inside some of them, walk over the uneven planks, look up into the smoke-blackened rafters and consider how it would have been to spend your time in such a home. If there's a fire burning in any of the hearths, the smell will bring the Anglo-Saxons back through your nostrils.

What's quite obvious as you walk around is that all the buildings are different: this is deliberate. The archaeologists have been experimenting with various construction solutions to see which seems the best fit for the evidence they've dug up. Remember that they are working from the imprints of wooden posts left in outline in the soil, supplemented with some burnt remains of building materials from a couple of houses that went up in flames. It's not that much to go on, so they have tried different ways of interpreting how the houses might have been made.

One of the biggest debates in Anglo-Saxon archaeology has raged over the question of sunken-featured buildings. Excavations have shown that in some structures the floor area inside had been dug out to below ground level. At one time this was assumed to be evidence that the inhabitants were ignorant sorts who were happy to wallow in muddy slop. That's very much the picture you get when you peer into the only house in the village that has its thatched roof running right down to the ground. Inside, with a bare, sandy floor and not much space to stand and walk around, it doesn't present a very desirable residence.

That view of squat and squalid living has been challenged, though, and the houses next to the sunken one have been constructed with an alternative take on the pit – that it was dug for either storage or insulation and would have been planked over. The homes thus created look decidedly more enticing. In the last half-century or so, the Anglo-Saxons have been rehabilitated somewhat from Dark Age savages on the very edge of

West Stow: the reconstructed houses give a taste of life for the early Anglo-Saxons

civilisation. Now there is a nuanced view, which has them enjoying a much more cultured and better-quality way of life. The differing ways of interpreting what the pits under their houses meant is the result of this academic Anglo-Saxon renaissance.

Equally, if you think that the houses look a little on the small side by today's standards, it's worth noting the theory of how they were used. The idea is that there would have been a large hall in the village for communal gatherings of each family group, along with smaller houses for sleeping, working and storage. In other words, their accommodation worked much like ours, but with separate buildings rather than separate rooms.

Although we don't know of any particular momentous events that occurred in West Stow in its 200-year life as a settlement from around AD 450, it does open a door for us back to an ill-documented time. Sitting on the benches around the edge of a great hall, looking into a fire and casting your mind back to how the Anglo-Saxons might have done something similar, listening perhaps to a storyteller reciting tales of Beowulf, is a tremendous way to visit the past.

'The reconstructed houses and sheds at West Stow give you a great feeling for what everyday life must have been like in the 6th and 7th centuries,' agrees Callow. 'You get a real sense of the skills these people had, in the way they built their houses or made their clothes, for example.'

The excellent small museum here showcases the finds that were dug up from the site, and takes you through the story of the early Anglo-Saxon period. Although there's nothing like the riches of nearby Sutton Hoo on display, West Stow is a marvellous place to consider the early days of the unheralded settlers who laid the foundations of what was to become England.

West Stow

Anglo-Saxon Village and Country Park, Icklingham Road, West Stow, Bury St Edmunds, Suffolk IP28 6HG

01284 728718

www.stedmundsbury.gov.uk

Iona Abbey, Argyll

Nominated by Clare Downham, lecturer, Institute of Irish Studies, University of Liverpool

'Where Christianity started its comeback in Britain'

Iona Abbey is not a particularly easy place to get to. It sits to the west of the island of Mull in the Inner Hebrides, so two ferries are required to reach it from the Scottish mainland. The island's most famous inhabitant, St Columba, wouldn't have been able to rely on the regular timetables of Caledonian MacBrayne to get him to and from the place in the 6th century AD, but Irish monks are noted for appreciating the solitude of island retreats.

However, Iona was far from cut off from the world around it in Columba's day. Sea travel was in many ways a more reliable method of getting about than travelling overland, and the Hebridean islands formed part of a maritime kingdom that stretched from Ireland across to south-west Scotland. The name of that kingdom was Dalriada.

In the aftermath of the Roman withdrawal from Britain, while the Anglo-Saxons were establishing themselves in southern and eastern England (see West Stow, page 26), Celtic British kingdoms, such as Dalriada, were emerging to the west and north. In Ireland, Roman occupation had never taken place, but although the Irish Sea held back the arrival of the legionaries, it didn't staunch the flow of ideas between the two islands, notably the spread of Christianity.

It is thought that British missionaries took the religion to Ireland in the early part of the 5th century. The most famous of these missionaries was St Patrick, a man born into an established Romano-British family in the late 4th or early 5th century. We don't know exactly where he lived, but it must have been somewhere not too far from the western coast of Britain as his family's estates were raided and the young Patrick, along with many others, was carried off into slavery in Ireland. He escaped and eventually returned to Ireland as a missionary, playing a substantial role in the development of early Irish Christianity.

Given the actions of St Patrick and other British missionaries, Dalriada may well have been mainly Christian by the time of Columba. Elsewhere in 5th- and 6th-century Britain, the end of the Roman occupation (which had sanctioned Christian worship – see York Minster, page 22) handed the religion a serious reverse, particularly in the lands populated by incoming pagan Anglo-Saxons.

Columba was born into royalty in Ireland and spent his early years there. We know little about what he got up to, but the assumption is that he was a churchman of some repute. Columba went to Iona in the year 563, and his arrival helped to revitalise Christianity in Britain. His royal connections seemingly opened doors for him with kings across northern Britain, and enabled him to found churches across the land. 'Iona is one of the most important early centres of Christianity in Britain and Ireland,' notes Clare Downham. 'It's from there that a lot of the Christianisation of north Britain took place.'

Columba and his followers spread the message of their faith from the base on Iona, but it was a slightly different brand of Christianity from that propagated by the mission led by Augustine from Rome (see Canterbury Cathedral, page 84), which arrived in 597, the year of Columba's death, and worked its way up from southern England. When the Synod of Whitby (see Whitby Abbey, page 38) concluded that the Roman rather than the Irish line of thinking was correct, Iona lost some of its cachet and power. Its monks were expelled from parts of northern Britain, but it still maintained a network around the Irish Sea over the following centuries, during which time Columba's posthumous reputation grew more powerful. Iona's continuing significance explains why visitors today view a 20th-century restoration of a 13th-century Benedictine monastery built on the site of the original 6th-century foundations.

Of Columba's monastery, there is now little to see. The raised bank of earth that surrounded it is still visible in parts, while tradition has it that the rocky knoll beside the current church is where Columba went to write, and that the building known now as Columba's shrine is where he was buried. Other than that, there is little tangible remaining. Probably the closest you can get to those early days of religious activity are the beautifully carved stone High Crosses, which are thought to have been erected within the monastic enclosure in the 8th and 9th centuries. One still stands, along with a 19th-century replica, while other pieces are on display in the abbey museum, which is a very rewarding place to explore. 'To my mind the sculpture is how you get back to the Middle Ages,' says Downham. 'The monks' world view was embedded in sculpture. A lot of this sort of sculpture has been taken away from its original site, but it's still there at Iona.'

The lack of much else to see from that early period stems in part from the fact that the first buildings were probably not of stone, and partly from the impact of invaders: 'It was completely hammered by the Vikings from the end of the 8th century because it was seen as an important target. They attacked in 795, 802 and 806, and they came back in 825. Iona must have been a wealthy place, but there wouldn't have been enough time for it to recover between raids, so I think the Vikings were motivated by more than lust for booty. They probably also saw it as a spiritual powerbase and a blow against the morale of the people they were trying to conquer. However, a few centuries on, Viking descendants were enthusiastic patrons of the Church of Iona and they adopted the cult of Columba.'

It was these Viking descendants who, as lords of the isles, invited Benedictine monks to re-establish the monastery on Iona in the 13th century, and it's a Benedictine church and cloisters that you tour today (though with a considerable daub of Victorian restoration thrown in too). If you want to see more authentic ruins, the nearby nunnery is the place to go, though it doesn't benefit from quite such a compelling position over the Hebridean Sea.

The stream of tour buses offloading passengers from the Iona ferry at the end of the road on Mull confirms that Iona's place in the creation of Christian Scotland is now well attested. Iona continues to draw pilgrims from around the world, but whether your interest is primarily historical or spiritual, you can't help but be enchanted by the view of the monastery across the water.

Iona Abbey
Isle of Iona, Argyll PA76 6SQ
01681 700512
www.historic-scotland.gov.uk

Sutton Hoo, Suffolk
Nominated by Julian D. Richards, professor of archaeology, University of York
'Where we can see Anglo-Saxon England coming out of the Dark Ages'

Sutton Hoo is perhaps Britain's most famous archaeological site. It was here in 1939 that an astonishingly rich Anglo-Saxon boat burial was unearthed, complete with a now iconic and entirely fabulous visored helmet. That helmet has become the symbol of the raw and alien power of the Anglo-Saxons, and its arresting visage has since graced the covers of most books and magazines devoted to the period.

Along with the helmet were found beautiful pieces of Anglo-Saxon metalwork, weapons, armour, bowls, cups, dishes and even musical instruments. Some of the objects had come from Europe, and as far away as exotic Byzantium (now Istanbul). All the treasures are now held in London, handsomely displayed in the British Museum. Meanwhile, the site of the ship burial itself, now known prosaically as Mound One, has reverted to being just one grassy lump among a field of grassy lumps. You might be inclined to think it doesn't sound too encouraging for a visit. I'll declare my interest now as a lifelong aficionado of mounds, so perhaps I'm biased, but I'd say that there is something very special about this particular lumpy patch of grass.

There are nearly 20 mounds in the place that we now know as the burial ground at Sutton Hoo. One of them has been raised up in modern times to the sort of height it might have achieved in the Anglo-Saxon period, while the rest, in part due to centuries of grave-robbing and antiquarian investigation, are much less noticeable features. Nevertheless, it's still abundantly clear that this neck of sandy land on a prominent bluff overlooking the tidal waters of the river Deben was a place that mattered in the past.

'It's a mysterious landscape in a way,' says Julian D. Richards. 'It feels quite alien to the English countryside and would be more at home in Scandinavia.'

Of course, that's no great surprise. The Anglo-Saxons were the peoples who came by sea from Scandinavia and northwest Europe to Britain at the end of the Roman period. It's only natural that they would have sought out sites that reminded them of home and offered access to the sea that had borne them here.

Decades of research on the Sutton Hoo burial site have taught us much. We know that it was in use for about 50 years in the early 7th century. We know that there were at least two ship burials, where complete wooden boats were interred in separate and substantial earthen mounds, along with numerous other cremations and burials under the other barrows. We can see, particularly from the finds in Mound One, that the burials were made at a time of tension between the Anglo-Saxons' old pagan ways and the tenets of Christianity, which would have been a novelty to them at the time. With items such as christening spoons jostling for space in the grave with swords and buckles carved with dragons, it's clear that there was an accommodation being sought between old and new religions and ways of life. The long-term research here has greatly expanded knowledge of the period, but it was the immediate impact of the excavation in 1939 that perhaps did more than anything to change perceptions of the Anglo-Saxons.

'Until the discovery of Sutton Hoo, historians and archaeologists had taken rather a dim view of the Anglo-Saxon barbarians who had stepped into the power vacuum after the departure of the legions. Sutton Hoo shows that there was a very vibrant culture, and the beginnings of English culture emerging. It's also important for the development of archaeology in this country. It was an iconic excavation, done in difficult conditions on the eve of the Second World War,' comments Richards.

The ship burial was discovered by a local Suffolk man, Basil Brown, who'd been asked to investigate what was in the mounds by the landowner, Mrs Edith Pretty. Brown's meticulous approach ensured that the outline of the ship, marked by iron rivets and the imprint of the long-since rotted wooden planks, was spotted and traced. When he got down to the burial chamber and started to unearth the precious finds inside, Mrs Pretty called the British Museum. Poor Basil was relegated to digging out the rest of the ship, while a crack team of archaeologists was parachuted in to excavate the burial chamber. They just managed to retrieve the finds and store them in the British Museum for safekeeping before Hitler brought war down across Europe.

The dramatic story of the excavation is told in the modern visitor centre on the site. Although you won't see all the original finds from the burial here, there are some excellent replicas on display, along with a complete re-creation of the burial scene in the ship, with the body of a man laid down amongst his grave goods. Curiously, no actual body was ever found in the ship, so it's fitting that the man in the model is an opaque and forgettable sort of chap. A corpse may have never been buried in the ship originally, but it's more likely that it simply rotted away in the acidic soil.

The lack of a body hasn't stopped decades of speculation over whose grave this was. The strongest case has been made for Raedwald, King of the East Anglians, who died around AD 625. The majority view probably sides with Raedwald today, but the link to him is far from watertight. In a sense, the identity of the interred is incidental to the bigger picture and what the grave reveals about the early Anglo-Saxons.

'It's the site where we see England coming out from the Dark Ages. We can see the emergence of Anglo-Saxon kingship and what it means to be a warrior king in the 7th century, with all the trappings and power that go with that,' says Richards.

You can, and should, go to the British Museum to see the original finds, but you should also go to Sutton Hoo to see where the Anglo-Saxons chose to bury their riches and lay claim to their new land.

Sutton Hoo

Tranmer House, Sutton Hoo, Woodbridge, Suffolk IP12 3DJ

01394 389700

www.nationaltrust.org.uk

Whitby Abbey, North Yorkshire

Nominated by Sarah Foot, Regius Professor of Ecclesiastical History, University of Oxford
'Where England signed up to Rome's model of Christianity'

Whitby Abbey is surely one of the most evocative and dramatic remains in British history. It would be doing a disservice to describe the abbey as simply perched over the town and coast; rather, it commands the place from its windy headland. You can see the ruins from several miles distant. Up close, they are even more impressive: the glorious stonework, mottled by the salty air, but still as richly detailed as it would have been in the 13th century, stands stark against the Yorkshire sky and North Sea waves.

What you're looking at is the roofless remnant of a mighty medieval monastery, set up by a follower of William the Conqueror in the late 11th century, richly endowed and prosperous enough to embark on a major rebuilding in the 1220s, and then dissolved on the orders of Henry VIII in 1539. If this was all the place had going for it, a visit would still be worthwhile, but it's what went on before those events that gives the abbey real historical significance.

Whitby was the site of an Anglo-Saxon monastery from AD 657. It was founded on the instructions of King Oswy of Northumbria, an Anglo-Saxon ruler and a Christian. He had defeated a pagan adversary, Penda, in battle two years prior to founding Whitby, and in thanks to God for his victory he had dedicated some of his money and his daughter Aelfled to a life of monastic service. Thus, Aelfled found herself in the new royal monastery at Whitby under the leadership of Abbess Hild.

Hild must have done a good job in building up her monastery (housing both monks and nuns), for less than a decade after its foundation it was important enough, and presumably had buildings large and grand enough, to play host to a major Northumbrian church council, the Synod of Whitby in 664.

By that point, most of the Anglo-Saxon kingdoms of England were nominally Christian. The religion that had first been state-sanctioned in Roman times under Constantine (see York Minster, page 22) but had then been rather overwhelmed in the years after the Roman withdrawal, was back and now growing firmer roots. However, as is often the case with religious matters, there was more than one sort of faith being followed. In Northumbria, Oswy was an adherent of what we now call Celtic Christianity, which had been brought over from Ireland via Iona (page 30). Other, more southerly, Anglo-Saxon kingdoms followed the Roman model of the faith, which had arrived with the mission of Augustine to

Kent in 597. Oswy called the synod in 664 to decide on whether the Celtic or Roman strand was the right path to follow.

The great Anglo-Saxon historian Bede goes into some detail about the debate, which pitched leading churchmen against one another. There were two particular points of contention: one was the question of how monks should cut their hair (Celtic priests shaved the front of the head and let the back grow, while their Roman counterparts removed a circle on top of the pate) because then, as now, appearances were important. The second question was a rather more pressing personal concern for Oswy, as Sarah Foot explains.

'The argument was over how to calculate the date of Easter. King Oswy was following the Irish tradition, but his [southern Anglo-Saxon] wife was doing it differently, the Roman way, as she had been brought up by Roman missionaries. There was one year when the king had finished marking Easter, and was in a position to exercise his conjugal rights, having given them up for the 40 days of Lent, while his wife was still on Palm Sunday and had a further week of the fast to go. So Bede presents marital strife as one of the things that drove the argument.'

I think many people today remain confused about how Easter is worked out, scratching their heads over that movable bank holiday, but for Oswy it was a matter of considerably more import than when to pencil the long weekend into the diary. He needed the best minds in the early Church to help him decide whether to be Celtic or Roman. Having heard the theological wrangling from those minds, he came down on the side of the Romans, surmising that the authority of St Peter should not be chal-lenged, as it was St Peter who held the keys to heaven. Oswy did not want to run the risk of being locked out of that particular gate. The decision was something of a shock; most observers were probably not expecting the king to change his mind.

'It put England into the European mainstream, so instead of being an aberrant sect at the corner of the world, by 665 the whole of England all the way up to Lothian and the Scottish borders was worshipping in the same way as they were in Western Europe,' notes Foot. 'The decision made at Whitby to ally the Church in England with the Church of Rome, and therefore Christian practice on the rest of the European mainland, made England very firmly part of European Christendom. If the decision had gone the other way and they'd decided to plump for the Irish, they would have isolated themselves from the mainstream of Christian culture and possibly left themselves out on a limb for many centuries to come.'

In purely English terms, you can make a case for the Synod of Whitby as a formative moment in the development of a single English state because it meant that all the Anglo-Saxon kings were following the same way of worshipping. If they had still been at odds over haircuts and Easter 250 years later, it would have been much more difficult for Athelstan to have brought together Northumbria with Wessex and Mercia to become the first King of England (see Kingston Coronation Stone, page 50).

So Whitby's Anglo-Saxon significance cannot be underestimated. Sadly, there is very little left of Hild's monastery. The Anglo-Saxon foundation appears to have disappeared at some point in the mid 9th century due to the depredations of the Viking raids. The only evidence you'll see on the headland today are some tomb markers on the seaward side of the medieval ruins, and some inscribed stones in the splendid and airily modern visitor centre. The neglected memory of the abbey's past importance, though, was enough to convince the Normans that it should be refounded, so although you're not looking directly at 7th-century stones in the ruins today, they are, I think, in the tradition of that earlier Anglo-Saxon story.

Whitby Abbey
Abbey Lane, Whitby, North Yorkshire YO22 4JT
01947 603568
www.english-heritagee.org.uk/daysout

Lindisfarne Priory, Northumberland
Nominated by Barbara Yorke, professor of early medieval history, University of Winchester
'Where the Vikings began their onslaught on Britain'

Lindisfarne Priory, on the southwestern corner of Holy Island, is the sort of place that invites gentle reflection. You have to cross a causeway to get there, so by dint of its twice-daily tidal isolation, the island has a pleasantly calm feel to it. Although the priory itself is in ruins, it retains something of the contemplative atmosphere that comes from centuries of monastic meditation.

What you'll see today are the remains of the 12th-century priory church. Its ruddy-coloured stones occupy a delightful site at the edge of the island's village, with a fine view across the sea to the crag on which sits Lindisfarne Castle. The scene practically demands that you find a quiet patch

An engraving of the remarkable rainbow arch at Lindisfarne
by S. Rawle, after a drawing by William Westall

of grass on which to sit and mull over the long span of history set out before you. The problem is that you can't see much of the priory's really interesting history, as that goes back earlier than the medieval buildings there now.

The first monastery was founded here in 635, when the Anglo-Saxon king of Northumbria, Oswald, converted to Christianity and invited Irish monks from Iona to set up a church on this island just off the coast. Lindisfarne became particularly important for the spread of the Irish brand of Christianity among the Anglo-Saxons, as Barbara Yorke explains: 'It was the main base of the Irish influence in Northumbria, so it was the centre from which they fanned out into many areas of England and established churches.'

The first three bishops of Lindisfarne – Aidan, Finan and Colman – were all Irish monks who came directly from Iona. Under them, the community prospered, but in 664 King Oswald's brother and successor, Oswy, decided that the right sort of Christianity was not the Irish version but the Roman one (see Whitby Abbey, page 38). Shortly afterwards, the man who was to become Lindisfarne's most famous resident, Cuthbert, arrived from Melrose Priory in the Scottish borders. In the 670s he set about reforming the place in the Roman model. Some of his monks didn't like it, but Cuthbert acquired a particular reputation as a man of God. After his death in 687, miracles were reported at his shrine, and Lindisfarne shone in the light of Cuthbert's saintly reputation.

Further cementing the significance of the place, the fabulous illuminated Lindisfarne Gospels were made here in the early 8th century. The island was a great cultural centre at the time, with a reputation as a leading place of Christian learning, but the Anglo-Saxon monastery is no more, and there is a clue to the reason why in the museum next door to the medieval ruins. 'The site of the later priory contains some wonderful sculptures that came from the original Irish and Anglo-Saxon priory,' says Yorke. These sculpted stones, dating from the 7th century through to the 10th, were discovered around the priory site. The most impressive one is the so-called Viking Domesday Stone, which is a 9th-century grave marker with carvings on both sides. On one face there's a cross with some praying supplicants beneath it, and on the other a relief of seven furious-looking warriors, weapons raised in what appears to be a wild assault. The flattened perspective gives the impression that these attackers are one-eyed fiends. Even on a grey stone surface (though it might originally have been luridly painted), and with over a millennium separating the stonemason from us today, they have an inhuman look that is disquieting.

This frightful scene has been interpreted as a 9th-century commentary on the looming arrival of the biblical Judgement Day, as evidenced by the coming of the Vikings. The Scandinavian raiders first made their appearance on the shores at Lindisfarne in AD 793, with a bloodthirsty and sacrilegious assault that heralded the start of the Viking age, with subsequent raids carried out on monasteries throughout northern Britain, the northern isles and Ireland. So are those Vikings the alien ogres depicted on the grave marker? We can't be sure, but certainly the Lindisfarne attack caused a flood of fear to wash over the Christian Anglo-Saxons. The failure of Cuthbert's saintly presence to protect this most holy of Anglo-Saxon Christian sites led to widespread consternation.

The Vikings first raided and then came to settle, establishing kingdoms, and evicting the existing Anglo-Saxon and British rulers. We don't know for certain why they came. Some theories have it that they were driven out of the fjords by poverty and over-population, others that trading economics led to a need for silver so great among Viking elites that it could be satisfied only by plunder, while another idea is that they were actually trying to protect their pagan identity from the advance of Christianity. Whatever prompted them, their legacy is a long one. Some of their number settled in northern France, coming to rule what we now call Normandy, and it was from there of course that William the Conqueror led his invasion fleet to England in 1066.

While the pagan Viking raiders were at large on Britain's seaboard, Lindisfarne was not a safe place for monks to be. The community abandoned their church in the 9th century, taking the relics of St Cuthbert with them. However, the Vikings' Norman descendants were keen adherents to the Christian religion and enthusiastic promoters of monastic institutions, so when they arrived on the scene they were keen to see such an important site as Lindisfarne refounded. Once more there were monks here in the 12th century. The ruins of their Norman church are what you see today. The tantalising sight of the delicate rib of the rainbow arch suspended (perhaps miraculously, if you're of a religious persuasion) over what was the central crossing of the church is a hint of what would have been here had the monastery not lost its purpose in the Reformation. There's still lots to see and explore among the remains, but now you're more likely to hear barking seals than chanting monks. Personally, I think they make a suitably surreal soundtrack for the moment of contemplation that the ruins require.

Lindisfarne Priory

Holy Island, Berwick-upon-Tweed, Northumberland TD15 2RX

01289 389200

www.english-heritage.org.uk/daysout

Athelney Island, Somerset
Nominated by David Allan, reader in history,
University of St Andrews
'Where King Alfred rescued England from the Vikings'

England was saved by a little island on the edge of the Somerset Levels. It doesn't look like much today, and in fact it doesn't particularly look like an island, unless you catch it in a wet winter when the river has overtopped its banks and the fields have returned to their natural state of being mostly under water.

This flat, low-lying patch of Somerset has always been susceptible to flooding. The monks of Glastonbury Abbey began to put some concerted effort into draining the area in the medieval period, but prior to that the Isle of Athelney would have been altogether more difficult to get to than it is today.

Now the A361 runs past the place, and there's a handy lay-by shielded from the road, where you can stop and take a look. If you're coming from the north, from the heart of the Levels, it's just a little way on from the intersection of the rivers Tone and Parrett at Burrowbridge, where the enigmatic Burrow Mump rises up from the lowlands and is crested by a ruined medieval church. The Isle of Athelney is much less pronounced than Burrow Mump, but it is still a noticeable area of raised ground, with a monument on it. A signboard near the lay-by reveals that the monument is to King Alfred. David Allan explains: 'This is where Alfred the Great, king of the West Saxons and the last English political leader holding out against the Viking invaders in 878, holed up to plot his counter-attack. The latter culminated at a place called Ethandun, where Alfred defeated

Guthrum and his Danes, converting them to Christianity and, it is usually said, effectively ensuring that the English would continue to develop a state called England.'

The decade or so leading up to this point had not been a good one for the various Anglo-Saxon kingdoms (there was as yet no England as such). Viking invaders from Scandinavia had overrun Northumbria in 866–7, East Anglia in 869–70, and then mauled Mercia in the Midlands. Danish and Norwegian armies appear to have settled in the areas they'd conquered and replaced the Anglo-Saxon rulers with their own kings and earls. The Anglo-Saxons very much had their backs to the wall, their Christianity at risk from the pagan Vikings, whose treatment of churches was not at all respectful.

The kingdom of Wessex, in the south of England, had also been badly battered in 870–1, but it was not yet subjugated, and it remained the last bastion of the Anglo-Saxons, under the leadership of the very godly Alfred, who had been king since 871. For the first few years of his reign the Vikings stayed away, but in 876 they were back in Wessex, attacking Wareham and Exeter. After a close-run thing at Chippenham, where Alfred was nearly captured, he retired to Athelney, from where he conducted a guerrilla campaign against the invaders, before managing to regroup enough of an army to take the fight to the Vikings at Ethandun.

Ethandun was a turning point. It enabled Alfred to push the Vikings out of Wessex (though they took a while leaving), and then it bought him enough time to reorganise the defences of his kingdom to better fend off the attentions of the northern invaders. He famously restructured his army in such a way that he had a more reliable supply of fighting men, he expanded his navy and introduced bigger ships, and he built a chain of forts around his kingdom. It was enough to convince future Viking raiders that easier pickings were to be had elsewhere. This all meant that when he died in 899, Alfred was able to pass on a much more secure realm, and a base from which his successors could go on to push back the extent of Viking power and eventually bring all the Anglo-Saxon peoples together in one kingdom called England.

We don't actually know where Ethandun was fought; some scholars say Edington in Wiltshire, others plump for Edington just over the northern side of the Polden Hills in Somerset. The lack of a firm location for the battle site is a familiar problem for most fields of conflict from this period. 'It's difficult not to conclude that in early British history the modern obscurity of a site is in inverse proportion to its likely historical importance,' notes Allan.

Yet at Athelney we can be more certain of Alfred's presence. And without Athelney, Ethandun would probably never have been fought, and the subsequent securing of Wessex never have been carried out. Without Athelney we'd also not have a schoolroom story to tell about an absent-minded king burning cakes, as it was here that Alfred reputedly forgot the baking he'd been entrusted with by a swineherd. The story is supposed to demonstrate that the mind of this deep-thinking monarch was on weightier matters.

Sadly, there are no great evocative remains on the island; it's just a raised lump of ground surrounded by grazing farmland, with the monument, which was erected in 1801, sitting on its saddleback. It's on private fields, but you're not missing that much if you don't venture from the lay-by. The monument itself is not the most uplifting piece of architecture you'll ever come across; it's rather squat, has been ravaged by two centuries of weathering and it's difficult to make out the wording on it. There's nothing to see of the abbey that Alfred founded in the 880s in gratitude for his refuge (it survived until the Dissolution, but it was always a small community, so it was thoroughly dissolved). As a result, you have to try to conjure up an image of this island surrounded by reedy marsh, where a desperate and damp ruler searched for inspiration to save his kingdom from obliteration.

'All in all, it requires a bit of imagination to get a real appreciation for Athelney's importance when one visits, and it won't detain anyone for very long, given the lack of visitor attractions,' concludes Allan. 'But the fact that it's so understated, beyond a patient explanation in a lay-by, is in itself a rather English approach to such a defining moment in the nation's history.'

Athelney Island
Lay-by on the A361 between East Lyng and Burrowbridge, Somerset
Grid reference: ST 3456 2924 (ST 32 NW)
www.visitsomerset.co.uk

Kingston Coronation Stone, Surrey
Nominated by Seán Lang, senior lecturer in history, Anglia Ruskin University
'Where Saxon kings were crowned'

There is a large grey stone, several feet high, which from a certain angle resembles nothing more than an oversized and very off-colour molar, that sits just outside the Guildhall in Kingston upon Thames. It is, in truth, not that much of a spectacle, particularly if you, as I did, happen to visit the town on a typically English grey day. The blue decorative railings around the stone do add a splash of colour, but other than that, this is an eminently missable artefact.

The three American tourists who stopped to investigate while I was there looked in turn bemused and then disappointed. I'm guessing they had been diverted off the main road by the beckoning 'Coronation Stone' sign. Yet, despite its somewhat unprepossessing nature and inauspicious location, this stone has an important story to tell. It was supposedly the stone upon which a number of Anglo-Saxon kings of England were crowned. The names of the kings, seven in total, are inscribed on the plinth beneath the stone. Their names are evocative but probably unfamiliar – Eadred and Eadwig, for example – and they speak of an age that many of us know little about.

For Seán Lang, that's the point: 'I've always felt that Saxon history gets rather short shrift in this country. We number our kings from 1066. It's such an effective cut-off point that the Normans introduced, and was ratified by the Whigs for their own purposes later on, that it's only Saxon enthusiasts who get to know the period. Otherwise people only learn about it when they're very young – in primary school – and it's written off as a childish period in history. I think that an artefact like the stone is a reminder of just how sophisticated and advanced Saxon England was.'

All seven kings who were apparently crowned on the stone ruled in the 10th century, a formative period in the development of the kingdom of England. At the end of the 9th century, Alfred the Great's successful campaign against the Viking armies (see Athelney Island, page 47) meant that although he was King of Wessex, in his lifetime he was also acknowl-edged as overlord or king of neighbouring Mercia. He died in AD 899, and it was Alfred's legacy that his successors were able to rule over both Wessex and Mercia, thereby becoming kings of England. We only have firm evidence, however, for the coronation in Kingston of two of the seven: Athelstan and Aethelred.

Athelstan is a particularly notable figure. *The Anglo-Saxon Chronicle* records that his consecration took place here in AD 925, and the site was chosen, over Alfred's capital of Winchester, because it was on the border of Wessex and Mercia (marked by the Thames). Athelstan, after some initial confusion, was crowned king of both kingdoms. Later in his reign he went on to take over the kingdom of Northumbria, thereby becoming the first real King of England. His coronation, therefore, is a truly pivotal moment in English history.

What we don't know is the role played, if any, by the Coronation Stone. Its history is shadowy and we cannot say for certain if it was actually used in any 10th-century ceremonies. If it were, the king would perhaps have stood on top of it (that's what he did in a re-enactment of the cere-mony in Kingston in the 1950s). What we can be more certain about is that no coronations took place where the stone currently sits. It has been moved around Kingston several times in the past 150 years as the town's burghers have looked for a suitable site for their royal memorial.

It's fair to say that the stone's current location does it no favours, so it's pleasing to note that there are plans afoot to have it moved back to its likely original position, in the churchyard of All Saints Church, just a short stroll away. All Saints is not a Saxon church: it has some Norman fabric, but it is mostly a later construction. It might sit on top of an earlier Saxon foundation, and there is certainly evidence for a Saxon chapel in the churchyard (you can see a plaque to it today). Inside the church there are one or two bits of masonry that may once have been associated with the Saxon building, but the real story is one that looks to the future. If the stone is brought back to the churchyard and given some decent interpretation facilities and a more attractive backdrop, as is envisaged, that presents a good opportunity for more people to find out about the important role played by Kingston upon Thames in the formation of a polity called England.

Lang even wonders if it might have a part to play in future coronation ceremonies for British monarchs: 'From a national point of view, especially now that the Stone of Scone has gone back to Edinburgh, I've always thought that there's a good case for using it again as a coronation stone. At a time when the unity of the United Kingdom is under strain, it's worth reminding ourselves of how the Saxon monarchy forged a single kingdom out of different ones.'

The Stone of Scone, of course, is the Scottish equivalent that was removed and brought to England by Edward I, and only recently returned north of the border. The deal is that the stone is supposed to be brought down to London for future coronations. Were it ever to happen that Kingston's Coronation Stone displaced the Stone of Scone, the coronation chair, which you can currently see in Westminster Abbey, would need to have something of a redesign, as this stone would certainly not fit in the cavity under the seat that the Stone of Scone slots into.

As it stands, Kingston's Coronation Stone continues to occupy its rather lonely, unloved and peripheral location. Until and unless it is moved into more salubrious surroundings, you'd be well advised to pop into

Kingston's pleasant museum for a bit more information about the Saxon history and later story of this royal borough. As you walk to the museum, you might pass the jolly pictorial plaque on the side of the Eden Walk shopping centre, depicting the lives of the various kings associated with Kingston coronations. Other than that, there isn't much left to remind the casual visitor of this London suburb's Saxon story.

Kingston Coronation Stone
Outside the Guildhall, High Street, Kingston upon Thames, Surrey KT1 1EU
www.kingston.gov.uk

All Saints Church
Market Place, Kingston upon Thames, Surrey KT1 1JP
020 8546 5964
www.allsaintskingston.co.uk

Scutchamer Knob, Oxfordshire

Nominated by Ryan Lavelle, lecturer in history, University of Winchester
'Where you can see how the Vikings challenged the Anglo-Saxon order'

People have been walking along the Ridgeway for a long time, so much so that it's been dubbed 'Britain's Oldest Road', which is quite a grand title and rather depends on your view of what a road amounts to. Certainly, the route across the chalk ridge of southern England has been an obvious and attractive path for some millennia, as evidenced by the wealth of prehistoric burial mounds, hill forts and defensive ditches along its length, and, indeed, one large white horse at Uffington.

Scutchamer Knob is one of these prehistoric sites, a Bronze Age round barrow, also known as Cwichelm's Barrow or Cuckhamsley Hill. It sits by the side of the Ridgeway a little to the south of the very pleasant thatched and half-timbered village of East Hendred. If you're driving, there is a car park right next to the site, but a much more invigorating way to approach would be to combine it with a hike along this section of the Ridgeway, which is now a well-signposted national trail. Unless you're an extremely early riser, its current popularity does mean that any hopes you might harbour of having the place to yourself are likely to be dashed by the regular army of dog walkers and cyclists enjoying the splendid path.

Aficionados of Bronze Age round barrows might be disappointed on arrival to note that this one is missing its middle. Its current horseshoe-shaped appearance derives from the fact that in the mid 19th century it was subject to an over-vigorous antiquarian inspection, which resulted in the centre of the mound being carted away. When the gentlemen of the Newbury District Field Club came to dig here once more in the 1930s, there wasn't that much left for them to investigate, though they did report that they were unable to locate any evidence to verify the tradition that King Cwichelm, or indeed anyone else, was buried inside.

Cwichelm, who lived in the early 7th century, was a king of the West Saxons and notable for being the man who sent an assassin to kill the first Christian king of Northumbria. Whether or not Scutchamer Knob is Cwichelm's final resting place, it was certainly an important site for the

Anglo-Saxons. We know from documentary evidence that it was an assembly place – the meeting point for the shire of Berkshire. The Anglo-Saxons often appear to have reused prehistoric mounds for this purpose, though we don't know whether they appreciated the historic dimension or simply found them useful raised platforms in generally accessible locations.

Assembly places like this probably began to be used soon after the Anglo-Saxons got established in an area, becoming centres for administration and justice, where the local inhabitants were required to attend regular meetings. Thus they would have been an important part of the landscape. They continued in use right down to the later Anglo-Saxon period, and that's where Scutchamer Knob's story really gets interesting.

At the start of the 11th century, the very existence of the Anglo-Saxon kingdom was under threat from Viking raiders. After Alfred the Great had famously fought off the Vikings in the 9th century and established the kingdom of England (see Athelney Island, page 47), some stability was given to the Anglo-Saxon state, but the Viking raids started up again in the latter part of the 10th century. Alfred's descendant as King of England, Aethelred, had mounted a lacklustre defence. In fact, by 1006 he'd been forced to beat a retreat westwards from his heartland in Wessex, as Ryan Lavelle explains: 'In 1006 the Vikings were devastating Wessex; they were marching up and down with impunity. The king, Aethelred, had gone off to Shropshire and was getting all his food and income from there, while the Vikings were getting what the king should have got from Wessex.'

Scutchamer Knob lay right at the heart of Wessex. With Aethelred nowhere to be seen, the Vikings were able to pierce their way to it and encamp themselves on this key Anglo-Saxon administrative site. In so doing, they cocked a snook at the defenders who, according to *The Anglo-Saxon Chronicle*, had boasted that 'if they [the Vikings] sought out Cwichelm's Barrow they would never get to the sea'.

'Warfare in this period was a series of posturing and counter-posturing, and is summed up beautifully here,' explains Lavelle. 'So the Vikings headed to this place and challenged the Anglo-Saxon army in Wessex to fight. They didn't respond to the challenge, but there was eventually a battle in Wiltshire where the English were beaten. Probably the reason why the English didn't respond to the Viking challenge was because it was an assembly site, and if they did respond, they would effectively have been summoned to an assembly by the Vikings. That would have shown that the Vikings held the Wessex countryside. There is a series of meanings to places.'

So Scutchamer Knob gives us an insight into how warfare was conducted in the later Anglo-Saxon period, and it sheds light on how closely interweaved are the stories of the Anglo-Saxons and the Vikings. King Aethelred, who has since been tainted with the nickname 'the Unready' (though actually the original meaning was 'ill-advised') for his conduct in the war, was unable to counter the Viking threat. He was eventually replaced on the throne by the Danish king Swein Forkbeard in 1013, and forced to flee to Normandy. Although he briefly returned from exile after Swein's death, Aethelred was succeeded not by an Anglo-Saxon, but by Swein's son, Cnut.

It's interesting to think of what would have gone on at Scutchamer Knob in 1006. The mound would have looked much more mound-like then, and presumably the Vikings, in some numbers, would have been encamped in what are now the woods and fields surrounding it. The one thing that the early excavations do appear to have found in the mound is evidence of some sort of burnt oak stake within. Scutchamer

Knob seems to have been part of the Anglo-Saxon beacon system across southern England, and *The Anglo-Saxon Chronicle* states that the Viking army similarly ignited beacons as they advanced through Wessex. One can imagine an army settled in here, a fire lit on top of the old barrow to announce its presence, and awaiting the Anglo-Saxon response to its power-posturing. Now, of course, any beacon here would be rather over-shadowed by the clouds pumping out from Didcot Power Station in the near distance, but look the other way, over the fields of southern England, and you can more readily appreciate how the Anglo-Saxons must have felt about the presence of a foreign force sitting provocatively in their midst.

Scutchamer Knob

3 km (2 miles) south of East Hendred, off the A417 east of Wantage,

Oxfordshire

Grid reference: SU 458851

www.nationaltrail.co.uk/ridgeway

Battle Abbey and the Battlefield of Hastings, East Sussex

Nominated by Thomas Asbridge, reader in medieval history, Queen Mary, University of London
'Where the Norman Conquest began'

The blood and the gore, and the dead bodies of the warriors of Anglo-Saxon England, have long since gone. But the site of the Battle of Hastings retains a resonance in our history that few other sites can match. This was, of course, where William the Conqueror, Duke of Normandy, defeated King Harold, last Anglo-Saxon ruler of England, in 1066.

You can walk along the ridge where Harold's army locked their shields together and, as they would have done, you can look down on the valley where the Norman forces were massed below. The beauty of this particular battlefield is that you can be reasonably sure that you're standing in the thick of where the action took place. Thomas Asbridge feels that this adds considerably to the allure of the place. 'One of the reasons I think Battle Abbey and the site surrounding it is important is that, unlike other battle-field sites, where we can't be precise over the exact shape of events, we have a pretty shrewd idea of what went on at the battle of Hastings. That's because the battlefield is in close proximity to the abbey later founded by William, supposedly in the area where Harold fell. I love being able to go to places where we can really get a sense of what went on. It adds elec-tricity to being in that place.'

Battle Abbey was a very rich monastery until Henry VIII's time, when it was dissolved, partly demolished, then converted into a private house and subsequently a school, a purpose it still retains. However, some of the abbey ruins are now in the care of English Heritage. The great gatehouse stands sentinel over the abbey, and in there you'll find an interesting little exhibition about the history of the buildings and life in a monastery. Then, in a separate centre, English Heritage has created a very smart interpreta-tion base, complete with a short film on the battle, narrated by no less a historical luminary than David Starkey.

Of course, all the modern interpretation in the world pales into insignificance beside the glorious historical record of the campaign and battle, the Bayeux Tapestry, the stunning piece of art that was probably created not long after 1066 and provides a colourfully vivid, if slightly one-dimensional, picture of what went on. You can see it in Bayeux in Normandy today, or Reading Museum has a very passable replica made by the hands of Victorian ladies from Leek.

Nevertheless, the battlefield centre does provide a lively introduction to the battle and the views of modern scholarship. There's a particularly jaunty interactive map board that allows you to trace, with a joystick, Harold's less than ideal preparation for the clash with William. In the month before the battle of Hastings (on 14 October), Harold's army had marched up to Yorkshire to fight and defeat another pretender to his throne, the Viking Harold Hadrada, at Stamford Bridge. They then had to hotfoot it back down the length of the country when they heard that the Normans had arrived on the south coast. Unsurprisingly, the Anglo-Saxons weren't as fresh as they might have been when they took to the field.

When you visit the battle site, you can limit your own marching to a short walk along the ridge where the Anglo-Saxons assembled, or take a longer path down into the valley to review the Norman positions. Either way, you should take advantage of the audio guide that comes free with your entrance fee. Combined with the information panels scattered around the site, it's not too hard to get an idea of what happened where and to whom. The numbers involved in the battle were not huge – perhaps 7000 or so on each side – but in a fairly well-contained field of conflict, you can easily imagine what sort of carnage unfolded here.

'You can try to look at the lie of the land and get a feel for what that encounter might have been like. Harold appears to have had his troops on the upper ground. There are two things that meant he wasn't able to capitalise on that advantage – one is that William managed to turn the battle round by intervening personally, charging to the front of the fray and stopping his troops from retreating when they'd been trying to get up the hill and been beaten back down,' explains Asbridge. 'The second thing, which always strikes me as an extraordinary feature of Anglo-Saxon warfare, was that the Anglo-Saxons didn't know how to fight on horses. They rode around on them, but as soon as they got to the battle, they dismounted and fought on foot. If they had been able to mount some sort of downhill charge, they might have been able to scatter William's troops.'

Probably the best place to mull over all this is up on the ridge, with added historic interest provided by the ruins of the abbey and the plaque on the altar of the abbey's church, which marks the spot where Harold supposedly fell. Whether or not it is actually the site of Harold's death, and whether – as the story goes – he was killed as the result of an arrow in the eye is disputed, but the outcome isn't. Harold was deposed and the Norman William took the throne in his stead. This was a transformational moment in English, and latterly British, history. In the short term, quite apart from the turbulence of having a foreign king on the throne, it led to the wholesale replacement of the Anglo-Saxon ruling elite and a thoroughgoing revolution in landholding in the country.

In the long term, it realigned the nation's geopolitical outlook: 'Before Hastings the major axis of contact in terms of culture, economy, politics and military alliance was horizontal – it was connecting the British Isles to the Scandinavian world. If Hastings had gone the other way, or the time had been reversed and William the Conqueror had landed before Harold Hadrada, perhaps he'd have been defeated at Hastings and we'd have seen a victory up in the north. The fact that William was triumphant and did manage to hold on to and then expand his foothold, creating this

Anglo-Norman world, transforms this axis of contact. It goes from being horizontal to vertical. For the rest of the Middle Ages that's the major form of contact, politically, culturally and economically.'

If the Norman Conquest turned English eyes towards France for inspiration, it also tempted them to look immediately north and west with covetous intent. After Hastings, William amassed a huge amount of power in the hands of the Crown, which, as Asbridge notes, had potentially seismic consequences. 'This led to a very powerful English monarchy and a very administratively effective English monarch. And I think over time those things led to the ability to threaten Scotland and overwhelm Wales. You could argue that the ability to forge a united kingdom stemmed in part from that centralisation of power after the Norman Conquest.'

Battle Abbey and Battlefield of Hastings
Battle, East Sussex TN33 0AD
01424 775705
www.english-heritage.org.uk/daysout

Winchester Cathedral, Hampshire

Nominated by Andrew Abram, lecturer in medieval history, University of Wales Trinity Saint David
'Where the Norman kings set themselves as heirs to the Anglo-Saxons'

In the centre of Winchester Cathedral, on top of the intricately carved stonework of the screens that surround the quire, are six colourfully painted wooden chests. They are mortuary boxes, and are said to contain the bones of William the Conqueror's son, William Rufus, along with several earlier Anglo-Saxon kings boasting such arcane and probably unfamiliar names as Cenwalh, Ethelwulf and Cynegils, plus, more famously, the Anglo-Danish monarch Cnut (whose name is forever linked with an effort to hold back the advancing sea) and his queen, Emma.

If your Latin is rusty, there is a helpful wooden plaque on the outer wall of the quire, explaining whose bones are reputedly in which box, but don't take this as gospel because the contents were jumbled up in later centuries. Everything is, in fact, a little out of place here. The building that the boxes are housed in post-dates most of the Anglo-Saxon kings and queens inside by a considerable margin. For Winchester Cathedral, as we see it today, was a Norman foundation, begun in 1079 during the reign of William I, the conqueror, the man who famously removed the last Anglo-Saxon king, Harold, from his throne.

There is a good reason for this. The Norman cathedral sits atop earlier Anglo-Saxon remains – indeed, you can see the lines of the Saxon Old Minster laid out in brickwork on the green just next to the present cathedral. This, according to Andrew Abram, is a recognisable Norman strategy. 'If you look at the way that the Normans operated, it's in a very familiar model – they went out of their way to justify themselves. The cathedral supplanted this early, much smaller Anglo-Saxon Benedictine monastery. The person they saw themselves as the natural successor of – the last legal Anglo-Saxon king – was Edward the Confessor [who was crowned in Winchester in 1043], and they played on that, promoting themselves as the new, justifiable legal successors to the Anglo-Saxons. It was very clever, very manipulative.'

So why did the Normans take a particular interest in Winchester? Because it was, says Abram, 'the spiritual centre of the earldom of Wessex and, by extension, the Anglo-Saxon kingdoms'. Cenwalh, an early king of Wessex (he's in one of the boxes), built the Old Minster church way back in 648. Thereafter it appears to have been an important site for the West Saxon kings. But it was under the most famous of their line, King Alfred, the ruler of Wessex who became king of the Anglo-Saxons through his military success in fending off the Vikings in the late 9th century, that Winchester became nationally significant. His son Edward had a New Minster built, right next to the Old Minster. Alfred himself was buried in both (his remains were transferred from the Old to the New Minster when the latter building was completed), as were many of his successors, including the Danish kings Cnut and Harthacnut. It's the bones of these kings that have now found their way into the mortuary boxes.

So from at least Alfred's time until the coming of the Normans, Winchester was England's capital, and it was only after 1066 that it was supplanted by London. In the years before the Conquest, Winchester was one of the largest towns in the country, with planned streets, refortified Roman walls, and major buildings like the minsters. Winchester was also home to the treasury, thus making it a doubly important site for William the Conqueror. He maintained Winchester's role as the home to the royal treasury, so when his son William Rufus was attempting to secure the crown after his father's death in 1087, he too came to Winchester, as indeed did his brother and successor to the throne, Henry I, in 1100: 'With William the Conqueror and his sons, the first place they made for was Winchester to seize the treasury and the spiritual centre. The Anglo-

The atmospheric crypt of Winchester Cathedral,
complete with modern Gormley sculpture

Normans copied the Anglo-Saxons and continued what they were about.'

You can see this thread of continual significance in and around the cathedral, with those foundation lines of the Anglo-Saxon royal cult centre underlying the stones of the Norman cathedral, and the bones of Anglo-Saxon kings jumbled up inside, along with the remains of William Rufus. So it's a great place to visit to get a feel for the Anglo-Saxon story of England, and the way that power was transferred from the Anglo-Saxon kings to the Normans.

Of course, there is a whole lot more to see in the cathedral than this. The place does, after all, have another nine centuries of history to plough through after the Anglo-Saxon and Anglo-Norman period. Your eyes might well be diverted from the mortuary boxes to the astonishing Great

Screen at the end of the quire. The Norman parts of the building are limited mostly to the area around the quire and the transepts. The Holy Sepulchre Chapel is definitely worth a look for its tremendous 12th-century wall paintings. You certainly shouldn't miss a trip down to the crypt below the north transept, which dates from the 11th century, and is now enlivened by an Antony Gormley sculpture, particularly impressive in winter when the place gets flooded.

The central tower that stood above the quire collapsed in 1107, so its rather squat replacement, along with the entire east–west length of the cathedral, is all post-Norman. You shouldn't, and indeed can't really, miss the nave, which for its length alone demands respect, notwithstanding its sweeping vault high above you. Nor should you pass up the opportunity to have a wander around the cathedral close outside, and the rest of historic Winchester. The excellent City Museum, between the High Street and the cathedral, will give you a good insight into the Anglo-Saxon history of the whole city, while at the bottom of the High Street is the Hamo Thorny-croft statue of King Alfred, which rounds off the story nicely.

Winchester Cathedral
9 The Close, Winchester, Hampshire SO23 9LS
01962 857200
www.winchester-cathedral.org.uk

The Tower of London, London

Nominated by Helen Castor, fellow in medieval history,
University of Cambridge
'Where the Norman kings imposed themselves on
England'

When William the Conqueror was crowned in Westminster Abbey on Christmas Day 1066, his position as king of England was far from secure. Although the Norman duke had won his great victory over the English king Harold at Hastings (see Battle Abbey, page 58) in October, and spent the rest of the autumn and early winter securing a powerbase in the southeast, resistance to his new regime was not stamped out. In fact, when the assembled knights raised a shout of acclamation at William's coronation, the guards outside the abbey feared a rebellion was afoot, and in the ensuing panic, a fire started that burnt down a number of houses in the city.

Unsurprisingly, William did not linger in London. He retreated to somewhere that didn't seem quite so volatile, and ordered the building of several strongholds in the city to keep the population in order. One of these forts was probably erected on the site of the Tower of London. Shortly after, construction work began on the great stone keep, the White Tower, which still forms the heart of the place today. It was probably complete by the year 1100. As there have been nearly a thousand years of change and development here since William's time, it's startling that the tower is still standing, a big square brute of a building, still able to dominate the mass of later fortifications, ramparts and buildings that now encircle it.

The tower today isn't exactly the Norman original. In the 11th century it would have been a two-storey keep over a basement. The layout of each floor would have been basically open, though a separate chapel was on the upper level. In the 15th century a third floor was added, while the onion turrets on the four corners were added later still, in Henry VIII's time in the 16th century. It didn't actually become a white tower until the reign of Henry III, when, in March 1240, he had the building coated with whitewash. The tower hasn't been painted since the 17th century, so it's more of a mellow beige than bright white on the outside nowadays.

Despite the later alterations and additions, the exterior of the building remains broadly true to the Norman concept of the keep, or great tower. This was an idea imported from William's lands in northern France, and the Tower of London was the first example of this sort of architecture of power in England. It was designed as a fortress, but also as a centre for ceremony and, crucially, a very vivid statement of who was in charge. It spawned Norman keeps across the land as William and his successors made their mark on their new territory.

'If you want to get a sense of the Norman Conquest and what that meant, a building like the Tower tells you a lot about the imposition of a new regime on a subject people,' says Helen Castor. 'These great fortresses went up all over the country, but this was a particularly important one at the water entrance to the city of London, which had, after all, had Viking ships sailing into it less than a century before. Internal control and defence were going on at the same time when William started building this extraordinary place. It gives you a real sense of the city of London and how important it was.'

The White Tower provides a very clear expression in stone of the transfer in power that took place in the aftermath of the Norman Conquest. We know from another remarkable survival of William's time – the 1086 survey

A medieval depiction of the bright white Tower of London

of England known as the Domesday Book – that by the end of his reign, almost all of the English nobility had been wiped out as a landowning class. The wholesale replacement of English landholders by new men from France was accompanied by a programme of castle-building across the land to keep the restless natives in order. It was places like the Tower of London that enabled the Norman kings to maintain their grip on England.

Inside the tower today are reminders of its later history as the head-quarters of the Office of Ordnance. From the late 17th century through to the mid 19th, the castle was a supply depot for munitions and arma-ments, and you can see all manner of arms and armour on display in the tower now. There is one place where the Norman atmosphere still lingers, however, and that's in the lovely St John's Chapel on the first floor. With its semicircular design, barrel vaulting, arcaded gallery and characteristic round arches, it's a tremendous example of surviving Norman architec-ture, and a pleasant place to gather your thoughts, as most of the visiting crowd tends to rush past this quiet corner.

Of course, a visit to the White Tower is but one aspect of a day out at the Tower of London. You've got the medieval ramparts and towers of Henry III and Edward I to explore (bear in mind that much of what's there today is the result of Victorian renovations, however), and all the echoes of Tudor life in the place, when it became a place of imprisonment, torture and execution for those on the wrong side of the religious divide imposed by the Reformation. It's particularly gripping to look at the graf-fiti of those who were locked up in the various towers around the place, and to dwell on the horrors they endured.

Famously, three Tudor queens were executed inside the perimeter of the castle, and you can look at the scaffold site where Anne Boleyn,

Katherine Howard and Jane Grey lost their lives on Tower Green, commemorated by a striking modern sculpture. The Chapel Royal on the edge of that green is another remarkable reminder of the bloody history of the place. As Castor notes, 'It makes you think about individuals and the human reality of history. The first thing that got me into history as a child was Anne Boleyn standing alone before the scaffold in the tower. The tower remains as a symbol of that extraordinary outpouring of political violence in the 16th century. People and power are what I'm interested in, and you get such a sense of both the human scale and the grand scale here.'

All this would be enough to merit a visit, and that's without even thinking about the Roman origins of the place (part of the Roman city wall stands to an impressive height just outside Tower Hill tube station), its role as a Royal Mint (Isaac Newton worked here as warden of the mint for a time), royal menagerie (lions, elephants and polar bears were caged here), nor indeed most famously its position as home to the Crown Jewels (now housed in a barracks building created by the Duke of Wellington).

There's so much to see here that you certainly need half a day at least to do the place justice. Bear in mind that this is a very popular attraction, particularly if you go in summer, when a lengthy queue tends to snake out from the entrance to the Crown Jewels display. If you do find yourself waiting in line to see the royal regalia, at least you have the opportunity to take a good look at the walls of William's mighty tower, a lasting legacy of his statement of regal power over nine centuries ago.

Tower of London
Tower Hill, London EC3N 4AB
0844 482 7777
www.hrp.co.uk/toweroflondon

Dunfermline Abbey, Fife

Nominated by Michael Penman, senior lecturer in
history, University of Stirling
'Where Anglo-Scottish harmony was almost born'

If you've ever wondered what Robert the Bruce's skull looks like, Dunfermline Abbey is the place to go. A plaster cast of it lives there in a glass box. This oddly ghoulish artefact exists because in 1818 the remains of Scotland's hero king were discovered here during building works. The cast was made before Robert the Bruce's remains were reburied with great ceremony, and 80 years later a magnificent memorial brass, a good Victorian effort at a medieval design, was placed on top of his re-interred body.

With his skull and his memorial plaque on display, Robert the Bruce, first buried here in 1329, is well remembered in the Abbey Church. The same can't be said of the numerous other early medieval Scottish monarchs and their consorts also interred in this place. As Michael Penman explains, 'This is Scotland's Westminster, the burial site of Scotland's kings both before and after the Wars of Independence.'

Robert the Bruce was a pivotal figure in the recognition of Scottish independence at the end of those wars, during which England, under Edward I and his son Edward II, had attempted to invade and conquer Scotland in the late 13th and early 14th centuries. Prior to that, Scotland had been developing as an independent nation, often on relatively friendly terms with its southern neighbour. It had its own line of kings stretching back to the mid 9th century, when Kenneth MacAlpin united much of what is now Scotland under his rule.

The list of monarchs known to have been buried in Dunfermline's royal mausoleum does not go quite that far back. It reaches only to 1093, when Margaret, queen of Malcolm III, King of Scots, was buried here. Margaret had invited a community of Benedictine monks to set up a priory at Dunfermline, and she was buried in the monastery that she founded, as was her husband and later their son, King David I. For the next two centuries, successive Scottish kings and queens were buried here, until the most famous incumbent, Robert the Bruce, was laid to rest within the walls.

Other than Robert the Bruce and Queen Margaret, none of the graves of the other kings and queens interred here is marked. That's because the abbey and its church have been substantially knocked about since the Reformation – so much so that the church you can visit today is two buildings in one. The old church is a beautiful piece of 12th-century architecture, built on the orders of David I, and the only intact remains of the early abbey. The monastic choir has long since fallen, and the new church that squats on its foundations, abutting the old nave, is a 19th-century creation.

If you want to see Robert the Bruce's memorial, you'll find it under the pulpit of the new church. However, if, like me, you prefer your arches round and Romanesque, you'll find more to divert you in the old church. Some of the decoration on the columns there is quite lovely and, unsurprisingly, given the age difference, there's much more of a sense of history to be found in this part of the abbey. Queen Margaret's original 11th-century church lies directly underneath the building, and you can see the foundations through grilles in the floor.

Margaret's memorial, oddly enough, is not in the church at all. Rather, it's around the back, immediately behind the new church. Margaret, for her notable piety, was canonised in 1249, and the following year a shrine was established for her saintly remains, of which only the outline and the plinth survive today. The shrine, as a relic of Catholic days, didn't fit with the 19th-century attitudes of the church builders, explains Penman: 'It being a Protestant church at that point, the only thing they made certain to keep outside the walls of this new church was the shrine of this queen who became a saint. She's since been marginalised, but in Scotland in the medieval period she was hugely important, and could have been such for medieval Britain had the monarchies continued to intermarry.'

What's interesting about Queen Margaret is that she was an English princess, granddaughter of the Anglo-Saxon king Edmund II. She was forced to flee England after the Norman Conquest and took refuge in the court of Malcolm III, eventually becoming his wife. Penman observes, 'Dunfermline Abbey is underestimated as possibly the place that would have become pre-eminent had England and Scotland remained more friendly and their monarchies continued to intermarry, which they did do in the 13th century and occasionally thereafter, usually to stop war. If the monarchies had continued to intermarry, would they have looked back on this saint and her husband as their founding couple?'

Perhaps because he was of mixed Scottish and English blood, their son David imported ideas and practices from the Norman kingdom to the south (it was probably Norman-English craftsmen who built his abbey here). However, the intermarrying couldn't stop hostility between the two countries. Trouble boiled over in the reign of Edward I of England, who made the abbey his winter campaign headquarters in 1303 as he drove his army into Scotland. He ordered that the monks' domestic buildings be destroyed, and the place was apparently in a parlous state when he left. It was Robert the Bruce, the man who fought back against the English incursions and famously won the battle at Bannockburn in 1314, who had Dunfermline Abbey rebuilt in readiness for his burial here. Today he is by far the most famous royal resident. Indeed, the tower of the new church has his name writ large at its apex so you can't be in any doubt as to who lies inside.

There's a lot to see beside the Abbey Church. The remains of the abbey and its accompanying guest quarters are still visible, with a particularly handsome gatehouse that now serves as the visitor entrance to the ruins. These domestic buildings are mostly 14th century, owing to the depredations visited on Dunfermline by Edward I. The monastic guest house would have been a grand place, fit for a Scottish king or queen to stay in. And stay they did – indeed, King James VI's wife Anna gave birth to their son Charles in one of the rooms here in 1600. Three years later, James VI of Scotland became also James I of England when he succeeded to the throne of the childless Elizabeth I in the Union of the Crowns of 1603. His Dunfermline-born son followed him as Charles I of England and Scotland, thereby rekindling the Anglo-Scottish links that lay at the heart of the abbey's foundation.

Dunfermline Abbey
Dunfermline, Fife KY12 7PE
01383 724586
www.dunfermlineabbey.co.uk

St Davids Cathedral and Bishops' Palace, Pembrokeshire

Nominated by Ralph Griffiths, professor emeritus of history, Swansea University

'Where Welsh Christianity and nationalism are entwined'

Christianity has shaped British history. In the view of Ralph Griffiths, St Davids, with its beautiful cathedral, ruined bishops' palace and delightful medieval city, is 'one of the most significant sites in the history of Christianity in the British Isles, and one of the earliest'.

According to legend and his later *Life*, St David was born around 600 in this southwestern extremity of Wales and later died here, having founded his monastery in the interim on the current cathedral site in St Davids. Firm details of his life are scarce. He has come down to us as a Christian prophet and miracle worker, who was involved in the conversion of pagans across Britain in the 6th century. A cult grew up around him after his death, and by the 10th century, he appears to have been viewed as the leading Welsh saint. Indeed, his successors at his church in St Davids were often regarded as archbishops in the early medieval period.

As with other important Christian coastal sites, St Davids was a regular target for Viking attacks from the late 8th century onwards, and, interestingly, King Alfred in Wessex called upon Asser, the Bishop of St Davids, to help him re-establish intellectual life in his kingdom after his Viking trouble in the 9th century. Rulers in England had long recognised the significance of this place. So as well as being a focus for Welsh identity, St Davids was also used in England's colonisation (both physical and intellectual) of

Wales. The first Norman king in England, William the Conqueror, wisely recognised its importance and came here to pray in 1081. William's son Henry I encouraged English settlement in South Wales during the early 12th century, so Anglo-Norman influence was pressed west. In the 1120s a new Norman cathedral was built on the site, but that itself was replaced by the present structure, which was begun in 1182.

'I suppose the Normans regarded it as important to their religion, but they also saw it as a means of helping to exert their control in Wales after the conquest,' says Griffiths. 'I think it might have helped. The diocese covers primarily central and southern Wales, where the bulk of the immigrant settlers would have made for. A fair proportion of the bishops of St Davids would have been of English or immigrant stock.'

Those bishops, after the Norman Conquest, were given the status of Marcher Lords, and thus a range of independent powers. While they harboured ambitions to regain their pre-Conquest archbishop status, they did not actually manage it. However, as Marcher Lords, they did have a reasonably free hand in their affairs, as they were afforded substantial concessions by the Anglo-Norman kings in return for their help in imposing, spreading and consolidating their rule over Wales. What you see with the cathedral at St Davids is, in a sense, a demonstration in stone of the spread of influence from England into Wales.

That influence, of course, has not gone unchallenged. Both St David and St Davids have, says Griffiths, 'become a talisman for Welsh identity and nationhood'. The Welsh leader Owain Glyndŵr, who rebelled against the English king Henry IV, outlined a blueprint for his independent nation against the 'fury of the barbarous Saxons' in 1406. This would have had St Davids as the archbishopric of the Welsh Church. He also perhaps had St Davids in mind as the site for one of the two universities that he envisaged for Wales.

Glyndŵr's rebellion did not free Wales from the English, but St Davids continued to be an important spiritual centre, attracting a steady stream of pilgrims. It is said that, back in the 12th century, Bishop Bernard, the first Norman bishop of St Davids, secured a papal privilege that meant two pilgrimages to St Davids were equal to a single one to Rome. From then until the break from Rome in the mid 16th century, a steady stream of pilgrims made their way to west Wales, bringing with them money and stature.

You can see evidence of this wealth in the cathedral gatehouse. This would have been part of the 14th-century enclosure of the cathedral city and is the only survivor of the four gatehouses that originally guarded the city walls. In the gatehouse now is a decent exhibition that takes you through the story of St David, the cathedral and the city. On the other side of it, the 13th- and 14th-century Bishops' Palace, though now ruined following the decline in pilgrims after the Reformation, still demonstrates the power and wealth of the medieval bishops here.

Nothing remains of St David's early chapels now, but the cathedral itself has some marvellous medieval survivals, now handsomely presented after an extensive conservation project. The nave is a particularly interesting place if you crane your neck upwards beyond the Norman walls to the wooden ceiling. Norman churches tended to have stone-vaulted ceilings, but here the foundations weren't as deep as they might have been, and a 13th-century earthquake exposed the problem, so a wooden roof was erected instead.

One aspect of the cathedral, which strikes you as you approach, is that it's in a dip, hidden from view almost until you come upon it at the foot of a valley. Churches tend to be more prominent in the landscape than this, but being so close to the sea, and so handily positioned for Viking raiders to descend upon, made lying low a sensible position. The medieval settlement that grew up around the cathedral would have blown its cover somewhat, but by then the Vikings were no longer marauding through the Irish Sea.

It would be folly not to make at least a quick trip to the stunningly beautiful Pembrokeshire coast to see from where those Vikings would have approached. Aside from taking in the view, you get a sense of how strategically positioned St Davids was. Although perhaps now it seems a little out of the way, in the medieval period it was on a major land–sea route linking Ireland, Wales and England. A good place to make for is the nearby headland, where you can see St Non's Chapel and Well (St Non being St David's mother). Your peace may be disturbed by drenched and excitable gangs coming up from the cliffs, but do not fear – it's not the Vikings returning, but rather the local adventure centres bringing back their clients from a spell leaping off the cliffs into the foam below. St Davids has morphed now from religious capital to adrenalin capital of Wales, but its historical and spiritual significance remains.

St Davids Cathedral
The Close, St Davids, Pembrokeshire SA62 6RH
01437 720202
www.stdavidscathedral.org.uk

Tintagel Castle, Cornwall

*Nominated by Nicholas Orme, emeritus professor
of history, University of Exeter*

'Where Britain got a national myth to believe in'

With a casual glance, you could be deceived into thinking that Tintagel is
nothing more than a tacky tribute to teashops and trinkets. Well, it is all
that, but beyond the village it's a beautiful place, with an evocative castle
on a peninsula jutting out from Cornwall's Atlantic north coast.

The reason behind the tourist trappings is also why Tintagel is
included in this selection of sites, for the place reeks of the legends of King
Arthur. This is all down to one man, Geoffrey of Monmouth, who in his
very creative 12th-century *History of the Kings of Britain* wrote that
Arthur was conceived at Tintagel. He doesn't give dates, but the backdrop
is the troubled times after the Roman withdrawal from Britain in the 5th
century AD, when the native Celtic people were locked in conflict with
incoming Anglo-Saxon invaders. Geoffrey's Arthur was the son of the
Celtic lord Uther Pendragon, who had an illicit liaison with Igerna, wife
of the Duke of Cornwall.

Hold on, you might be thinking. Arthur was a quasi-historical figure
at best, and a complete fabrication at worst. Whatever the historical truth
behind the story, Nicholas Orme believes that the legend of Arthur, as
devised by Geoffrey of Monmouth, holds an important place in the long
process of binding together the disparate peoples of the British Isles.

'Geoffrey didn't invent Arthur,' points out Orme. 'He had been
around earlier in Welsh literature, but Geoffrey made him a hero for the
whole of Britain and gave the island a figure around whom they could

Tintagel has been attracting Arthurian-inspired tourists for centuries

all rally. The genius of Geoffrey was that he managed to invent a celebrity with whom everybody could identify. In 12th-century Britain, there were several different races or nations – Normans, Anglo-Saxons, Cornish, Welsh and Scots – but he started to project an idea of Britain as one area, one nation and one kingdom, an idea into which everyone could buy, even the Scots. Long before there was a United Kingdom, Geoffrey invited them all to rally around a single great historical figure: King Arthur.

Geoffrey of Monmouth was a Welsh churchman whom we don't know much about. He wrote several books, of which his *History of the Kings of Britain* is the most enduring. It charts the story of Britain from its earliest foundations to the coming of the Saxons, including Arthur's reign. Many of the events he describes appear to be pure fantasy to the modern reader, but for medieval audiences they struck a chord.

He lived in the first half of the 12th century, at a time when the Norman Conquest was becoming a distant memory and the barriers between the Normans and the English they conquered were breaking down. Indeed, another writer at the time said that you could no longer tell who was Norman and who was English.

So his *History* appeared at a time when Britain had different peoples coming together, sometimes forcibly, but without a national story that they could all subscribe to. Geoffrey provided one. In his Arthur he gives us a king of Celtic origin, who marries a woman of noble Roman descent, binds the Anglo-Saxons under his rule with his wise but firm kingship, brings Scotland under his control, and then goes off around Europe conquering various places before eventually defeating the forces of Rome itself. It's a story that not only gave all the various peoples of Britain a king they could 'own', but also one who put the British centre-stage in Europe. The Arthur story was so compelling that it soon became a Europe-wide hit.

Henry II, the King of England in Geoffrey's time, was no doubt delighted at the European prestige this new Arthur afforded the English monarchy. The monks of Glastonbury obligingly produced Arthur's tomb for him. And Henry was not alone in spotting the potential. Edward III was a notable Arthurian devotee, making Windsor his new Camelot in the 14th century, and Henry VIII, when breaking from Rome, referred to Geoffrey's Arthurian empire as justification for his creation of an independent sovereign English empire in the 1530s.

We don't know why Geoffrey settled on Tintagel to play such a key role in his story. However, we do know that the place was a centre of some importance in the post-Roman period, possibly the base of a local chieftain. The large number of buildings and the huge amount of imported 5th- and 6th-century Mediterranean pottery dug up in excavations here is evidence at least of some source of power and wealth. It's quite possible that legends of a great man having once lived at Tintagel reached Geoffrey's ears and inspired him to put two and two together and make it Arthur's Tintagel.

Geoffrey's stories were so popular that it wasn't long before Tintagel fulfilled its own prophecy and got the castle it deserved. In Geoffrey's time, the place belonged to a local gentleman of little importance, but by the 13th century the link between Arthur and Tintagel was so entrenched that Earl Richard of Cornwall, second son of King John, bought the land and built a castle there to match the stories. It's his castle, or at least its ruins, that you see today.

Richard, by dint of the peculiarities of mid-13th-century European politics, was both Earl of Cornwall and claimant to be King of Germany. By this time the Germans had become as keen on Arthur as everyone else, so it was politically a great boon for Richard to be able to portray himself as Arthur's heir, with the castle to prove it.

So go to Tintagel, visit Earl Richard's castle, enjoy the view out to sea, breathe in the salty atmosphere of Merlin's Cave below, and revel in the power of King Arthur, the legend who began to bind Britons together with a common national story. And if you don't much like the touristy side of Tintagel village, just remember that this is all part of the Arthur phenomenon too. Geoffrey was the first man to positively put Arthur on the map and link events with places, thereby creating the Arthur Trail. Places such as Glastonbury, Winchester, London and Caerleon, all became places of interest to Arthur's devotees on Geoffrey's say-so. The trinkets on sale in Tintagel's shops today are just the latest in a long line of Arthurian relics that have been peddled for centuries.

Tintagel Castle

Bossiney Road, Tintagel, Cornwall PL34 0HE

01840 770328

www.english-heritage.or.uk/daysout

Canterbury Cathedral, Kent

Nominated by Alixe Bovey, lecturer in medieval history, University of Kent

'Where the medieval clash between king and Church got bloody'

Down the steps in the northwest transept of Canterbury Cathedral, out of view of the stunning parallel columns and swooping vault of the nave, is the site of one of the all-time great stories of medieval history. It was here on 29 December 1170 that Thomas Becket, Archbishop of Canterbury and primary churchman in England, was murdered by knights acting on what they thought were the orders of England's King Henry II.

How did it come to this? Thomas Becket had been on a collision course with the king ever since his investiture as archbishop in 1162. Up to that point, Becket and Henry had been on good terms, and the king was expecting a pliable ally at the head of the Church. Becket turned out to be nothing of the sort, and the next years saw a power struggle between king and prelate. Becket managed to alienate most of his supporters and ended up in exile in France. The reconciliation in 1170 between the two went wrong, with Henry publicly expressing his fury at the archbishop's continued inflexibility in the now famous question, 'Who will rid me of this turbulent priest?' (or something along those lines). The knights took him at his word, and thus Becket was murdered.

You can visit where Becket died, the Martyrdom as it's known today, and you'll find it a suitably dark corner of this magnificent, multi-period structure. Standing there, it's not hard to visualise the gory episode when Becket's blood and brains were spattered across the flagstones by the swords of the four knights. If you open the wooden door to your left as you've descended the steps, you'll see the route that the archbishop would have taken on a dark and wintry afternoon from his palace and through the cloisters to seek refuge in his church from his angry assailants.

The murder of the archbishop is a story that's almost as well worn as the stones on which it occurred, but what happened next is surprising. Says Alixe Bovey, 'What's interesting is how fast news of it spread across Europe and how it scandalised everybody. Almost immediately, people started to report cures of things like blindness through the touch of Becket's blood. It was exciting in the medieval period to have an actual martyr (the great age of martyrs was the early Christian period), so Becket's murder harked back to the glory days of Christian oppression.'

The place where these miracles happened was the crypt, where the Canterbury monks placed Becket's body. You can head down into that tremendously well-preserved vaulted Norman space from the Martyrdom. Becket was declared a saint in 1173, so this was where the first cult visitors would have come. However, in 1174 the east end of the church was ravaged by a fire. The subsequent rebuilding, which led to the first major construction project in the new Gothic style, was made with the burgeoning power of Becket's cult firmly in mind.

'The chain of events from December 1170 to the fire of 1174 is really interesting. There has been some speculation by modern historians about the curious coincidence between the arrival of the new Gothic style and fires that destroyed Romanesque buildings,' remarks Bovey. 'It's been suggested that these fires might have been deliberate. Obviously medieval buildings were a lot more flammable than you might think. One historian, Peter Kidson, has written a provocative article suggesting that the monks themselves might have set fire to the building and engaged in a cover-up. Their motive might have been to reconstruct the building to accommodate the pilgrims that were coming. They didn't add a lot of square feet, but they did add an ambulatory around the east end and a very glamorous shrine for Becket. A pilgrim could make a journey around the building looking at various bits of his body.'

You can't make a similar pilgrimage around the church now because the great shrine that was constructed as the central part of the new east end was entirely removed on the orders of Henry VIII – a king who was not one to suffer dissent from the Church. However, you can see the place where Becket's body lay from 1174 until 1220 in the Trinity Chapel crypt of the church (and note the windows above the spot, from which the monks could keep an eye on the pilgrims below). You can also view the place where the shrine was from 1220 until 1538, directly above the crypt. It's now marked by a single burning candle, with a grand mosaic floor in front. To get there you come up the Pilgrim's Steps, then progress around the ambulatory with the medieval stained-glass windows your constant companions on the way. The chapel at the very back of the church, the Corona, would once have housed a rather grisly relic: part of Becket's skull. Apparently, the red sections of the pillars in front of the Corona were so coloured in order to signify the martyr's blood.

So despite the discouragements of Henry VIII, it's still possible to see how the whole building was dominated by the cult of the martyred St Thomas Becket. Henry II wisely dissociated himself from the murder and made a great play of his repentance and acceptance of the saintly power of his dead archbishop. He visited Canterbury ten times after the murder, on the first occasion, Bovey notes, 'completing the journey on foot and allowing himself to be ceremonially flogged, which is a fairly remarkable thing for a medieval king to submit to'.

The great rebuilding of the castle at Canterbury's nearest port, Dover, in the 1180s has been interpreted recently by the historian John Gillingham as a move by Henry to take firmer control of the pilgrim trade from the Continent, giving him a place to impress the stream of important dignitaries who were arriving from across the Channel to pay their respects to the martyr's memorial. So, rather perversely given the circumstances, the king managed to find a way to harness the power of the cult to his advantage.

To see the story of this dramatic moment in medieval history makes Canterbury Cathedral worth visiting, but there are other glories to enjoy at this site. Do take a wander around the walled precinct, which is a wondrous place of forgotten crumbling structures. Then perhaps pop into the Hospital of St Thomas the Martyr on the High Street to get a taste of the accommodation afforded to medieval pilgrims. But, of course, Canterbury has much more to offer. This was first a Roman city (and the excellent little Roman Museum will tell you about that), then a Saxon settlement, and notably, in 597, the site of the mission by St Augustine to bring Christianity back to Britain. And that brings us nicely back to the cathedral, for Augustine founded it, along with the nearby ruined St Augustine's Abbey, in his effort to restore the faith of the nation. The whole area has been designated a World Heritage Site, along with the little church of St Martin's, a short walk from the cathedral, which claims to be the oldest parish church in England still in use.

Canterbury Cathedral
11 The Precincts, Canterbury, Kent CT1 2EH
01227 762862
www.canterbury-cathedral.org

Runnymede, Berkshire
Nominated by Joanna Bourke, professor of history, Birkbeck College, University of London
'Where ideas of law and freedom were written down'

There's something very English about Runnymede. Perhaps it's the 1930s' tearooms and the National Trust car park; possibly it's the sight of the Thames flowing slowly past; or maybe it's the pleasant combination of oak woodland and buttercup meadow. Or perhaps it is linked to the signing of the Magna Carta, and all that implies for some of our national obsessions – liberty and democracy – which is so ingrained that it can't help but exude Englishness.

It was in these meadows, just down the road from Windsor Castle, that in 1215 King John put his seal to the Magna Carta, a document that has a continuing resonance far beyond its original intention. The great charter laid out ideas on human rights that have since provided the bedrock for civil liberties across the world.

According to Joanna Bourke, 'The document is an expression of feudal customs, but it retains its importance. The rhetoric of the Magna Carta is absolutely crucial to every period of history, including today, in terms of habeas corpus, trial by jury, prohibition of torture, due process of law, and the right of resistance. These are things that still preoccupy us.'

In the short term, this was an important moment. By 1215 King John had, for several years, been in conflict with his barons over taxation, foreign policy and his arbitrary government. Finding himself running out of allies, money and time, John was forced into making an accommodation with his rebellious barons that curbed his powers substantially. The provisions were contained in the charter that he agreed to at Runnymede on 15 June. With 63 clauses, it was a substantial document, known at the time as the Charter of Liberties, and designed both to solve the immediate problems of John's reign and to try to keep him to his word, which was something the king had no intention of doing. In fact, by mid July John had written to the pope asking him to annul it. That he died of dysentery in 1216, universally disliked by his barons, probably did more to fix the failings of his reign than the Magna Carta ever did.

However, the charter was not destined to become a mere footnote to an early 13th-century political crisis. It was reissued by John's successor Henry III and was passed into English law during Edward I's reign. Since then, it has been used as the basis for constitutional and political discourse down the centuries and across the world, taken up by those fighting for civil rights against despotism and slavery. Although some of the clauses in the document appear distinctly parochial today, and most have no continuing legal significance, it's probably the following words that continue to attract the most attention: 'No free man shall be seized or imprisoned, or stripped of his rights or possessions, or outlawed or exiled. Nor will we proceed with force against him, except by the lawful judgement of his equals or by the law of the land. To no one will we sell, to no one deny or delay right or justice.'

The idea of putting the law above the king has meant that campaigners throughout history have been able to use the Magna Carta for their own purposes. Interestingly, Bourke thinks that many people have missed a key point about the link between politics and economics: 'Everyone talks about the Magna Carta, which gives political and legal rights, but actually there's a second charter that I think needs to be more widely known, and that's the Charter of the Forest. This second charter gave economic rights – the freedom of the commons and the right to subsistence. There is a clear distinction made between political rights and economic rights, yet the two can only really work together.'

To see one of the original copies of Magna Carta itself you need to make the trip to the British Library in London, where it's on permanent display (or use its excellent website to see a virtual version), or go to Lincoln Castle or Salisbury Cathedral. There are other, later, copies scattered around the country too.

What's curious about visiting Runnymede today is that, despite its surface Englishness, there is a firm strand of American history present too. It's a pleasant walk from the car park to the Magna Carta memorial pagoda, which was established by the American Bar Association in 1957. On the way you pass by the Memorial Garden for the American President John F. Kennedy, which is in fact now American property, and between the two is a small oak tree with a plaque declaring that it was 'planted with soil from Jamestown, Virginia ... on the bicentenary of the Constitution of the United States of America'. The American Constitution, framed in 1787, looked to the Magna Carta as a template for stating rights and liberties.

You might want to round off your Runnymede trip with a walk up to the Commonwealth Air Forces Memorial on the hill overlooking the meadow. Opened in 1953 to commemorate the Allied Air Force casualties of the Second World War, it's a beautiful and sobering place, where you could let your thoughts run to those who have died fighting for the freedoms that were encapsulated 800 years earlier on the meadow below.

Runnymede
Near Old Windsor, Surrey
01784 432891
www.nationaltrust.org.uk

Dolbadarn Castle, Gwynedd
Nominated by Huw Pryce, professor of Welsh history, Bangor University
'Where the Welsh princes demonstrated their authority'

In the mid 13th century, Dolbadarn Castle was an obvious statement of power, particularly for anyone harbouring intentions of making uninvited inroads into Snowdonia via the Llanberis Pass. The castle sits on a rocky outcrop at the foot of the pass, its commanding position now somewhat overshadowed by the presence of the small tourist town of Llanberis just down-valley. Although its strategic importance has long been surpassed – an invading army could now just get the mountain train from the town to the top of Snowdon if they felt so inclined – its location remains magnificent.

Beneath the castle is a narrow spur of land that separates the twin lakes Padarn and Peris, while across Llyn Peris, on the far side of the valley, are the huge and darkly grey steps of the former Dinorwig slate mine (which itself has a fascinating and important story). Looking up the valley you see the crags and scree of the Snowdonian mountains. This all provides for a very photogenic backdrop to the castle's single, slate, round tower perched atop its crag. The tower survives to a height of several storeys, while the other buildings and walls that once surrounded it are now reduced to foundation level.

Without any surviving documentation, we can't be entirely sure about who built the castle, but it was most probably Llywelyn the Great, Prince of Gwynedd, who died in 1240. Llywelyn is thought to have been behind several castles in and around Snowdonia, which was the heart of his domain. The architecture is characteristic of other 13th-century Welsh fortifications, and the location of Dolbadarn fits the political scene in Llywelyn's time.

Llywelyn was born *c*.1173 into the ruling family of Gwynedd in north-west Wales. By this time, Anglo-Norman lords had taken possession of much of south Wales (see St Davids, page 76), while to the north, the area still in the hands of the native Welsh was divided under numerous princes. By the close of the 12th century, after several years of conflict with his relatives, Llywelyn had conquered Gwynedd and was addressing himself in charters as 'Prince of all north Wales'. Then, in 1201, he made an agreement with King John of England. Llywelyn agreed to do homage to the English ruler, while John acknowledged the territorial gains made by Llywelyn. This was the first written treaty between a Welsh ruler and an English king.

In the following decades Llywelyn successively clashed and made peace with the English, while expanding his powerbase in Wales. He led invasions into south and west Wales, and by 1216 was acknowledged as overlord of the other native Welsh rulers. In 1218 he made peace with the new English king Henry III at Worcester, where he did homage to Henry and undertook to get the other Welsh rulers to do the same.

Llywelyn emphasised his position as the leading man in Wales by building castles, and in this he followed the styles and technology employed by the Marcher Lords on the Welsh frontier. Castell y Bere further to the south and Degannwy to the north are both considered to have been Llywelyn's work, and in the 1230s he's thought to have sent his builders to Dolbadarn.

'In the longer story of British history, it captures a moment when there was still a powerful political entity in the west of Britain,' says Huw Pryce. 'It's a symbol of the power of the princes of Gwynedd in the 13th century. This wasn't a castle that was aimed at stopping mass invasion from England, but more about proclaiming authority over its own people. It was a sign of status, showing that they were up-to-date rulers adopting the latest technology. In the 13th century the number of stone buildings, especially on that scale, were few in Gwynedd, so its erection there would have made a very dramatic statement in its own right.'

Llywelyn was one of the greatest rulers of independent Wales and he certainly established himself as the pre-eminent Welsh prince. However, his wider pre-eminence died with him, as he did not succeed in getting England's Henry III to recognise his son and heir Dafydd as anything more than Prince of Gwynedd. When Dafydd himself died childless in 1246, Gwynedd suffered the regular fate of Welsh princedoms: division among rival claimants for the succession. Yet by the 1250s, Llywelyn ap Gruffudd, the grandson of Llywelyn the Great, had defeated his brothers and emerged as the next Prince of Gwynedd. As Pryce points out, Dolbadarn re-enters the story here: 'Dolbadarn also shows how the princes' power depended on defeating their kinsmen, as Llywelyn the Great's grandson, Llywelyn ap Gruffudd almost certainly imprisoned his brother Owain there from 1255 to 1277 – a fate recalled in antiquarian tradition from the 16th century onwards.'

Visiting Dolbadarn, you quickly realise that imprisonment in the perhaps comfortable, but certainly cramped, round tower must have been a suffocating experience for Owain. Nevertheless, Llywelyn ap Gruffudd couldn't afford to have potentially rebellious brothers on the loose while he endeavoured to regain his grandfather's mantle as leader of all the native Welsh. By 1258 he had succeeded, through force and alliance, and having probably received the allegiance of all the Welsh princes, in doing just that. He was styling himself Prince of Wales, a title that was formally acknowledged by Henry III in 1267. The control of Wales by a native Welsh prince was, however, a short-lived episode. The conquest of the principality in the 1280s by Henry III's successor in England, Edward I, was just around the corner (see Conwy Castle, page 99).

Edward's victory over the Welsh spelt the end of Dolbadarn's significance. By building the huge and magnificent Caernarfon Castle downstream of it (and adding insult to injury by reusing Dolbadarn timbers in its construction), the English king deleted any military potency it had possessed. Certainly, it was a pointed gesture by Edward to slight the princely castle and make it part of his new house of power.

Centuries later, the dilapidated castle enjoyed a renaissance of sorts. By the 18th century, romantic ruins were all the rage as subjects for landscape painters. Famously, J.M.W. Turner exhibited his *Dolbadern Castle* (sic) at the Royal Academy in 1802, and once more brought the place to the attention of the public. The message his painting imparts is one of melancholy rather than majesty. No doubt that wouldn't have been the legacy Llywelyn the Great hoped for when he built it in the 1230s. Despite that, it remains a powerful reminder of a time when the Welsh princes were a force to be reckoned with.

Dolbadarn Castle
500 metres (½ mile) southeast of Llanberis on the A4086, Gwynedd
Grid reference: SH 5859
www.cadw.wales.gov.uk

Westminster Abbey, London

Nominated by David Carpenter, professor of medieval history, King's College London

'Where an English king brought God on to his side'

Westminster Abbey is, says David Carpenter, 'a great national church, the coronation church and the centre of the nation'. Today packs of visitors, with audio guides clamped firmly to their ears, vie for space with the assembled statuary of the great and the good of Britain's past as they funnel around the one-way system. There is so much to see here, so many memorials worth noting, so many royal tombs, so many echoes of great events, and so many architectural highlights to enjoy that it perhaps doesn't do the place justice to focus on just one aspect. Yet there is one particular reason for visiting, and that is to understand what King Henry III was trying to achieve with the abbey in the mid 13th century.

Edward the Confessor, the penultimate Anglo-Saxon king before the arrival of the Normans under William the Conqueror, had a church built here in 1065. It was called the West Minster to distinguish it from the East Minster – St Paul's Cathedral. Edward was buried in this church when he died in 1066. However, much of the current structure dates from 1245 to 1272, when Henry III had the place rebuilt with a specific plan in mind.

First, he was endeavouring to create 'the most magnificent church in the world'. The abbey is acknowledged as a Gothic masterpiece, and the view as you enter through the great north door is indeed a sight to behold – in Carpenter's opinion 'one of the most breathtakingly beautiful in the world'.

But his second reason, and the motive for the magnificence, is the interesting one, as it gives us a window into the world of this particular medieval period. Henry III had the church built essentially to win the favour of a saint, none other than Edward the Confessor, who had been canonised in 1161. 'Henry III in the 1230s became passionately devoted to Edward and adopted him as his patron saint,' explains Carpenter. 'He believed Edward was a saint of mighty power sitting at God's right hand.'

Henry's view was that if he won the dead king's saintly favour, Edward would support him in this life and shepherd him into the next. The king, and all medieval people, would have believed that God intervened directly in day-to-day affairs, so Henry was banking on Edward being able to intercede with God on his behalf. The way he intended to win Edward's favour was to build this magnificent abbey as a great offering to him. It was an enormous gesture of gratitude, and a very clear statement to everyone who saw the abbey being built, right in the centre of his realm, that Henry was backed by his saintly predecessor.

Immediately as you enter the abbey today, if you look straight across the church into the south transept you can see evidence of Henry's homage to the Confessor. Directly underneath the Rose Window, you'll see four sculptures high up on the wall. The two flanking figures are angels, and the two central figures are Edward the Confessor on the left and a pilgrim with his hand outstretched on the right. This scene would have been pivotal in Henry III's designs, as it depicts a story from the life of Edward, where he met a pilgrim and gave him a ring. The pilgrim transpired to be none other than St John the Evangelist, who later told two English pilgrims that he would be escorting Edward up to heaven, and asked them to take the ring back to England with them as proof of his message. The story underlined the key idea that Henry needed to get across to visitors to his church, as it was in essence a guarantee of the saintly power of Edward: a demonstration to all who entered the building of the power of the saint behind the throne. The sculpture no longer carries such a powerful message as it would have done in the 13th century, first because most visitors are no longer familiar with the story, and second because the sculptures have at some point in the ensuing seven and a half centuries lost their heads.

What hasn't lost its power is the shrine to the Confessor, which was to be the centrepoint of Henry's new church. It is a potent monument, but also a fragile one, so public access is restricted, though certain tours will allow you entrance. If you can't get in, you can catch a glimpse as you pass along the South Ambulatory. Within the shrine is the Confessor's coffin inside a stone casing, and on top of that a towering wooden canopy. Around the shrine are the tombs of several English kings and queens, Henry III included. The stone base of Edward's tomb would originally have been decorated with Cosmati work, a luxurious, expensive and intricate 13th-century mosaic style. Most of that work has been lost, but happily, just on the other side of Edward's shrine, on the High Altar, the Cosmati pavement has just been restored after decades hiding under a carpet, so you can look at that to get a sense of the former magnificence of the tomb.

The pavement is stunning. It depicts the universe and includes a riddling inscription (of which only part survives) that enables one to work out the date of its end – the Last Judgement. The idea was that anyone who stood in front of the pavement would be awed and alarmed at the threat of judgement to come, then look past the pavement to the shrine of the Confessor and realise that through the intercession of the saint one could gain salvation. Sadly, the 15th-century screen now blocks the view from the pavement to the shrine, so the effect is somewhat lost, even in the unlikely circumstance of a modern visitor being able to unravel the universal riddle before them.

The presence of the highly prized Cosmati work illustrates the lengths to which Henry went in his quest for magnificence in the abbey. He certainly achieved that, but he failed in his larger ambition, which was for all his people to share in the patronage of Edward the Confessor. He hoped that pilgrims would flood to the shrine with gifts to the saint, but they didn't. 'The whole thing was a flop,' notes Carpenter, and Edward never became a popular saint.

Despite this, Westminster Abbey continued to grow and prosper, albeit with some hairy moments during the Reformation and Common-wealth, as the coronation church and principal royal burial place for English monarchs. That, combined with its role as memorial site for centuries of very important people, means that a single trip will not be enough to take it all in. A good place to start, though, is to whip back to the 13th century and take a tour into the medieval mindset and motives of Henry III.

Westminster Abbey

20 Dean's Yard, London SWIP 3PA

020 7222 5152

www.westminster-abbey.org

Conwy Castle, Conwy

Nominated by Deborah Youngs, lecturer in medieval history, Swansea University

'Where Edward I imposed his rule on the Welsh'

You can't fail to be impressed by Conwy Castle today, a romantic vision of medieval masonry framed by the racing river Conwy below and the mountains of Snowdonia behind. Remember, though, that in the 13th century it was even more imposing than it is today. Its now grit-grey stonework would have been painted dazzling white, and of course it wasn't so much of a ruin back then. Its purpose was to dominate and cow the locals, and emphasise the power of the king who built it.

That king was Edward I, the English ruler who led armies into both Wales and Scotland in pursuit of dominance over his neighbours (see Stirling Castle, page 103). In Wales, Edward's opponent was Llywelyn ap Gruffudd, Prince of Gwynedd. Edward's father Henry III had recognised Llywelyn as Prince of Wales in 1267 (see Dolbadarn Castle, page 91), but Llywelyn was not one to bow to English overlordship. When Edward came to the throne in 1272, the Welshman did not attend his coronation or pay homage. Edward could not let this slight pass unattended, so in 1277 he sent his troops into Wales. The English quickly overwhelmed the Welsh, and Llywelyn was forced to sign a very severe peace settlement.

However, that wasn't the end of the matter. Llywelyn rose up in revolt in 1282, after his brother Dafydd had provoked the English with a surprise attack. Once more, Edward's men marched west, and once more they were victorious. Llywelyn was killed at the end of the year, while Dafydd was captured the following summer and afforded a very unpleasant traitor's execution.

During the revolt, while Dafydd was still at large in Snowdonia, Edward had his campaign headquarters at the strategically important and symbolically vital site of Aberconwy, which commanded the Conwy valley and routes into the mountains, and was home to a Cistercian abbey where Llewelyn's ancestors were buried. Even before Dafydd's capture, Edward started building at Aberconwy, and soon the settlement was over-looked by Conwy Castle and ringed by the great town wall. Construction was rapid; it's thought that the work was finished by 1287, at which point

Edward's victory was complete. By then, the Statute of Rhuddlan in 1284 had placed the conquered principality under English rule and English law.

'When you go to the castle, you see a magnificent building that poets and painters have called sublime and picturesque,' notes Deborah Youngs. 'Because we have that romantic view, we tend to forget that the castle was there for the subjugation of a people. It was an integral part of the conquest that spelt the end of an independent native Wales. King Edward was making sure that it was the end of the princely dynasties. English rule would dominate in Wales from then on.'

Conwy was just one of a network of castles erected by Edward to cement his grip in north Wales. Caernarfon was the royal centre, while Harlech and Beaumaris were also notably impressive constructions. Edward's aim, says Youngs, was to remove any doubt as to who was in charge: 'You can see how psychologically this was going to have a damaging impact. They were put up very quickly and on a scale never seen here before. It said to the Welsh, "This is a power far superior to you." They were also placed strategically next to the sea so they could always be supplied and the garrisons fed.'

Conwy's self-sufficiency was further enhanced by the planted, defended town that was built along with it. The place was designed to be a centre of administration, and the civilians, most of whom were English people brought in from Lancashire and Cheshire, needed security as much as the soldiers. The uniformity and fantastic preservation of both castle and town walls are what make the place such a draw today. You can still walk along most of the length of the town wall, and if you make your way to the Upper Gate, you have a cracking view down towards the castle.

The castle itself sits on a natural rock outcrop right next to the river. Externally, the round towers and ramparts are in good shape, but inside the buildings have lost their roofs, so you can look down into the shell of the great hall from the wall walk. There are eight towers, all of which you can clamber up, so you can be assured of some good exercise here, as well as a series of bracingly good views from the top. Both exercise and views would have been in short supply for anyone unfortunate enough to have found themselves holed up in the prison tower. The basement here, with its doorless, windowless dungeon cut down into the rock below the castle, offers a disturbing glimpse of medieval punishment. Other parts of the castle offered considerably more appealing quarters, befitting its role as a royal residence. The King's Tower, great chamber and royal chapel give a sense of the former majesty of the place.

Conwy, and the other castles in Edward's iron chain around Snowdonia, have been designated a World Heritage Site, and rightly receive a lot of visitors. They represent some of the finest survivals of medieval fortifications, and speak of a vital period in Anglo-Welsh relations. For some today, they remain an unwelcome reminder of English imperialism over Wales, and of course they weren't much loved by the Welsh when they were built. However, as Youngs points out: 'Through the 14th century there was accommodation and cooperation. Occupation could still generate tension, but you get a sense of a Welsh acceptance of the status quo.'

Owain Glyndŵr challenged that status quo when he led the Welsh revolt against the English at the start of the 15th century (see Harlech Castle, page 122). Conwy was captured and the medieval town buildings completely burnt down. Despite this, the medieval street layout does survive quite well today, and the half-timbered Aberconwy House deserves a visit as one of the first generation of houses built after Owain's uprising. The medieval St Mary's and All Saints Church in the centre of the town is also worth exploring. This was the former Cistercian abbey that once housed the mortal remains of native Welsh princes. Edward I forced the monks to uproot and set up a new abbey 13 km (8 miles) away at Maenan. A master of the symbolic, the English king marked the end of the Gwynedd princely dynasty by depriving them of their burial place and imposing his bright white castle over their sacred ground.

Conwy Castle
Conwy LL32 8AY
01492 592358
www.cadw.wales.gov.uk

Stirling Castle, Stirling

Nominated by Michael Brown, lecturer in history, University of St Andrews

'Where Scottish independence survived and prospered'

Stand on the battlements of Stirling Castle and you can see various monuments to the Scottish fight for independence against the English in the late 13th and early 14th centuries. Its elevated position on a rocky crag over the valley of the river Forth means that you can view Stirling Bridge, not far from where Scotland's braveheart William Wallace and Andrew Murray defeated an English army in 1297. Beyond is the Victorian monument raised to Wallace, a huge tower on the skyline. Swing your eyes right and, if the weather's on your side, you might be able to catch a glimpse of the flagpole that marks the spot where Robert the Bruce defeated Edward II at Bannockburn in 1314.

As Michael Brown explains, geography is the key: 'If you look at the way Scotland develops, in terms of the early kingdom, it's a frontier post – Scotland starts at the Forth. The bridge over the river at Stirling is a boundary point, so the castle on this huge outcrop of volcanic rock right next to the bridge is in a hugely significant strategic location. In the wars from 1296 onwards, and particularly in the 20 years after then, Stirling was repeatedly taken and retaken. The battles of 1297 at Stirling Bridge, 1298 at Falkirk, 1314 at Bannockburn, the big clashes in that first period of warfare, are all about the custody and control of Stirling and the crossing.'

The Wars of Independence commenced after the untimely death of the Scottish king Alexander III in 1286, and his heir Margaret of Norway in 1290. King Edward I of England was asked to adjudicate between the rival claimants to the vacant throne, Robert Brus and John Balliol. He took the opportunity to press the case for his overlordship of the Scottish Crown, and Edward's choice, Balliol, acknowledged the English king as such. The Scots, none too happy with this outcome, concluded a treaty with France, England's enemy, for protection against Edward's advances. Riled, Edward immediately marched north and crushed the Scottish army at Dunbar in 1296, deposing Balliol and sending him into captivity. Stirling Castle was soon in English hands.

William Wallace and Andrew Murray led the resistance against the English, recording their notable victory at Stirling Bridge in 1297, but their success was short lived: they were defeated by Edward at Falkirk the following year. Nevertheless, Edward was unable to clamp down comprehensively on the Scots, who retook Stirling Castle in 1299. English armies marched north in 1300, 1301 and 1303, but it was their recapture of Stirling Castle in 1304 that marked an end to the first phase of the Wars of Independence.

'If you're looking for one set piece for Stirling's significance,' says Brown, 'that's the siege of 1304, when it was blockaded for months. Edward I finally drew together his siege engines from across Scotland. The surrender of Stirling was, from Edward's perspective, the end of the war. From the other side, it was an indication of what Edward was up against. An English chronicler reported the Scots as saying that they weren't holding out for any king – there was no active king – they were fighting for the lion, the symbol of Scottish kingship.'

So with those sentiments in mind, it's no surprise to note that 1304 wasn't the end of the matter. In 1306 Robert the Bruce, grandson of the overlooked Brus claimant to the throne of the 1290s, had himself crowned at Scone Palace. Edward I died of dysentery the year after, and Robert I, King of Scots, spent the next few years consolidating his position and ejecting English garrisons. It wasn't until 1314 that Edward II of England arrived to exert his authority, with the English soldiers holding out in Stirling Castle committed to surrender to the Scots by midsummer unless they were relieved. Battle was joined at Bannockburn: Edward lost, though Robert I's position wasn't secured until later in his reign, helped in some measure by the issuing of the Declaration of Arbroath (see Arbroath Abbey, page 111).

All this action revolved around Stirling Castle, yet there is little left in the fabric today that dates back to the Wars of Independence. Robert the Bruce had the place slighted to prevent it falling back into English hands.

'In its interior the castle is a Renaissance palace,' says Brown. 'Because of its military importance and its historical connections, it's a place where the Scottish kings continued to invest a lot of money. When you go inside the castle, and partly because of the damage done to it by Bruce and others, there's practically nothing you can see dating from the Wars of Independence period. What you see is a castle modified for use as a living space for the Stuart kings of the 15th and 16th centuries. You get a sense of the development of Scotland, its survival following the Wars of Independence, and its flowering as a late medieval/early modern monarchy. That's what people going to Stirling will see. It's not like the Tudor palaces; it's much more like the French chateaux.'

The best place to appreciate this continuing story is to go and stand in the centre of the Inner Close. There you are surrounded on all sides by architectural monuments to the Stuart kings of the 16th century. James IV, King of Scots from 1488 to 1513, built the Great Hall and the Old Building; his son James V built the Royal Palace; and his grandson James VI built the Chapel Royal in 1594. All these buildings are worth a look. The Great Hall has been renovated and replastered to present it as it might have been when constructed. It's the largest great hall ever built in Scotland, and boasts an impressive new hammerbeam roof. Inside, the Chapel Royal feels like it's been plucked out of Renaissance Italy, while the exterior of the Royal Palace does indeed resemble a French chateau, withstatuary lining its walls and ornate decoration throughout.

The Stuart dynasty took on the baton of an independent Scotland from Robert I and his successors, and Stirling Castle was safe ground for them. The place was a nursery for several future Stuart kings, and a major royal residence for sitting monarchs. Through the grand buildings they had built here, you can plainly see the power and confidence they came to gain. It was James VI, the chapel builder, who came to the throne of England as James I following the death of Queen Elizabeth in 1603, thereby putting the two nations on a road to union that would not have seemed likely in the time of Robert the Bruce.

Stirling Castle
Castle Wynd, Stirling FK8 1EJ
01786 450000
www.stirlingcastle.gov.uk

Longthorpe Tower, Cambridgeshire
Nominated by Richard Jones, lecturer in landscape history, University of Leicester
'Where you can peek into the medieval mind'

Neither a great sweeping drive through manicured parkland nor a rural ramble along disued paths is needed to take you to Longthorpe Tower. This medieval building must have one of the most incongruous settings of all the places featured in this book, squatting as it does among houses in suburban obscurity on the edge of Peterborough. On the outside it's a fairly unremarkable place: a small, square, though clearly venerable stone tower, almost hidden by the modern residential scatter around it. Inside, however, it's a different matter. Climb a few steps to the door that opens into the first floor and smack, you're back in the Middle Ages.

The tower isn't big enough to accommodate more than one small room on each floor, but when you step into that first floor chamber, you'll see that the walls are alive with medieval paintings. Richard Jones describes it: 'We're dealing here with a very small room, but one with extraordinarily wide horizons. It takes us into the whole mental world of the medieval period. It's a cosmology. If you are interested in medieval ideas about the macrocosm and the microcosm, the big being reflected in the little, this one chamber does that, because the murals that adorn all four sides of this space and the ceiling as well reflect how people were trying to explain the world around them in the 14th century. It's a tiny space that takes you everywhere.'

What you're looking at is a remarkable survival of 14th-century domestic decoration, the like of which you won't find anywhere else in England. The tower is part of a larger house (which still survives but is not open to the public), probably built in the late 13th or early 14th century by a steward of Peterborough Abbey. The first floor of the tower is thought to have been the lord's private apartment. At some point in the first half of the 14th century, he had his chamber painted. We don't know too much about the later history of the tower, but the walls were subsequently whitewashed and the painting beneath forgotten. During the Second World War, the tower was requisitioned for the Home Guard. Once peace resumed, a man whose name deserves to be celebrated, Mr Hugh Horrell, was going to redecorate the place after the soldiers had departed. He noticed that there was something unusual under the whitewash, called in the experts, and so the whole amazing artistic spectacle was revealed and saved.

What you can see today are paintings that cut across the breadth of the medieval existence, from spirituality to everyday life. A large part of the imagery is devoted to biblical figures and scenes, but there are also portrayals of morality messages, and some murals that appear to show purely secular themes and stories. It's high-quality, characteristically medieval artwork, and the preservation is exceptional. The colours would have been crisper back in the 14th century, and there are a few patches where the paintings have not survived, but for the most part, you're looking at exactly the same decorative scheme that the minor medieval lord who commissioned the decoration would have enjoyed.

You will be able to make out the images and admire the workmanship, but unless you're a medieval scholar, you probably won't get the messages that underpin the murals. Happily, you can only visit the tower as part of a guided tour on certain Sundays, so there will be someone there to explain what you're looking at. What will surely strike you, as you try to understand what the paintings are all about, is the distance that they highlight between the average person today and the average person in the Middle Ages.

'Here we're dealing with a world that isn't fully literate,' explains Jones, 'where images have more power than the written word. With Longthorpe we're not dealing with top-ranking members of the seigneury. We're talking about ordinary people. Here a minor local lord is playing with the big scholastic, philosophical and theological questions, having these ideas represented to him in this mural. One of the things that should be of interest to us is how far these big ideas might have percolated down through the social orders. Did peasants, I ask myself, understand the world in the same way as scholars? For me, Longthorpe is a lynchpin in that chain. If these ideas have got down to a local lord acting as a steward of an estate, it's possible they could easily have been communicated to those who worked the fields. And suddenly you realise that the way they are thinking about how to get their crops to grow is being informed by some really big, powerful, but not very modern, ideas. Sometimes I suspect that because we can visit where these people lived, we think that they were like us, but they weren't. Their points of reference that helped them to orientate themselves in the world were entirely different from ours. Consequently, despite the short distance of time that separates us from them, what the murals at Longthorpe remind us is that their world view is entirely alien to the way we think about things.'

Alien views they may have had, but some things at least don't need any explanation. The portrayals of bitterns and curlews on the north wall, for example, are clearly depictions of local fenland birds. In stark contrast to that familiarity, you probably won't recognise the creature on the panel opposite, which is graphically releasing the contents of its bowels on to an unfortunate individual standing to its rear. This is the mythical bonnacon, a curious and rather unpleasant creature that (I hope) you won't find in the fens along with the bitterns and curlews.

The walls on the upper floor of the tower are not painted, so you have to content yourself with the one room of riches. It is an extraordinary survival, though, and a hint at what might have been a much broader trend. A fair amount of medieval painting has come down to us in churches and cathedrals, but it's very rare to find it in private, secular houses. Therefore, if you want to get a handle on how the medieval man in the street might have thought, Longthorpe Tower is a perfect place to go – all the more so for the fact that the moment you step outside you'll probably bump into the modern man on the street, which will make for a handy comparison.

Longthorpe Tower

Thorpe Road, Peterborough, Cambridgeshire PE3 6XP

01536 203230

www.english-heritage.org.uk/daysout

Arbroath Abbey, Angus

Nominated by Ted Cowan, emeritus professor of Scottish history, University of Glasgow

'Where the Scots articulated a vision of liberty'

In 1951 the Stone of Scone, the Scottish Stone of Destiny, was left near the High Altar of Arbroath Abbey. Four Scottish students had previously extricated it from Westminster Abbey. It was the first time that the sacred artefact on which medieval Scottish kings were crowned had been north of the border since 1296, when Edward I of England had brought it south in triumph after his victorious Scottish campaign (see Stirling Castle, page 103). Arbroath Abbey was just as much a ruin in 1951 as it is today, but back then the students wouldn't have had to sneak the stone through the smart new visitor centre that now welcomes you to the site.

That visitor centre provides a fantastic first-floor viewing gallery from which you can survey the broken walls and pillar bases outside. The exhibition tells the story behind the ruins, dwelling particularly on the moment that inspired those students to choose this abbey as the appropriate place to deposit the Stone of Scone – the issuing in 1320 of the document that we now call the Declaration of Arbroath.

When the declaration was being drawn up, Arbroath Abbey would have been a mighty church, already venerable and rich. The Scottish king William I founded the place in 1178 in memory of the martyred Thomas Becket (see Canterbury Cathedral, page 84) and was buried there in 1214. In between times, he granted the new abbey custody of the Monymusk Reliquary, a casket that contained the relics of St Columba (see Iona, page 30), and that lent the foundation particular national resonance. A century later, that casket was carried into battle at Bannockburn in 1314 to offer saintly support to the Scots under Robert the Bruce against the English led by Edward II. It worked. The Scots won. Bannockburn, fought within view of the walls of Stirling Castle, was a great victory in the Scottish Wars of Independence. Edward II fled south, and English inroads into Scotland were significantly undone. Robert the Bruce became Scotland's hero of independence.

However, Edward refused to accept Robert as the rightful king of the Scots, so the Scots decided to write to the pope to back up their claim to autonomy from England, and at the same time to ask him to rescind the excommunication that had been placed on Robert the Bruce back in 1306 for the murder of a rival to the Scottish throne, John Comyn. And that's where the Declaration of Arbroath comes in, because this is the letter that the nobles of Scotland sent to Rome. It was probably written by clerks in Arbroath Abbey, whose Abbot Bernard was chancellor to Robert the Bruce. Given Arbroath's location on the east coast, it was a good place from which to get the letter to the Continent without fear of interference from the English.

The eloquence of the document is its shining asset. Its language and sentiments sound surprisingly modern in parts. It first details the pedigree of the Scots, before launching into an attack on Edward for unjustly laying claim to their land, then goes on to talk about Robert the Bruce, whose rule, it says, is based 'on right according to our laws and customs … [and] the due consent and assent of us all'. Curiously, the letter then moves on to explain that even though Robert the Bruce is ruling by right and in right-eous style, if he ever agrees to make Scotland subject to the English, the letter-writing barons will drive him out and put another man on the throne.

'The interesting thing about that clause is that it seems to be the first European articulation of the contractual theory of monarchy in an abstract context. They are articulating what much later becomes known as the doctrine of popular sovereignty,' says Ted Cowan. 'Then they go on to say something that everybody of a certain persuasion in Scotland knows about: "For as long as a hundred of us remain alive we shall never surrender; it is not for glory, nor riches nor honours, that we are fighting but for freedom alone, which no honest person will lose but with life itself." In the first part you've got an appeal to constitutionalism, and in the second an appeal to the dignity of freedom. That is now turned into something called Tartan Day. So on every 6 April the declaration is memorialised in various coun-tries around the world. It's become something that is para-historical.'

Para-historical it may be, but back in the 1320s, the letter was a public relations success that did have an impact on the politics of its day. It brought about a truce in the first place, and then a treaty with England in 1328, which recognised the right of Scotland to be free and ruled by its own lawful king. That makes it an important part of the story of Scotland's firm resistance to English efforts to control and subdue it.

The rather magnificent ruin that you'll find today is in its present condition because of the Scottish Reformation, which in 1560 effectively ended monastic life here. From that point until the early 19th century, the abbey buildings became a useful source of construction material for the people of Arbroath. Nevertheless, there's still enough upstanding for you to get a sense of what it once was. The large, circular window sitting high in the lonely wall of the south transept is particularly attention-grabbing. Below that lie the pointed arches in the wall that once formed the base of the east end of the church, and just in front of that is where the high altar would have been, and where the Stone of Scone found its way in 1951.

Given the past significance and continued modern resonance of the document that bears its name, Arbroath Abbey holds a particular place in Scottish history. To understand better how and why the Scots were able to fend off the martial advances of the English in the Wars of Independence, and why the sentiments in the Declaration of Arbroath continue to excite passions today, the abbey's elegant remains are the place to visit. As Cowan notes: 'If you're looking for somewhere iconic and of national importance in Scotland, that's Arbroath.'

Arbroath Abbey
Abbey Street, Arbroath, Angus DD11 1EG
01241 878756
www.historic-scotland.gov.uk

Lincoln's Inn, London

Nominated by John Hudson, professor of legal history,
University of St Andrews
'Where English law has taken shape'

Charles Dickens fixed the Old Hall of Lincoln's Inn at the heart of a London-wide fog in the opening of his Victorian epic *Bleak House*, his point being to mount an attack on lawyerly obfuscation and the failings of the legal system at the time. The Old Hall today is free of any such fog, as it is no longer the High Court of Chancery (civil law) as it was in Dickens' day. Major civil cases are now decided across the road from Lincoln's Inn, at the Royal Courts of Justice, leaving the Old Hall as a venue for conferences and events, as well as being open to tourists (at least to those who have joined a tour of the inn).

The hall certainly merits a peek inside. For the most part it dates back to 1490, making it the oldest surviving building here. It boasts a fine original timber roof (for a long time lost behind a Georgian ceiling), plus a fabulous wooden screen. Impressive though it is, the Old Hall is but one element of the architectural mash that makes up Lincoln's Inn. You'll also find a 17th-century chapel and brick-built central courtyard, plus the 18th-century white Stone Buildings, and the 19th-century Victorian Gothic New Hall and Library. It's a fascinating mix, which inspires John Hudson. 'As far as the buildings are concerned, Lincoln's Inn is incredibly atmospheric. It's like putting an Oxford or Cambridge college in the middle of central London, in Holborn. You walk in through a gatehouse and you move back many centuries to historic buildings, some of the late 15th century, some of the early 16th century, and some impressive mock-Gothic buildings as well. It's a wonderful, quiet area of elegant architecture with very beautiful gardens as well.'

The comparison with Oxbridge colleges is apposite. London had no universities of its own until the 19th century, so the Inns of Court, of which Lincoln's Inn is one of four surviving institutions, stood in their place, providing a legal education for prospective lawyers, but also a general education for sons of gentry and nobility who were never truly destined for the law. These four inns (the others being Middle Temple, Inner Temple and Gray's Inn) appear to have come into existence at some time around the middle of the 14th century, though precisely when is not known. Certainly, Lincoln's Inn boasts the first written records, in the form of its Black Books, which start in 1422.

'All four of the present surviving Inns of Court seem to date from the same time; from roughly the 1340s. They have some sort of prehistory as well,' says Hudson. 'It seems likely that students stayed in the area earlier, certainly when the royal courts were being held in London. There were phases during the reigns of Edward I and Edward III when the courts were being held in York, and all the students of law travelled with the courts. But from the 1340s they have a continuous history in London. At that time too they stopped just being places where students lodged, but became responsible for teaching as well.'

The term 'inn' denotes the fact that the buildings were originally lodgings, and the Lincoln in question is thought to refer to a noted mid 14th-century legal figure called Thomas de Lincoln. The site of that earliest Lincoln's Inn may not be exactly where the current place stands, but it was close by. As we don't have the original student lodgings any more, the Old Hall is the closest you can get to the earliest phase of the inn. Presumably it was here that lectures and moots (legal debates) were held. The key element in the education provided was that student lawyers were trained by working lawyers, a practice that has continued ever since. Indeed, the legal training offered here has, according to Hudson, been instrumental in the way that law has developed in England since the Middle Ages.

'The Inns of Court in London have always been the centre of legal education, and it's a form of education that is characteristically English. If you ask why law hasn't traditionally been a university subject in Britain until the 20th century, it's because it was taught in the Inns of Court. That has been fundamental to England and English-speaking parts of the world having a common law rather than a Roman and canon law culture, which is what existed elsewhere in Europe. The distinctive difference of English law is that it's something developed through practitioners – people who practise the law – teaching future practitioners. It's based on the idea of common learning amongst a legal profession rather than being a university subject with set texts, as in Roman law systems. This now goes right through to modern British and American law.'

Today, student lawyers are expected to complete some of their training outside the inns, but they are still required to attend a set number of dinners in the grand New Hall before they are eligible to be called to the bar. The New Hall is a huge and very Victorian space, dominated by an enormous fresco at one end, which was built in 1843. Lincoln's Inn lawyers also congregate in the handsome chapel, which is notable for its original 1620s' pews and for its links with the poet John Donne, who was a preacher here in the 17th century. He is thought to have coined the term 'For whom the bell tolls' in reference to the practice of announcing the death of senior inn members (benchers) by the tolling of the chapel bells.

The chapel is open to the public for services at certain times, but to gain entry to the Old and New Halls, you do need to be on an organised tour, and of course most of the other buildings within the inn are either used as chambers by barristers or accommodation for members. There is pedestrian access to the inn via the great gate and several other entrances, so you can walk through the compound and see the architectural jumble from the outside at your leisure. As you do so, you can dwell on the fact that it was here, and the other Inns of Court in London, where law has been shaped for centuries.

Lincoln's Inn

The Treasury Office, Lincoln's Inn, London WC2A 3TL

020 7405 1393

www.lincolnsinn.org.uk

Windsor Castle, Berkshire

Nominated by Mark Ormrod, professor of history, University of York

'Where the majesty of monarchy is on display'

Windsor Castle has been the home of 39 kings and queens since William the Conqueror founded it in the 11th century. It is redolent of royalty. That's why it's such a tourist magnet. If you're going to visit, you have to accept that you won't be able to savour the place alone. Queues are an unavoidable annoyance, but here's my tip: arrive early, get in front of the first coach parties of the day, and head straight for St George's Chapel in the Lower Ward. While everyone else makes a beeline for the State Apartments in the Upper Ward, you should have a few minutes to enjoy this medieval masterpiece. It's a magnificent space, constructed mostly by the English King Edward IV in the late 15th century, with a gorgeous vaulted roof that you can't help but gawp at.

It's an earlier Edward we have to thank for the message that's been delivered here, though, as Mark Ormrod explains: 'In the 14th century, Edward III set out to make Windsor his new Camelot. Very deliberately, he aimed to associate the place with King Arthur and thus bring to himself all the glamour and honour that came with that connection. So the monumental nature of the castle, the look of it from at least the 14th century onwards, was designed to send a public message about the strength, power and magnificence of monarchy.'

Edward III was one of England's great warrior kings, who pursued a policy of ruthless imperial expansion to unite the British Isles, subdue the Scots and boldly claim the French throne. He took the fight to the French in the Hundred Years War and scored a famous victory at Crécy in 1346, before capturing Calais in 1347. He didn't want just to win in war, though; he wanted to win with glory and honour. Edward was steeped in the idea of chivalry as portrayed in the Arthurian legends, which had become a fixation among Europe's elite since Geoffrey of Monmouth's 12th-century retelling of the story (see Tintagel Castle, page 80). That's why in 1348 he established the Order of the Garter, now the oldest order of chivalry in the world, in celebration of his French successes. While the order was underpinned by Arthurian imagery, it was dedicated to another of Edward's heroes, St George, and its home was St George's Chapel in Windsor Castle. Edward spent £50,000 rebuilding

Windsor, part of which was allocated to transforming the existing chapel, built by Henry III in honour of Edward the Confessor, into a chapel for St George. It was Edward's admiration of St George that spelt an end to Henry III's ambition that Edward the Confessor be patron saint of England (see Westminster Abbey, page 95).

Although the chapel was rebuilt by Edward IV, it has always remained the spiritual heart of the order. The quire at the centre of the chapel is quite a sight, with its ornately carved wooden stalls on which the Knights of the Garter were to sit, their banners suspended above their helmets, shields and swords, which are mounted just below. Behind the stalls are the brass plates of the 700 or so past members of the order. It's an extraordinary monument to medieval chivalry, the sort of thing you'd expect to see in an Arthurian fantasy today.

'Arthur was Edward III's number one model of successful kingship,' says Ormrod. 'To emulate him was considered by Edward to be the duty and destiny of all monarchs. But, in particular, this was about military glory. It was about demonstrating that Edward's achievement through his wars and great victories in Britain and France was a fulfilment of the Arthurian destiny that very clearly by the 14th century had come to be seen as turning the English monarchy into the greatest political power in Christendom. That's why Edward was interested in associating himself with Arthur – as a means of explaining and justifying to a wider public why they were having to pay so many taxes to finance his wars.'

Outside the quire, you can see Edward's enormous sword, 2 metres (6½ feet) long, and a 17th-century likeness of the man himself. You'll find that St George and the Order of the Garter pervade the rest of the castle too. In particular, there's the cavernous St George's Hall in the

Upper Ward, which was consumed by fire in 1992, but has now been renovated to its former glory. Its walls are studded with the coats of arms of all the past Knights of the Garter, and their names are inscribed on the wooden panels.

St George's Hall was created for George IV in the early 19th century. By this point Windsor Castle had returned to royal favour after a period when Hampton Court and Kensington Palace were preferred by the monarchy. Under Georges III and IV, Windsor was remodelled once more and, in the view of Mark Ormrod, 'there's a strong sense that the Crown is acting out its medieval glories by "performing" monarchy at Windsor'. Certainly, there was a renewed emphasis on the medieval Gothic style and on the Order of the Garter at the time of the Georgian renovations. Queen Victoria accepted the Gothic transformation of the castle that George IV had implemented, and very much made Windsor the heart of her reign.

This return to Windsor by the later Hanoverians and Victoria, and the harking back to medieval chivalry and majesty, have been interpreted as the British monarchy's response to the threat of republicanism from across the Channel after the French Revolution of 1789. If that's so, it's indicative of the versatility of the monarchy in Britain and why it has endured where others have failed. For a more recent example of that, you need look no further than the name of the current ruling dynasty, the House of Windsor. During the First World War, George V wisely dispensed with his Saxe-Coburg-Gotha family name in favour of the more English-sounding Windsor, taken from his principal royal residence, as it was clearly no longer politically expedient to have a Germanic-sounding royal family on the British throne.

As Ormrod concludes, 'Windsor represents the long history of both the monarchy and the country right through from the Normans. It's been such a focus of royal interest that it's become an icon of both the Crown and the kingdom in that time.'

Windsor Castle
Windsor, Berkshire SL4 1NJ
020 7766 7304
www.windsor.gov.uk

Harlech Castle, Gwynedd

Nominated by Ronald Hutton, professor of history, Bristol University

'Where Owain Glyndŵr made a last stand for Welsh independence'

There's always a risk if you build yourself a really good stronghold that your opponent might at some point capture it and use it against you. Harlech Castle was one of Edward I's ring of English fortresses built to consolidate his conquest of north Wales in the 1280s (see Conwy Castle, page 99). But English overlordship continued to rankle long after Edward's death. At the start of the 15th century Owain Glyndŵr became the leader of a renewed attempt to rid Wales of the English. Rebellion rumbled around northern and central Wales for the first few years of the revolt, then in 1404 things got really serious when, after a long siege, Harlech Castle fell to Glyndŵr.

As you'll see if you visit the place, this was no inconsiderable capture for the Welsh rebels. Harlech is imposing – a square of grey stone, with strong round towers at each corner and an enormous gatehouse that entirely dominates the rest of the structure. It stands on a crag overlooking the sea (which when it was built would have come much closer to the foot of the cliff on which the castle stands), with the mountains of Snowdonia providing the landward background.

It is, in short, a great place to hold out, even when your back is against the wall (or the sea in this instance). As Ronald Hutton notes, you can see Harlech as 'the castle of lost causes. It was the last place to hold out for Welsh independence in the Middle Ages, it was the last place to hold for the House of Lancaster in the Wars of the Roses, and it was the last place to hold out for the cavaliers in the English Civil War.'

To start with, however, Harlech (along with Aberystwyth Castle, which was also captured in 1404) gave Glyndŵr an excellent base from which to extend his authority over central Wales. The castle was home to his court and family, the site of his parliaments, and perhaps the place where he was crowned Prince of Wales. It was the heart of the Welsh revolt, but not long after its capture, the impetus of the rebellion faltered, and in 1408 Harlech was once more under siege. This time the army at the gates was English, its leader a rival prince of Wales, Harry of Monmouth, the future King Henry V. The English bombarded their former castle with cannons (and, indeed, the battering might account for the fine collection of cannon balls to be seen today on the floor of one of the guardrooms in the gatehouse). Eventually, in February 1409, Harlech fell once more, and although Glyndŵr lived on until 1416 and continued to lead resistance around Wales, it was the loss of his capital here that effectively ended his rebellion. His was the last major attempt to fight the English presence on Welsh soil. A century or so later, in the 1530 and 1540s, Wales was formally joined in union with England (see Ludlow Castle, page 153).

In between those two events, however, Harlech was subject to yet another assault, this time in the Wars of the Roses, when in 1468, after a seven-year siege (traditionally the inspiration for the song 'Men of Harlech'), the Yorkist forces of Edward IV finally shattered the resistance of the Lancastrian force within. The last great stand that Harlech made was during the English Civil War, when it was surrendered to parliamentary forces on 15 March 1647 after a stout defence over several months by a small group of Royalist officers and soldiers. It was the last castle to fly the flag for Charles I. Its fall signified the end of the civil war.

Despite this series of defeats for Harlech's defenders, perhaps it wasn't quite the bastion of futile resistance that it appears to be. 'You could make a case that every one of those causes managed to win its way in the end, thereby showing the British genius for compromise,' argues Hutton. 'Wales has got devolution, the house of Lancaster produced the Tudors, and the civil war cavaliers wanted a constitutional monarchy, and that's what we've had ever since 1660.'

Castle of lost causes or centre of sage compromise, Harlech is certainly a fine example of the art of fortification. Despite the succession of batterings it has received over the centuries, it's still in remarkably good colour, and probably the best way to appreciate the place is to take to the ramparts. The castle is now besieged not by cannons, but by caravans on the coastal plain below its much-mistreated walls. If you overlook them, the views from the walls out to sea, or across to the mountains of Snowdonia, are magnificent.

Harlech Castle: surely one of the most photogenic,
and most fought-over, castles in Britain

The stroll around the ramparts probably isn't the greatest for people
troubled by heights, as there's no railing on the castle side; you're but a
short trip from an untimely end if you take too much interest in the vista.
Personal safety considerations aside, it is worth diverting your eyes to look
back inside the castle occasionally because the inner façade of the great gatehouse is a remarkable piece of monumental medieval military architecture.
It's a solid mass of stone, interrupted by two rows of huge windows, and
with an external staircase up to the first-floor doorway that invites Holly-
wood visions of swashbuckling swordsmen duelling up the steps.

If you're still feeling spritely after climbing the spiral staircases of the
castle's towers, you could descend the steps to the Watergate, via which
defenders would have been resupplied during those sieges. Remember
that what goes down must in this case come back up again, and it's a

pretty steep hike. You'll want to leave enough time and energy to head out to the south of the town and look back towards Harlech. This is the vantage point from which hundreds of picture postcard photographs must have been composed, with the 13th-century walls of Edward I's castle framed handsomely against a mountain backdrop. Edward, or at least his mason, Master James of St George, knew how to build a castle that draws the eye and makes an impact. Of all his Welsh castles, perhaps Harlech is the one with the most presence.

Harlech Castle

Castle Square, Harlech, Gwynedd LL46 2YH

01766 780552

www.cadw.wales.gov.uk

Blackfriars' Hall, Norwich

Nominated by Carole Rawcliffe, professor of medieval history, University of East Anglia

'Where you can see how central Christianity was to medieval life'

If you want to get an idea of how far Christianity permeated everyday life in the Middle Ages, go to Norwich. It was a city made rich by the wool and cloth trade, and a lot of its money was diverted into the service of God through buildings devoted to him. By the mid 13th century it had something in the order of 60 churches, so Norwich's citizens would have had little excuse for not finding time to pray.

Aside from the churches, there was also the cathedral, with an associated community of monks, as well as a nunnery just outside the walls; and then there were the friaries. Norwich boasted four friaries by the end of the 13th century, and one of their number, Blackfriars, still survives with its medieval layout broadly intact.

Today Blackfriars is a civic building run by Norwich City Council and known as The Halls. It is hired out for concerts, dinners and the like. If no event is taking place, visitors are at liberty to wander around freely. There are two main spaces to explore: St Andrew's Hall and Blackfriars' Hall. St Andrew's, the larger of the two, was the friary nave, where the friars would preach to the assembled throng. When it was built in the mid 15th century (replacing an earlier 14th-century church that burnt down in 1413), it was designed to be a great open space for preaching to as many people as possible. It still retains that open feel today, despite having the trappings of a modern concert venue inserted within.

The smaller, but still sizeable, Blackfriars' Hall would have been the private chapel for the friars. Both these halls are grand and airy spaces, and both are remarkable 15th-century survivals, all the more so as a tower that stood between them collapsed in 1712. The cloisters that run around them are even older, dating back to the early 14th century, while the stone crypt (now home to a decent café) is more venerable still, from the mid 13th century.

You can nose around all these parts of the old friary, which makes it an interesting building with a different feeling to most historic sites, because it's still in public use today. The best place to linger is probably St Andrew's Hall. Its sheer size (it can accommodate 800 concert-goers) tells you something about the place of the friars in the medieval make-up.

Its generous capacity was because the mission of the Dominican Friars (known as the black friars because of the colour of their clothing) was to preach, and they needed as large a space as possible in which to do so. Unlike the monks, who closeted themselves away from the world, the friars mingled with the masses and taught them the word of God. They were nevertheless expected not to fall prey to the seductions of worldly life. Poverty and chastity were their watchwords. In fact, the friars were supposed to sustain themselves by begging, so local benefactors funded these mighty halls that they occupied.

'We have this remarkable building that testifies to the power of the Dominicans as a preaching order,' notes Carole Rawcliffe. 'You've got this vast nave, which would have been their theatre. You get a sense of what the Dominicans' urban mission would have been like that you don't get just by reading about it.'

The very fact that local worthies, such as the Agincourt knight Sir Thomas Erpingham and the Paston family, writers of celebrated letters, were willing to finance friaries like this demonstrates what they meant to the local community. They were, as Rawcliffe explains, integral to medieval urban life.

'It's a fascinating and beautiful building, but it's also very unusual because we have very few surviving friaries in England. This is an outstanding example and it gives you some sense of what a medieval town and city would have looked like because most would have had four of these for the major orders of friars. Norwich has lost its other three. The four principal orders performed different functions. They had an urban mission to spread knowledge, to inform the populace about the word of God. They were confessors to make sure that when people died they had pure and clean consciences. They were there also to educate and inform. You get a very clear sense of this here. They were knitted into civic life.'

What's noteworthy here is that the friary survives at all. When Henry VIII dissolved the monasteries in the 1530s, he also closed the friaries. Most were eventually pulled down, but the people of Norwich petitioned Henry to retain this friary and put it to public use, which is what it's been devoted to ever since. That's why there are four centuries of portraits of Norwich dignitaries adorning its walls.

It's intriguing to stand in the middle of St Andrew's Hall and think of a black-cloaked friar haranguing Norwich's cloth merchants about their worldly concerns in this very place 500 years ago. That this cavernous hall, with its fine arcading and rich, dark hammerbeam ceiling, was paid for by donations directly from the people of Norwich says something about the very central place that Christianity had for the average person in a medieval town.

If you want just a little more proof of that, take a gentle amble around the area. Walk in the general direction of the cathedral (five minutes away) and you're bound to pass at least two, if not more, of Norwich's 31 surviving medieval churches. The instruments of faith were everywhere, and whether or not you're a churchgoer today, you can't understand the Middle Ages without trying to get to grips with how central Christianity was to daily life in Britain. Norwich Blackfriars is a fine place to contemplate that.

Blackfriars' Hall
The Halls, St Andrews Plain, Norwich, Norfolk NR3 1AU
01603 628477
www.standrewshall.co.uk
www.norwichblackfriars.co.uk

Wharram Percy, North Yorkshire

Nominated by Christopher Dyer, professor of regional
and local history, University of Leicester
'Where you can see how wool shaped medieval
village life'

Some of the places in this book are out of the way, but Wharram Percy is
thoroughly isolated. That shouldn't surprise you: it is, after all, a deserted
medieval village (DMV). And what a beautiful, calm and delightful place
it is. You have to walk 500 metres (½ mile) or so to get to it from the
English Heritage car park, which means that there's a good chance you'll
be sharing your visit with just the cows and one or two other medieval
enthusiasts. The latter shouldn't disturb you, but the information boards
at the site do warn you to be mindful of the cows.

What you'll see when you get there is a wide path running along the
foot of a grassy hill towards a substantial and decidedly undeserted-looking
row of cottages, behind which rises the ruined tower of an emphatically
deserted-looking church. You don't need to have a trained archaeological
eye to note that you're standing on an unusually bumpy stretch of ground.
Christopher Dyer has some advice to understand what you're looking at:
'The thing to do is to go up on the little bank that runs beside the track
that was formerly the village street, and you will see the outline of foundations for a row of houses preserved in the turf. You can see where the doors
were and you can imagine yourself walking into a medieval house.'

If you keep in mind the aerial photograph that's reproduced on the
boards at the entrances to the site, that should help you to get a general
idea of what you're looking at. Further along the ridge, the outline of a

medieval longhouse (people slept at one end, livestock at the other) has been marked out in stone.

Where have all the houses gone, and, indeed, the people who lived in them? This was once a populous village, with houses that were reasonably well built, which seems to have flourished between the 12th and 13th centuries. It suffered somewhat with the Black Death in the mid 14th century, and from Scottish raids, famine and economic trouble thereafter, but the final cause of the desertion came later. It would appear that in the late 15th and early 16th centuries, the last few villagers were forced out by the landowners, the Hiltons, who wanted to turn the land over to sheep pasturing. This was a time when the wool industry was starting to blossom, and there was a lot more money to be had in sheep than people. You don't have to go too far away – to west Yorkshire and the Halifax Piece Hall (see page 256) – to be reminded of how potent the business of producing and selling wool was to become in later centuries. When we think of evictions, minds tend to flick to the Highland Clearances (see Badbea, page 261), but Wharram Percy is just one of many villages that were cleared of inhabitants to make space for sheep several centuries before those clearances began.

Aside from the lumpy ground, there are more visible remnants of the lost village. The church of St Martin stands roofless now, but you can get inside and enjoy its serenity. 'The church is a ruin and it's been carefully preserved as such by consolidating the collapsed tower,' explains Dyer. 'You also see the churchyard, which was still being used for burials one hundred years ago. It served one or two villages locally.'

Beyond the church are the restored medieval mill-streams and fish-pond. A lot of milling went on, harnessing the power of the Wharram stream to drive the watermills to grind the corn grown hereabouts. It's a lovely and memorable scene, with the ruined church and trickling waters; you'd be hard pressed to take a bad photograph of it.

And then there's the rather incongruous farmhouse, which is clearly much later than anything else on the site. Despite its boarded-up windows, it has obviously not long been empty. The building actually dates from the 18th century, when the landlord wanted to return the land to arable farming, so he put up the house for himself, and new stone buildings for his labourers. The reason the cottages don't look derelict is that they were in use quite recently, as a hostel and headquarters for the archaeologists who worked here from 1950 to 1990. They were engaged in a lengthy research project led by the scholars Maurice Beresford and John Hurst, and that is one of the reasons why Dyer has nominated the site: 'Wharram Percy is significant in the study of historic villages and settlements. It was here that Maurice Beresford began excavating a deserted village for the first time, and then, even more importantly, John Hurst took up the challenge of doing a large, long-running excavation.'

The work done here led to a burst of interest in the study of deserted medieval villages. We now know that there are around 3000 such sites across Britain. Wharram Percy, in purely historical terms, is perhaps no more significant than any of the others, though it is impressive in its state of preservation, its size and its magnificent isolated setting. However, in terms of the research that's been carried out here and the impact that has had on the wider development of landscape history, it's pre-eminent.

To visit it now, with a little imagination, enables you to conjure up a picture of life in a medieval village (and you can help yourself in that by downloading the helpful audio tour of the site from the English Heritage website, or visiting the nearby Malton Museum, where there is a Wharram

Percy exhibition). More broadly, it tells you of how the story of the rural landscape has been one of considerable change in the past, and gives a hint to the early years of the great British wool industry, and the way it shaped human lives long before the Industrial Revolution ushered in the days of mighty textile mills and factories.

Wharram Percy
Wharram, North Yorkshire YO17 9TW
www.english-heritage.org.uk/daysout

Bosworth Battlefield, Leicestershire
Nominated by David Musgrove, editor, BBC History Magazine
'Where the Tudor dynasty began'

There aren't that many battle sites in this book. In large part, that's because they tend not to be exciting places to visit. Often we can't be entirely sure of exactly where the action took place, or even the general vicinity of the battle – that's certainly true of many early fields of conflict. Others, where we are more sure of the site, are often in rather unprepossessing environments.

Bosworth is different for two reasons. First, because this was a clash where a king lost a horse, a crown, a kingdom and, indeed, his life. When Richard III died at Bosworth in 1485, he was to claim the distinction of being the last English king to die in battle. It was where the Plantagenet dynasty came to an end after 331 years. This was the battle that effectively concluded the Wars of the Roses, the 30-year conflict between a succession of protagonists belonging to the houses of York and Lancaster. Astutely, Bosworth's victorious Lancastrian claimant, Henry Tudor, sealed the deal by marrying Elizabeth of York and bringing together the two warring sides. As Henry VII, he had to see off several further challenges to his throne, including one that resulted in a further pitched battle at Stoke Field in 1487, but he resisted those who wanted to restore the Yorkist line.

If that isn't significant enough, the battle's recent history is more diverting than most. After several centuries of confusion about where the fighting actually took place, archaeologists have recently made some exciting finds that have enabled them to pinpoint things more accurately. The finds in question included a number of cannon balls. That might surprise you, but the late 15th century was the time when use of artillery in warfare started to make an impact. What's particularly disturbing is that archaeologists have carried out firing tests on the weaponry they believe was employed and it appears that the cannon balls may have bounced along on the ground at high speed. That seems to me a terrifying thought, a view shared no doubt by the massed ranks of the medieval soldiery, even those lucky enough to be wearing armour (and there wouldn't have been many). Some records of contemporary artillery use on the Continent state that the balls fired from the cannons could rip through six lines of infantry.

I suppose it's moot whether that's a more or less disturbing vision than the arrow storm that would also have been raining down on those unfortunate souls. The potency of the archer in 1485 had not yet been surpassed by the gunner. The archaeologists are still searching for evidence of where the arrows fell as they try to piece together the location of events that the written records mention. What they have found, though, aside from the cannon balls, is an intriguing silver badge with the emblem of a boar on it. Given that Richard III's personal device was the boar, the deduction is that the point where the badge was found might mark the place where the king made his last stand, having lost his horse in a desperate cavalry charge, and was then cut down in a marsh.

Cannon balls and boar badge were all found in farm fields a few kilometres away from the traditional location of the battle. You could view that as inconvenient for the curators of the recently built Bosworth Battlefield Heritage Centre, which sits, sensibly enough, near the traditional site. The staff at the centre take a more optimistic stance, noting that they wouldn't have built an interpretation facility slap bang on a battlefield anyway (the exhibition at the battlefield of Culloden has recently been moved for that very reason). They also point to the fact that you can see the new site from a vantage point on the hill near the centre, should you want a view of the field itself.

Whatever your opinion on its location, the interpretation centre is well worth a look. It's got a great interactive display that gives a very clear idea of what we know about how the battle progressed, and how the dynastic struggles of the Wars of the Roses reached the pitch that led to the clash in the first place. Interestingly, one of the first displays you get to is a video presentation on Richard III, sponsored by the Richard III Society. There are few other historic figures who have such vocal supporters as Richard III. The society considers him a wronged man, unfairly tarnished by, in particular, one William Shakespeare, whose influential hunchbacked portrayal of the last Yorkist ruler was simply pandering to the playwright's Tudor patrons. Their sponsored presentation puts the pro-Ricardian slant across.

There are plans for some sort of interpretation facilities at the new battlefield site itself, but as yet they are not confirmed. You could, if you wished, drive along the Roman road that cuts through the fields in question, but there isn't much to hold your attention if you do. For a more worthwhile diversion, you can still visit Crown Hill in the nearby village of Stoke Golding, where tradition, and now perhaps archaeological confirmation, suggests that Henry Tudor received Richard's crown after it had been hooked out of a hawthorn bush. Stoke Golding's signposts are annotated not with a 'Welcomes Careful Drivers' motto, but rather with the eminently more exciting 'Birthplace of the Tudor Dynasty', and there is a blue plaque on the side of a house in the village to say as much too.

The birth of that particular dynasty is a point of particular moment for British history, leading as it does from Henry VII to his son Henry VIII, and from there to the break with Rome, centuries of consequential turmoil between Catholics and Protestants, and Elizabeth I's long reign with the beginnings, after the defeat of the Spanish Armada, of a maritime supremacy that would eventually lead to empire. Every ruler, every dynasty, can point to being formative in some way, but the Tudors have better claim than most. Bosworth was where it began.

Bosworth Battlefield

Sutton Cheney, near Market Bosworth, Nuneaton, Leicestershire CV13 0AD

01455 290429

www.bosworthbattlefield.com

St John's College, Cambridge

Nominated by Phil Withington, lecturer in history,
Christ's College, University of Cambridge

'Where we start to leave the medieval period behind'

St John's is, perhaps, not the most physically imposing of Cambridge's 31 colleges, at least from the front. Its brickwork Great Gate, barricaded by tightly packed buildings and a narrow road, does not present a show-stopping façade like King's College, but St John's does, in the view of Phil Withington, have a particular importance in the development of ideas. 'The University of Cambridge was the centre of humanist ideology in 16th- and 17th-century England, and St John's was at its heart. The English Reformation, the Renaissance, colonial expansion, political reform – generations of its scholars were pivotal to all of these processes. If the birthplace of English modernity is anywhere, it's here.'

The humanist movement was essentially based on a rediscovery and new appreciation of ancient learning, the focus being on the study of classical works in their original form. This powered the rejuvenation of religious and political culture across Europe. It's one of the ideas that underpinned the Renaissance, and part of the process by which we move out of the medieval era and into the early modern one, linked to, but not necessarily in line with, the Reformation of the Church.

St John's College was founded in 1511, just as appreciation of human-ist ideas was gathering pace. It was created with the initial patronage of Lady Margaret Beaufort, the mother of King Henry VII and the early matriarch of the Tudor dynasty. When she died in 1509, it was left to her confessor John Fisher, Bishop of Rochester, to see the project through to fruition. Fisher was a friend of Europe's greatest humanist scholar Erasmus, and invited him over from the Continent to teach at Cambridge in the early years of the 16th century.

Cambridge University as an institution traces its history back much further than this, to 1209, in fact, when scholars from Oxford moved here after a town versus gown conflict. (The city celebrated the 800th anniversary in 2009 with some fanfare.) The colleges founded in the first few centuries of its existence were medieval institutions, but from the start St John's was designed to offer more of a Renaissance education. Indeed, in line with the humanists' stress on studying classical sources in the original, Bishop Fisher ruled that only Hebrew, Greek and Latin should be spoken within its walls.

You can still see those walls today. By 1516 the First Court of the new college was in place, and that Tudor brick quadrangle is what you enter once you've passed under the elaborate coat of arms (of Margaret Beaufort) on the Great Gate. It was here that the humanistic scholars brought to St John's by Bishop Fisher did much to advance the new approach to learning. Men such as Richard Croke and Robert Wakefield may not be household names today, but they were influential in moving the country out of the medieval mindset.

'From the start St John's had a very strong humanist curriculum,' says Withington. 'It was regarded as a centre for the new learning within the established educational structures. That ethos developed over the century and it combined with a particularly strong Calvinist Protestant reformatory edge. So many scholars from St John's went on to become reformers.'

The Reformation, the split in the Christian Church that led to the Catholic–Protestant divide, did not serve Bishop Fisher well, though. In the

1520s and 1530s he would not back Henry VIII in his 'great matter' – the question of whether he should be allowed to divorce Katherine of Aragon. As a result, he was executed in 1535, along with another notable humanist, Thomas More, for refusing to affirm Henry's new title as Supreme Head of the Church of England. Henry, of course, pushed through the break from the pope in Rome and established the separate Church of England.

Later notable scholars from St John's did support and encourage the growth of Protestantism in England. Most notable was William Cecil, Lord Burghley who was Elizabeth I's key adviser (see Hatfield House, page 178). Cecil was much influenced by the humanistic ethos he found at St John's, which through the rest of the 16th and 17th centuries became fused with a Puritan Protestant ethic.

Today the First Court is a pleasant and atmospheric quadrangle with cobbles underfoot, and a characteristic Tudor feel (though one side of the range has seen later modification). Statues of the founders, John Fisher and Margaret Beaufort, flank the door to the chapel in the far right corner as you look from the Great Gate, and the chapel itself is an impressive space, a Victorian Gothic replacement to a Tudor predecessor. The memorial plaques inside to notable St John's scholars are worth a few minutes before you head off into the later 16th-century and even more impressive Second Court.

The Third Court, which is crammed in hard to the river Cam behind, presents a completely different feel to the First and Second Courts, its Dutch-gabled buildings contrasting with their earlier Tudor style. It was built through the course of the 17th century, and perhaps it wouldn't be too much of a stretch to say that you can feel the changing nature of society as you progress through the three courts, advancing through architectural and ideological history as you go. St John's, in the view of Phil Withington, 'nicely encapsulates the cultural and social changes in the 16th and 17th centuries that took England from a medieval to a modern society', and though ideas are hard to see through buildings, walking through the three courts is perhaps as close as you can get.

That's not all you can see at St John's. It's a huge college, with much more lying beyond the Cam. To get to it you cross the river and have a fine view of the famous Bridge of Sighs. Then there's New Court, with its imposing 19th-century Gothic façade, and more modern college buildings behind that. The development of ideas has carried on here down the centuries, as of course it has throughout Cambridge's other colleges, which are mostly but a short stroll away from St John's.

St John's College
Cambridge CB2 1TP
01223 338600
www.joh.cam.ac.uk

Hampton Court, Surrey

Nominated by Eric Ives, emeritus professor of English history, University of Birmingham
'Where you can see how Henry VIII's court operated'

The biggest problem with Hampton Court is its size. You stroll in through the great brick gatehouse, past the ogling gargoyles manning the bridge over the moat, to be released into a great courtyard and myriad options: do you want to tackle Henry VIII's state rooms, investigate the extensive Tudor kitchens, plough on to William III's apartments, explore Queen Mary's chambers, or amble into the gardens? Once you have plumped for a course of action and marched through one of the beckoning doors or archways, it's hard to establish just exactly where you are in this expansive palace.

What you really need to do is review the site from the air, as that would very clearly demonstrate that the palace is made up of several open courtyards, all surrounded by brick squares of varying architectural styles. Assuming you're not arriving by private helicopter, the free map that you're given on arrival is an acceptable substitute. It is worth spending a minute with that before you make your first move. The excellent audio tour available on site is also worth listening to, as it details the various options on offer.

When most people think of Hampton Court, they probably think of the great Tudor monarch Henry VIII. He took possession of it in the late 1520s from his Lord Chancellor, Thomas Wolsey, who was always looking for ways to enhance his standing with the king. For Henry, the palace was a handy royal home near to London, with ready access to the city via the Thames, which runs past its walls. For Eric Ives, it's the perfect place to get into the Tudor spirit: 'I find that Hampton Court is the most imaginatively stimulating place for anyone who wants to understand Tudor society.'

Base Court, the first court you enter behind the great gatehouse, feels very Tudor indeed, though the chimneys on its roofs are actually Victorian replicas of Tudor designs. On the far side are Henry's apartments, of which the Great Hall, Chapel Royal and Watching Chamber survive today.

These rooms are well worth visiting, but you should linger in the court-yard first.

The buildings around the Base Court were where the royal courtiers and guests were accommodated. There were about 1000 people in Henry's court, so this was a crowded place and, says Ives, if you imagine them 'all herded in there, it explains all the backstabbing and all the galli-maufry that went on'. The low-ceilinged, interconnected rooms where the Tudor courtiers were housed were converted into grace and favour apartments in the mid 18th century, but are now mostly closed to the public. You can get a little taste of what was inside if you follow the route out of the court to the Orangery. It offers a sense of the claustrophobia that would have been an overarching feature of the Tudor lodgings.

A recent addition to the Base Court is the wine fountain, a newly erected structure in the middle of the courtyard. Although entirely modern, it is modelled on portrayals of such things in Tudor paintings and tapestries (of which there are many to enjoy in the various rooms of Hampton Court). If you visit at the weekend, you're able to partake of a glass of wine from the fountain (for an extra fee), and that's a little taste of what went on at Hampton Court in Henry's times, when feasting, revelry and drinking were the order of the day for the king and his courtiers.

Enormous quantities of food had to be prepared for the court, and the great Tudor kitchens, just behind Base Court, are a particular high-light of the palace today. In several large rooms you can get a sense of the huge logistical operation that was involved in keeping the court fed and watered. It's all very authentically recreated, with logs roaring away in the roasting fire, replica cuts of meat laid out on great wooden tables, and

Henry VIII stamped his mark on Hampton Court: he commissioned
the tapestries himself (this one hangs in the Great Hall)

tray upon tray of Tudor pies waiting to be devoured (only for those who can stomach plastic, though, I fear). The wine cellar opposite the kitchens is similarly capacious, and the whole impression is of a military catering operation. The food was carried up from the kitchens to the Great Hall, where up to 600 people (the lower tiers of the court hierarchy) would have eaten every day.

The tapestries that line of the walls of the Great Hall were commissioned by Henry himself (that's not unusual – the king was his own architect and site manager for work at Hampton Court), but they would only have been rolled out on special occasions, so consider yourself an important dignitary as you walk through the chamber with its highly decorated, wooden vaulted roof. The tapestries were just part of the majesty of the palace, designed to dominate and present Henry as a European monarch on a par with the King of France. And he was never satisfied, so Hampton Court always had the builders in.

It wasn't just the architecture and the decor that were there to impress: the king himself played his part in demonstrating his magnificence. You might well see a costumed interpreter dressed up as Henry as you wander around today, but don't be fooled into thinking that was normal in the 16th century. Even if you were a leading light at court, you wouldn't have seen much of the king unless you were truly well connected and attended him in his private chambers, which sadly no longer exist. 'The Tudors worked on the principle that the least said, the more exciting,' says Ives. 'The king came out only for formal occasions, which were in fact stage-managed.'

By far the showiest place in the Tudor palace is the Chapel Royal, which has a starry blue and gold roof that would surely have put all but the most godly off any sermon being delivered. Of course, in keeping with the theme of exclusivity, the royal family would not have sat with the rest of the congregation, but instead had a separate first-floor pew.

A visit to Hampton Court, then, will give you an insight into the life of Henry's court, and how it worked both practically and ideologically. Given Henry's pivotal role in English history as the monarch behind the break from the Roman Church, it's fascinating to see how he managed his image, although the part of the palace where he ran the government has, sadly, been demolished. Instead you have the later baroque buildings of William and Mary, which present an entirely different face to Hampton Court. And then there are the gardens, the real tennis courts and the famous maze in which to lose yourself.

Hampton Court Palace
East Molesey, Surrey KT8 9AU
0844 482 7777
www.hrp.org.uk/hamptoncourtpalace

Cartmel Priory Church, Cumbria
Nominated by Lucy Wooding, lecturer in early modern history, King's College London
'Where you can see the human impact of the Dissolution of the Monasteries'

For a small village in the Lake District, Cartmel's parish church is frankly out of all proportion. It is far too big. That much is obvious from the outside, with the tower rearing full and fat over the cluster of homes, pubs and shops that surround it. Behind the church's roundly arched Norman doorway, the effect is even more forceful: you might sense that you've stumbled on a small cathedral that's somehow lost its way and ended up in rural Cumbria.

The central crossing beneath the tower is high and mighty, handsomely flanked by the fine stonework of the north and south transepts. To the east is the choir, with some beautiful arcading high up on the walls, and an equally pleasing and richly carved wooden screen around it. Then there are two side chapels off the choir; and that's before you've even thought about the nave, which is a large enough space to house a bookshop today, and a scatter of tables and chairs for visiting tour groups, along with enough pews to seat, one suspects, the current congregation of Cartmel several times over.

What's going on? Well, this isn't just any parish church. As the name suggests, the Priory Church of St Mary and St Michael was originally part of a priory. A community of monks came here from Wiltshire at the end of the 12th century, under the patronage of the powerful knight William Marshal. Over the course of the next few centuries, they built up this church, along with a range of domestic buildings around it, so that they could fulfil their obligations for godly worship.

In common with most monastic houses, the monks of Cartmel grew rich through gifts of land from those who wanted to curry divine favour; thus they could afford such a grand house of prayer. The flow of money rather dried up after Scottish armies raided in 1316 and 1322, but the monks kept building despite their drop in income. Their straitened financial circumstances might explain why the nave, built in the 15th century, appears to have been constructed of a rather inferior rubble in contrast to the crisp stonework on display in the earlier parts of the church.

The priory's finances were not in such bad shape in the mid 16th century as to avoid the attention of Henry VIII's agents during the Dissolution of the Monasteries. This was the episode in the 1530s when the king shut down all the monastic houses, took their wealth for the Crown, and sold off or knocked down their buildings. Henry was in need of the money, and the sentiment that the religious orders were more worldly than godly afforded him the pretext to attack them. The Dissolution was part of the broader story of the Reformation, the reaction against the Catholic Church in favour of a more personal relationship with God.

The monasteries were unable to resist the king, and that's why many of them today survive only as romantic ruins, roofless haunts of tourists. That Cartmel's church did not suffer that fate is down to the villagers. Citing a clause in the foundation charter of William Marshal that reserved part of the church for the use of the local parishioners, they refused to let the priory be destroyed. As Lucy Wooding notes, their opposition was not entirely peaceful. 'It was closed down during the Dissolution and later reopened by the locals. Then, in early 1537, there was some violence, when the monks and the locals resisted the king's men. It shows you how passionately people felt about their monasteries. Four of the canons and ten of the villagers were hanged at Lancaster Castle. If you look at the war memorial in Cartmel churchyard, it tells you that 16 people died in the First World War, but 14 people died because of the Dissolution.'

What appears to have happened is that some of the roof of the church was removed in the 1540s, its lead and timber sold off, but that part of the building was saved from this ignominy and continued to be used as the parish church through the 16th century. In the 17th century the main roof was reinstalled and the renovation of the building commenced. It's possible that one of the side chapels to the choir, known as the Town Choir today, is where the parishioners met for those difficult years after the Dissolution. That chapel today is a lovely space, with a fine 14th-century tomb. The choir next to it boasts some surviving medieval woodwork in the form of the misericords, where the monks were allowed to rest their rears during long stints of standing devotion. Tradition has it that the ravaged state of the frame of the misericords is down to weather damage when that part of the church was open to the elements.

A visit to Cartmel gives you an inkling of the impact of the Dissolution that you don't get from taking yourself to one of the much grander, but now ruined, major monasteries. Wooding explains: 'It shows you the integration of monastic life with village life. It was a small monastery, but it was an essential part of the local community. The evidence suggests that monastic life was more crucial to the north of England, perhaps because life was tougher in the north. Monasteries were landlords, big farming concerns, the source of education and healthcare. They were the nearest thing you were going to get to a welfare state before 1945.'

The church at Cartmel continues to be integrated into village life today, both spiritually and practically, as some of the masonry from its domestic buildings has no doubt found its way into the houses around it. The priory gatehouse in the heart of the village is the largest intact reminder of the pre-Dissolution holdings of the monks (it's open to the public on rare afternoons during the year), but other buildings are thought to include monastic remains within their fabric. So for a dip into the Dissolution, Cartmel church and village are worth a visit.

Cartmel Priory Church
Priest Lane, Cartmel, Grange-over-Sands, Cumbria LA11 6PU
01539 536261
www.cartmelpriory.org.uk

Hever Castle, Kent

Nominated by Tracy Borman, chief executive,
Heritage Education Trust
'Where you can get close to Henry VIII's queens'

Hever looks like the perfect little castle. At the front it's medieval, with a water-filled moat guarding crenellated stone walls and a hefty gatehouse complete with wooden drawbridge. Behind that it's Tudor, with half-timbered walls and brick chimneys outside, dark wooden panelling, tapestries, four-poster beds and all the apparel you'd associate with that period within.

In fact, it's so good, so like a film set, that it might encourage a veteran heritage site visitor to raise a quizzical eyebrow. Such cynicism would be justified. Although the castle was begun in the 13th century, and expanded and altered in Tudor times, it's not quite what it seems, having been thoroughly restored and reconstructed in more recent times. At the start of the 20th century the castle, by now a little neglected, was acquired by the very wealthy American William Waldorf Astor. He spent a not inconsiderable part of his very considerable fortune on doing the place up, which is why it looks so shipshape today.

Its modern makeover aside, Hever Castle's historic credentials are impressive. Its main claim to fame is Anne Boleyn, perhaps the most famous of Henry VIII's six brides, whose childhood home it was. For Tracy Borman, however, it's the link to another of the king's wives that lends Hever its true significance: 'It has connections with Anne Boleyn, and is widely reputed to be her birthplace, but I think it's more likely she was born at Blickling Hall in Norfolk. Certainly, Henry VIII paid court to her at Hever, and it was pivotal in English history in that respect. The reason I've chosen it is the Anne of Cleves connection. I think she was quite possibly one of the greatest women in the 16th century. She was the queen who did the best out of Henry VIII because she gave him what he wanted, a divorce. He gave her Hever Castle and a few other nice little places. She spent lots of time there and created a very convivial household, entertaining many visitors. Hever almost became a rival to the court in London.'

Anne of Cleves was the fourth wife of Henry VIII (Anne Boleyn was the second). After the death of the third, Jane Seymour, Henry needed a new bride, and one who would give him an ally against his enemies in Europe. His courtiers set up the match with the German princess Anne of Cleves, and the first time the pair clapped eyes on each other was when she landed in England, ready to be wed (though Henry had seen a portrait of her by the celebrated painter Hans Holbein). Apparently, Henry was far from impressed by his potential new bride, but he couldn't immediately worm out of the deal. He married Anne in January 1540, but it wasn't long before the match was over – just seven months later, in fact.

We tend to think of the wives of King Henry as victims of the king's marital skullduggery, forever remembered with the following mnemonic: 'Divorced, beheaded, died, divorced, beheaded, survived.' For Borman, the experience of Anne of Cleves offers a more nuanced picture: 'She was this astoundingly independent woman for the 16th century. Most other rejected queens or women would have been looking out for another husband straight away, but Anne struck out on her own and was surprisingly successful. She was welcomed back at court, where she was known as the king's sister. Her discretion and good humour won her considerable popularity. She is often misrepresented as a poor, rejected, ugly woman, but I don't think she was any of those things. She got the upper hand on Henry, who had treated her pretty abysmally, and did very well out of the divorce.'

In terms of English history, the subject of Henry VIII and his numerous wives is one of the great stories. It's a Tudor touchstone, a subject that surely everyone has heard about, and it matters not just for the personal intrigue, but also for the bigger picture. It was Henry's desire for a divorce from his first wife, Katherine of Aragon (to enable him to wed Anne Boleyn), that led in part to the break with the pope in Rome and the establishment of the Church of England.

As Hever has such strong links with both Anne Boleyn and Anne of Cleves, it is an excellent place to get to grips with the story of Henry and his wives. It is Anne Boleyn who gets the lion's share of attention at the castle today. You walk through what tradition says was her childhood bedroom, view some prayer books that she owned, see her portrait, learn about Henry's numerous visits to Hever to woo her, and generally become suffused in the romance and tragedy of her time with the king.

Anne of Cleves gets far less of a look-in, but in the room now known as King Henry's Bedchamber (by dint of the fact that it's one of the largest rooms in the castle, so Astor guessed that it might have been where he stayed when he visited Hever), there is a splendid wooden fireplace with a carving that features the heads of both Queen Annes flanking a rather grumpy-looking King Henry.

Perhaps Anne of Cleves deserves a little more attention here. 'Hever is a great symbol of Anne's independence and her success, and those are the things she ought to be remembered for,' says Borman. 'She learnt from Katherine of Aragon's example because Katherine absolutely refused to give Henry a divorce and ended up shoved from pillar to post in the worst possible lodgings, and then died a miserable death, penniless and on her own.'

Anne of Cleves avoided that fate by immediately giving Henry what he wanted, and she was rewarded accordingly with an extremely generous divorce settlement that included Hever Castle. Her survival skills enabled her to become close to the young Princess Elizabeth (Henry and Anne Boleyn's daughter), and that affords Hever further Tudor import: 'I think it was Anne of Cleves who taught Elizabeth to be the pragmatist that she became. Elizabeth visited her former stepmother at Hever and wrote affectionate letters to her. Anne was enormously influential on Elizabeth, who of course was motherless by this stage, and she grew to share Anne's Protestant beliefs. For her part, Anne had been charmed by this precocious young girl from the beginning, and the pair remained close until Anne's death in 1557.'

Elizabeth went on to rule for almost half a century, and it was under her watch that the Protestant Reformation, initiated by her father, was

The famous cupid and dolphin mosaic at Fishbourne Palace is
proof of the former opulence of this early Roman site

The remains of the theatre of Verulamium: a quiet corner today,
but once the heart of the Roman town that became St Albans

The modern bronze statue of the Roman emperor Constantine the Great outside York Minster: his acceptance of Christianity had long-term implications for Britain, and the world

The romantically sited reminder of the ongoing importance of the patron saint of Wales at St Davids Cathedral

The nave of Winchester Cathedral: where Norman kings harnessed the legacy of their Anglo-Saxon predecessors

The heavy-handed rule of William the Conqueror is clearly demonstrated by the walls of the White Tower, heart of the Tower of London

The Welsh ruler Llywelyn the Great proved his credentials as a thoroughly modern leader with the round tower at Dolbadarn

The long walk up to Windsor Castle, sign of royal majesty for centuries, and Mecca for heritage tourists today

You'll struggle to find a more curious building than Rushton Triangular Lodge. Its 'three' motif is a hint of the religious troubles of the 16th century

Longthorpe Tower's medieval murals offer a very rare glimpse into the mindset of the Middle Ages

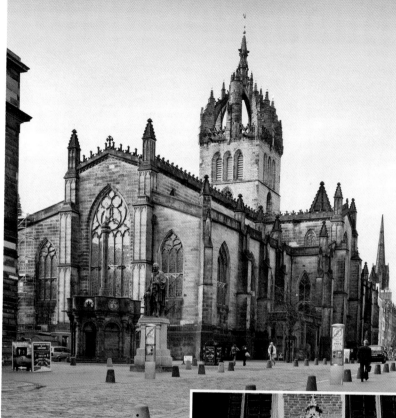

The Victorian exterior of St Giles'
Cathedral masks a medieval church,
inside which a stool-throwing
parishioner sparked civil war in
the mid 17th century

The ornate entrance to St John's
College, Cambridge: the humanist
scholars who worked here helped
move England from the medieval
to the early modern world

Roaring Meg, one of the many fine examples of Elizabethan and Jacobean cannons that line the 17th-century walls of Derry/Londonderry

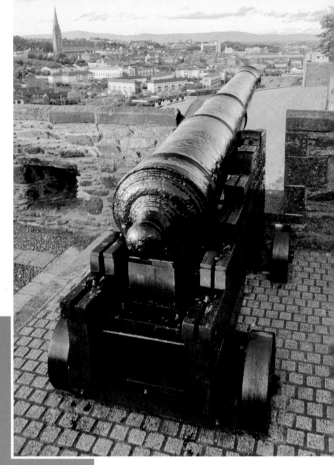

King William III stands sentinel on the quayside of Brixham harbour. His army landed here in 1688 en route to removing King James II from the throne

firmly implanted here. So with three Tudor queens, all of them significant in their own ways, all linked to Hever, it's well worth a visit.

Hever Castle

Hever, near Edenbridge, Kent TN8 7NG

01732 865224

www.hevercastle.co.uk

Ludlow Castle, Shropshire

Nominated by Lloyd Bowen, senior lecturer in early modern and Welsh history, Cardiff University

'Where Wales and England finally began to reach an accommodation'

England and Wales were not good neighbours in the medieval period. Theirs is a story of English and then Norman attempts to oppress the Welsh, and Welsh revolts against them. If you want to understand how Anglo-Welsh relations settled down to something more harmonious, you need to go to Ludlow Castle. In the view of Lloyd Bowen, 'It's a marginal place, but interesting because of that. It's a place of suppression, oppression, but also of meeting and where the bonds that make up Britain were forged.'

An extensive castle in its heyday, Ludlow is now a sprawling ruin, but a great one for exploring. It's not in the custody of one of our national heritage bodies, so it has a very different feel from your average National Trust, Cadw or English Heritage property. For one thing, some of the corridors and passages are genuinely challenging to navigate, particularly if your arms are full with camera, audio tour and guidebook, while others are so dark that you will find yourself slowing to a shuffle to ensure you keep your feet.

Since the conquest of Wales by Edward I of England at the end of the 13th century, Wales had been essentially annexed to England (physical proof of that being the ring of stone castles he constructed; see Conwy Castle, page 99). The rebellion of Owain Glyndŵr in the early 15th century (see Harlech Castle, page 122) was the last significant attempt at freeing Wales from English domination. It was henceforth ruled by the King of England, though Wales did not become part of England, and neither were the Welsh people on the same legal footing as the English.

Ludlow, with its strategic position in the borders, was always significant. According to Bowen, its castle affords an insight into English attitudes towards Wales: 'It shadows the relationship of the coalescing polity of England and how it deals with the peoples that it finds to its west. Beginning as a military establishment, it gives a sense of trying to police the borders in the medieval period; then, over a period of time, that policing role moves from suppression to interaction.'

Initially a Norman foundation in the 12th century, part of a chain of strongholds on the Anglo-Welsh border to keep the locals under control, Ludlow gradually became less of a fortress and more of a palace. It was the powerbase of Richard, Duke of York, who challenged for the throne in the Wars of the Roses in the mid 15th century. He died in 1460, unfulfilled in his ambition to be king, but his son did succeed, as Edward IV, in 1461. At that point Ludlow Castle became Crown property. His son, also Edward, became Prince of Wales and lived at Ludlow Castle. In 1473 the Prince's Council was established to advise the prince in matters of government. Significantly, this later developed into the Council of the Marches, which was responsible for the governance of Wales in the 16th and 17th centuries.

The prince was at Ludlow when Edward IV died in 1483, and his attempt to succeed to his father's crown was foiled by his uncle Richard, Duke of Gloucester. Edward was only 12 when his father died, but he was still due to be crowned immediately. Richard intercepted Edward's party en route from Ludlow to London for the coronation, had the ceremony delayed and himself named protector. Edward and his brother were incarcerated in the Tower of London (page 67). Then, once reinforcements had reached the city, Richard had himself crowned Richard III. The fate, and likely death, of the princes in the tower has excited commentators ever since. Richard's reign was cut short in 1485 by Henry Tudor, King Henry VII (see Bosworth, page 133).

The Tudor dynasty continued to look to Ludlow as the centre for the administration of Wales, though the Council of the Marches still had only limited powers. Henry VII's eldest son, Prince Arthur, was sent here in the 1490s, and you can see the chambers he apparently occupied in the solar tower of the castle. He died young (some at the time suspected due to premature sexual experience with his young wife Katherine of Aragon), allowing his brother, who would become Henry VIII, to take his place as heir to the throne and husband to his widow.

The Tudors had Welsh roots and were perhaps more favourably disposed to Wales than previous English dynasties. It was under Henry VIII that the two countries were formally joined in union through a series of Acts in the 1530s and 1540s. The status of the Council of the

Marches as the administrative and legal lead body for Wales and the borders was formally established by these Acts, and from that point until the end of the 17th century Wales was effectively run from Ludlow, as were the four English shires of Shropshire, Herefordshire, Worcestershire and Gloucestershire.

Visitors would have been reminded that they were entering a centre of power before they stepped inside the castle keep. As you cross the moat, look up and you see two coats of arms on the gatehouse, the upper one belonging to Henry VIII's daughter, Elizabeth I, and the one below, curiously featuring a chained porcupine, belonging to Sir Henry Sidney, who from 1559 to 1586 was Lord President of the Council of the Marches.

Just inside that gatehouse you have the Judge's Lodgings, which were erected during Elizabeth's reign to house the officials engaged in the increasing amount of judicial business being conducted in the castle. These lodgings have the feel of an Elizabethan stately home, in sharp contrast to the North Range of medieval buildings facing them across the inner bailey. Those starker 13th- and 14th-century buildings were to become the main centres of business for the Council of the Marches in the 16th century. With stained-glass windows and a timber roof, they would have been considerably more magnificent than the shell you see today. The huge Great Hall was used for entertaining and feasting by the Lord Presidents, while the council business was enacted on the first floor of the adjoining Great Chamber block.

'Ludlow was the focus for the royal administration of Wales in the 16th and 17th centuries,' notes Bowen. 'When London wanted to talk to Wales, it generally sent all its letters to Ludlow, and from there they were dispersed to the counties.'

You might think that the Welsh would have railed against this centre of colonial administration, but actually they were keen on it because it meant they were afforded legal privileges that had previously been denied to them. Ludlow became a place where justice could be had, and was much more convenient than a long trudge to London.

So for some in Wales at least, the Acts of Union and the establishment of Ludlow as the centre of law and governance were good things, as Bowen concludes: 'As the Council of the Marches at Ludlow was given statutory power, the union settlement gave the Welsh, particularly the gentry, participation in what seemed to be a much more stable, glittering, legally emancipatory and wealthier kingdom. There was also within Wales a particular appeal to history with the Acts of Union, allowing the Welsh to see themselves as the original inhabitants of Britain. One of the prophesies they clung to – which is why they supported Henry VII – was that they would regain their kingdom. In some senses the union was the confirmation of that, as it brought Britain back and returned the Welsh to the throne.'

Ludlow Castle
Castle Square, Ludlow, Shropshire SY8 1AY
01584 873355
www.ludlowcastle.com

Framlingham Castle, Suffolk

Nominated by Anna Whitelock, lecturer in early
modern history, Royal Holloway, University of London
'Where Mary raised her standard to preserve the
Tudor line'

When you visit a medieval castle with a perfectly preserved set of ramparts, as Framlingham has, it's only natural that you'd want to climb up and walk along the top. Happily, the 12th-century curtain wall here is in good enough shape for you to do just that.

As you might expect, the view over the pleasant town of Framlingham and the green fields that were once the castle's great park is impressive. Particularly pleasing is the lake just outside the bailey, which has provided generations of artists and photographers with the chance to catch the castle mirrored in the water. Curiously, the view inside the walls is, by comparison, a touch disappointing. There is no central stone keep to draw the eye, nor has there ever been. It's basically an empty, though pleasantly lawned place inside, with the exception of some 17th- and 18th-century buildings that made up Framlingham's Poor House. Now those rooms house the visitor exhibition and shop, and the entrance to the stairs that lead up on to the walls. All the medieval and Tudor structures that had occupied the castle's interior were pulled down in the 17th century to make way, and to provide materials for, this Poor House.

So as you're strolling along the wall-walk, in lieu of much to look down on within, you might find yourself diverted by the chimneys capping most of the towers. They appear both surprisingly numerous and oddly out of place. The stone ramparts and towers, with their crenellations and arrow loops, were clearly built with defence in mind, and look severe and imposing for that. Yet above them is a set of brick-built ornamental chimneys that look for all the world as if they've been swiped from Hampton Court and dropped down atop these medieval walls. They are, in fact, mostly decorative, each boasting a different intricate pattern zigzagging or spiralling around the flue. They shout of Tudor ostentation, and were indeed erected in the early 16th century when castles had begun to change from straight defensive fortifications to impressive homes for comfort and display.

The man responsible for the chimneys was probably Thomas Howard, Duke of Norfolk, who died at Framlingham in 1524. His son, also Thomas, was a notable scheming courtier in the reign of Henry VIII, who eventually overstepped himself and lost the king's favour. As a result, Framlingham, along with most of the Howard estates in East Anglia, came into the hands of Henry's daughter, Mary. She was to become queen, and to achieve infamy as Bloody Mary for her persecution of Protestants, after the death of her father in 1547 and the short reign of her brother Edward VI, who died six years later.

However, Mary's accession to the throne was far from a sure thing in 1553, even though her father's will acknowledged her as legal heir after Edward. The powerful Duke of Northumberland was plotting against her to install Lady Jane Grey as queen. When Mary heard that Northumberland was trying to capture her, explains Whitelock, Framlingham, with its thick stone walls, offered her the best hope of salvation.

'When Edward died and the Duke of Northumberland planned to capture Mary, who was then in Hertfordshire, she fled to Framlingham via Kenninghall in Norfolk under cover of darkness. There she raised her standard and rallied the local gentry and commons to her cause, staging a great scene where she came out of the castle, got down off her horse and walked around the mustered troops. It was an image of a female warrior figure that hadn't been seen before. When she was ready for battle, the Privy Council in London realised that the tide of popular support had turned in her favour, so members of the council went to Framlingham to submit to her and pledge their allegiance. It was the theatre of victory, where she won her throne.'

Framlingham Castle was therefore critical in Mary's accession to the throne. It was here that she was able to muster enough forces and demonstrate sufficient power to convince her opponents that she was a force to be reckoned with. If you look out over the deer park from the ramparts, you can imagine her supporters encamped there in their colourful thousands.

Mary played the crisis very well, underplaying the Catholic faith that was to become such a feature of her reign, and managing to acquire a broad spectrum of support. Her victory against the Duke of Northumberland was entirely against the odds, but the fact that she managed to secure the crown was important in the long run of English history, notes Whitelock: 'She preserved the line of Tudor succession. If Mary hadn't won the throne, Elizabeth wouldn't have followed. She broke the mould of male monarchy and set the stage for Elizabeth.'

Without Queen Elizabeth's long reign, the Protestant Church wouldn't have been so firmly established in England, so, ironically, that was Mary's legacy. There is a handsome small exhibition that charts Mary's rise to power in the old Poor House in the castle, while the audio tour that you're offered in the visitor centre also provides some useful context to the events of 1553 as you progress along the wall-walk.

When you descend from the ramparts, don't bypass the door off the stairs that opens into the delightful Lanman Museum. Harold Lanman was a Framlingham man who died in 1979, and this is his quirky collection of local memorabilia presented in splendidly Victorian style. Aside from being an unexpected hoard of minor treasures, it highlights how the castle has become integral to the fabric of the town down the centuries, and gives the local perspective on the national significance that Framlingham briefly attained during the mid 16th century, when it helped Mary to become Queen of England.

Framlingham Castle
Church Street, Framlingham, Suffolk IP13 9BP
01728 724189
www.english-heritage.org.uk/daysout

University Church, Oxford
Nominated by Diarmaid MacCulloch,
professor of the history of the Church, St Cross College,
University of Oxford
'Where the Church of England gathered martyrs'

Britain is a land of churches. They make up the lion's share of our listed buildings and they all have a story to tell. University Church, in the historic heart of a historic city, has seen many moments of note, but one in particular stands out as an event that went on to achieve national significance.

In 1555 Oxford's University Church of St Mary the Virgin played host to the trial of the Archbishop of Canterbury, Thomas Cranmer, for heresy. Cranmer had been one of the architects of the English Reformation, whereby the Church of England split from the control of the pope in Rome and placed Henry VIII at its head. He was the author of the Book of Common Prayer in 1549, and an instrumental figure in the replacement of Catholic ideas with Protestant ones during the reign of Henry's son Edward VI. But on Edward's early death, and following the failed attempt to place the Protestant Jane Grey on the throne, Cranmer found himself, in 1553, very much out of favour with the new queen, the Catholic Mary I (see Framlingham Castle, page 158).

So it was that this already ancient church of St Mary, the university's official place of worship since the 13th century, was the scene of the fallen archbishop's trial. Cranmer defended his theological position with vigour, but in the end was forced to proclaim that his support for Protestantism was wrong. He was made to watch the execution of his fellow Protestant bishops Hugh Latimer and Nicholas Ridley (who had also been tried in the church) from the window of his prison, Bocardo, and some months later shared their fate. In March 1556 the public crowded inside St Mary's, hoping and expecting to hear the man recant his beliefs, repent his Protestant sins and return to the Catholic fold before going to his death with a salved conscience. By this point Cranmer had already signed his confession, so the inquisitors no doubt felt confident that they had scored a major victory in the Catholic fight-back against the Reformation. But, as Diarmaid MacCulloch says, things didn't quite go to plan on the day: 'Hundreds of people were waiting for the man to recant. The church was packed to the rafters. It was the biggest show – the biggest scoop

Continent-wide for the Catholic Church. Cranmer had a prepared speech, which had been printed for him, but he changed the ending to deny everything that he'd recanted. Riots broke out in the church. He was dragged away to the stake and burnt. This was one of the most dramatic events to happen in any church in Britain.'

The drama didn't end there: when Cranmer was tied to the stake, he thrust his right hand, the one that had signed his confession, into the fire to demonstrate its disloyalty.

You can still see signs of these stirring moments in the church today. In the chancel are the wooden stalls, scarred with beetle borings and dark with age and damp, the self-same stalls on which the audience would have sat for Cranmer's trial. The basic fabric of the church is the same as it would have been in the 16th century, though there have been many alterations since then. In the nave is a modern memorial to those Oxford people who died on both sides of the religious divide during the Reformation. It has become a major attraction in its own right.

This all matters because of the way the events were viewed after Mary's death in 1558. Since she occupied the throne for only five years, Mary did not have a chance to restore the Catholic Church in the hearts and minds of her people. When her half-sister Elizabeth succeeded her, the Protestant vision resurfaced, and Cranmer's trial came to be seen as an important milestone in the story of England.

'It was the foundation of the English national identity as Protestant against a wicked, tyrannous, cruel Catholicism,' comments Diarmaid MacCulloch. 'So it's one of the foundational national self-image events and remained so until the 20th century. Tourists stand on the spot where Cranmer was burnt, which is marked on Broad Street.'

You can, in fact, follow an interesting trail from St Mary's, past the splendid Radcliffe Camera and the Bodleian Library, and left into Broad Street. Near the top of that wide thoroughfare, outside Balliol College, is a cross in the road that pinpoints where Cranmer was burnt. Walk on from there and turn right up Magdalen Street to reach the spire of the Martyrs' Memorial, the mid-19th-century monument to the Reformation, with statues of Cranmer, Latimer and Ridley. The north aisle of neighbouring St Mary Magdalen's Church is part of the same memorial and bears Cranmer's heraldry.

You wouldn't want to follow that little Reformation route without first having taken advantage of the excellent café in the Old Convocation House, which sits hard by St Mary's tower on the Radcliffe Square side. Not only does it provide fine sustenance, but it also sits in the first university building, dating back to 1320. Suitably refreshed, you ought then to climb the steps of the 14th-century tower of St Mary's to survey the tremendous scene below. If you do continue to the Martyrs' Memorial, you might find yourself in need of a second place to rest your legs, in which case pop into the newly refurbished Ashmolean Museum, just around the corner from the memorial. There you can revel in some of the many wonders inside, such as the beautiful Alfred Jewel (a bejewelled Gospel reading aid made for the pious Anglo-Saxon king Alfred), and also take tea in the rooftop café for an alternative but similarly elevated perspective over Oxford's spires.

University Church
High Street, Oxford OX1 4BJ
01865 279111
www.university-church.ox.ac.uk

Dunluce Castle, County Antrim

Nominated by Micheál Ó Siochrú,
lecturer in early modern Irish and British history,
Trinity College Dublin
'Where you can see how England and Scotland tried
to "civilise" Ireland'

Ruins don't come much more romantic than Dunluce: it has a prime location overlooking sharp cliffs on a beautiful stretch of Northern Ireland's
Antrim coastline, coupled with a fine range of walls and towers balanced
precariously on a dramatic promontory. This is not some pretty folly,
though: in the 17th century it was at the heart of the action as long-lasting
changes were being wrought in this part of Ireland.

The castle remains that you can see today are mostly 16th- and 17th-
century survivals, though there was probably some sort of fortification
here in much earlier times. The Anglo-Normans, never backward in building castles, no doubt recognised the defensible potential of Dunluce as
they looked to extend their influence into Ireland, following the invasion
in 1171 by King Henry II of England. Henry declared himself Lord of
Ireland, and for a century or so after that, thousands of emigrants from
England headed west to settle in this new English lordship – and such a
settlement was established somewhere in the area of Dunluce.

The English presence in Ireland waned after 1300, and although kings
of England continued to dub themselves Lords of Ireland, native rulers
across the island reasserted their power. For a couple of centuries following that, these local rulers fought amongst themselves for dominance. The
MacQuillans came to dominate this part of Antrim, and by the early 1500s

Dunluce had become their chief seat. Their regular feuding with other native Irish ruling families required reinforcements, and for this relied on mercenaries from the Scottish Highlands, known as Gallowglasses.

There is but a short stretch of sea between the northeast coast of Ireland and the isles of western Scotland, and long-held links existed between the peoples living in both areas. Indeed, a branch of the Scottish MacDonalds, who were Lords of the Isles, moved into the Antrim area, and in the early 16th century had become a powerful local force. Known as the MacDonnells in Ireland, they came to blows with the MacQuillans, and by the 1550s had taken possession of Dunluce Castle. It was the MacDonnells who built much of what you can see today, though there may be some fabric from the MacQuillan castle within it.

The rise of the MacDonnells coincided with renewed English interest in controlling Ireland. Following his break from Rome, Henry VIII came to view Ireland, peopled with wild and warlike Catholics, as a particular threat to his regime. His fear was heightened by the increasing presence of Scottish settlers, such as the MacDonnells, in the northeast. In 1541 he took to styling himself King rather than Lord of Ireland, and through the rest of the 16th century, the Tudors attempted to damp down the danger by making the island more English. The policy of 'surrender and regrant', whereby Irish lords handed over their lands to the Crown and then received them back with secure English titles, led to the creation of several Irish earldoms and a measure of success. But this cajoling went hand-in-hand with violent attempts to expel the Scots from Ireland during the reign of Elizabeth I. The leader of the MacDonnells, the wonderfully named Sorley Boy, found himself regularly in conflict with Elizabethan forces, and indeed in 1584 Dunluce was captured and then held by the English for a few years.

But Sorley Boy refused to be beaten. When he died in 1590, the MacDonnells were still entrenched in Antrim. His son Randal MacDonnell took over as head of the family, but after the death of Elizabeth I in 1603, he found himself facing a different set of circumstances from his father. As the queen's successor on the English throne was James VI of Scotland, the MacDonnells, with their Scottish heritage, were no longer enemies of the state.

'What's interesting about the MacDonnells is that they were originally a Highland family, who became a native Irish family,' notes Micheál Ó Siochrú. 'In the early 17th century they tried to adapt and get with the British programme and become "civilised". They adopted English customs and English laws.'

What you find when you visit Dunluce today, therefore, is not a rough frontier castle, but something surprisingly refined. Although it's now ruined, you can see that the large manor house at the centre of the place, probably built by Randal MacDonnell in the 1620s after he'd been made Earl of Antrim by King James, would have been quite a handsome building: 'The earl built this early Jacobean house there, which was one of the best examples of this new style of architecture coming to Ireland. It was moving away from the old castle style to something a bit more stylish,' says Ó Siochrú.

Outside the walls of the castle, Randal MacDonnell established a town in 1611. There's nothing to see of it now, but it's another indication of the way that this one-time Highland family was moving in a new direction. Excavations here have recently uncovered the remains of a Scottish merchant's house and some cobbled streets. The town was designed to mimic what was going on elsewhere in the north of Ireland, specifically in the Plantation of Ulster. This was a plan, implemented from 1609 onwards, whereby English and Scottish Protestant settlers were allocated land in Ireland. The native Irish were to be cleared from these areas and thus, hoped King James, the place could be subdued and civilised.

Randal MacDonnell's town at Dunluce was not part of the official plantation, but rather a private reaction to it. It's been estimated that some 100,000 Scots and 20,000 English settled in Ulster over the following century, despite a great Irish uprising against the process in 1641. The little town of Dunluce was burnt to the ground during that revolt, and the townspeople living there were ordered back to lowland Scotland from whence they had come 40 years previously. The castle, with its strong stone walls, has fared better than the town, even though it fell out of regular use soon after the civil wars of the mid 17th century.

'It's been a ruin for the last 350 years, but it's still very important for that part of the world,' comments Ó Siochrú. 'People regard the sea as a barrier, but in the 16th and 17th centuries it was very much a channel of communication. There was constant toing and froing between Scotland and the north of Ireland. From that point of view, Dunluce is an enormously significant site.'

As a final note on that, when you pass through the Scottish-style gatehouse into the ruins of Dunluce, do have a look for a faint carving in the corridor that leads into the castle. If you spot it, you'll see an archaic, Viking-style, galley that someone chose to chip into the stones, presumably in recognition of the importance of the sea in joining this part of Ireland to Scotland – and Britain.

Dunluce Castle

87 Dunluce Road, Bushmills, County Antrim BT57 8UY

028 2073 1938

www.doeni.gov.uk/niea

Plymouth Hoe, Devon

Nominated by Harry Bennett, reader in history,
University of Plymouth

'Where you can see how the victory against the
Spanish Armada helped foster a national image'

Whether or not there is any truth in the story of Sir Francis Drake insisting on completing his game of bowls on Plymouth Hoe before taking an interest in the news of the arrival of the Spanish Armada in 1588, it's a great story and one that no doubt draws a lot of visitors to the Hoe.

When you get there, you'll find both a memorial to the victory over the armada, and one to Drake himself. The surface of the Hoe probably wouldn't be ideal for that game of bowls any more, as it's now a tarmacked parade ground sloping away to the coast. Drake's memorial features a statue of the man himself, and he looks very much the Elizabethan gentleman.

When Elizabeth I came to the throne of England in 1558, Drake was a teenager, learning to be a pirate on the high seas. For the next couple of decades he made a name for himself harrying Spanish ships, and making a lot of money in the process. In 1577 he departed Plymouth on what turned out to be a three-year voyage that made him the first Englishman to circumnavigate the globe. On his return in 1580, his ship was packed to the gunwales with a huge bounty, much of it taken from Spanish ships and settlements. He gave a substantial portion of this to his queen, which pleased her enough to knight him on board his flagship, the *Golden Hind*. That act, however, very much displeased the King of Spain, Philip II, who took the view that Elizabeth was condoning attacks on his subjects.

Eight years later, relations between England and Spain had reached such a low (prompted by a raid on Cadiz by Drake) that Philip prepared an invasion army and sent his huge armada of ships to see to it that his English itch was scratched. Spain and England were by this time naturally disinclined to friendship as, in the light of the Reformation, Elizabeth had taken Protestantism to heart, while Spain remained firmly Catholic.

The Spanish fleet was famously rebuffed by England's navy, with the key encounter being the battle of Gravelines. Historians have actually tended to regard it as more of a draw than a clear-cut English victory, and certainly one that was weather-assisted. The Spanish fleet was blown northwards after Gravelines and was badly battered by an Atlantic storm as it tried to get home to Spain around the northwest coast of Britain and Ireland, losing many ships as a consequence. The intervention of the wind was seen at the time as evidence of divine support for the English cause, so the armada has become a defining point in the national maritime story – one that helped foster the image of a Protestant powerhouse protected by God.

Whatever the truth about the bowling game on the Hoe, what's certainly true is that the English fleet assembled in Plymouth Sound on 30 July 1588, and from there was able to outflank the Spanish fleet and harry its ships into a major engagement at Gravelines, near Calais. That's what's commemorated in the armada memorial on the Hoe. Along with a statue of Britannia, there is an inscription, 'He blew with His winds, and they were scattered'. These were the words used on medals struck in 1588 to commemorate the armada's failure and bolster the idea of divine protection for England.

Both the Drake and the armada memorials on the Hoe are overshadowed by the much larger Naval Memorial behind them. According to Harry

Plymouth Hoe is well-stocked with statues today; this is Sir Francis Drake, one of the heroes of the victory over the Spanish Armada

Bennett, Plymouth, as a key navy port for centuries, is a great place to see the bigger maritime picture. 'It's a superb vantage point, naturally, but also you see an incredible sweep of history – Plymouth's history, plus an intersection of Britain's history with world history, through the arrival of the Romans, the Spanish Armada, the Canadian Expeditionary Force on its way to the Front in 1914, the sailing of the Americans in 1944, ocean liners coming and going... It's like H.G. Wells's time traveller, where you're stuck in one location and you watch the passage of history go past you.'

That sense of seeing the long swathe of history is heightened when you look seaward from the clutch of memorials because immediately in front of you is half a lighthouse, the red-and-white-striped upper portion of John Smeaton's Eddystone Lighthouse. This once stood 20 km (14 miles) out to sea, and for over a hundred years, from the mid 18th century, it kept shipping off the Eddystone rocks. As Bennett notes, it's 'a key piece of Britain's industrial history', a piece of design that influenced many other lighthouses around the country, and was such a durable piece of engineering that it was taken down and then rebuilt on the Hoe at the end of the 19th century. Below that, on the seafront, is an art deco lido, which brings to mind the social history of Britain's love affair with the seaside. Meanwhile, on your left, with your back to the memorials, you've got the defensive importance of the coast in the form of the Royal Citadel, a 17th-century fortress that's still in military use today (it is open for occasional tours). Looking out across Plymouth Sound, you can see further evidence of the military significance of the place in the form of the blockhouses and forts on the headlands and islands.

'Don't just look out to sea,' advises Bennett. 'Turn around and look at the city too. It's the town that Drake knew and the town razed by the

Luftwaffe in the Second World War.' It was, of course, Plymouth's naval importance that made it a prime target for Hitler's air force, and the reason why the bombs rained down on it in 1941, causing the devastation of much of the city and the death of many of its citizens. Despite the destruction, Plymouth survived and was rebuilt, so it remains a place where Britain's maritime heritage is centre stage.

Plymouth Hoe
Plymouth PL1 2RH
www.plymouthbarbican.com

Hardwick Hall, Derbyshire
Nominated by Hannah Greig, lecturer in history,
University of York
'Where the power of women in Elizabethan society
is on show'

It's hard to know which way to look when you get to Hardwick Hall. As you step around the corner from the car park, the National Trust signs point to a sizeable window-filled wonder of a building to your left, yet plainly in front of you to your right is an equally large, and patently historic, ruin. Two grand houses shoulder to shoulder, but it's not like they are tight on space – they are surrounded by acres of beautiful gardens within rolling Derbyshire countryside.

The house that's still intact is probably the best place to start. This is Hardwick Hall, as opposed to the ruined Hardwick Old Hall. By far the most striking aspect of its exterior is the glut of windows it boasts.

'Hardwick Hall, more glass than wall' is how the old ditty goes. Built at a time when glass was expensive, it was a clear indication of the wealth and status of its builder.

In what we might consider today as something of a showy statement, that builder's initials 'ES' are emblazoned above those huge windows in stone carvings atop the several turrets of the house. ES stands for Elizabeth of Shrewsbury, but the woman in question is more commonly known as Bess of Hardwick. Born in 1527, Bess married four times to a succession of rich and influential men, the last of whom was the Earl of Shrewsbury. She outlived them all and died in 1608 as one of the richest people in England. She built both halls at Hardwick, in the 1580s and 1590s, and the New Hall remains as one of the most admired Elizabethan great houses still standing.

'The hall is a remarkable statement of female authority,' says Hannah Greig. 'It's associated with Bess of Hardwick, who was fantastically wealthy in the 16th century. She married multiple times, so she has an amazing story of success in manipulating the marriage market in the Elizabethan era. But what's so fantastic about the property she built is that she claimed it so completely as her own. On top of the building are these huge initials, and when you go into the house it's full of her. I don't know of any other property where you get such a strong sense of a single person, and that's partly because of the amazing collection of textiles they have there.'

The floor-to-ceiling tapestries that hang in most of the rooms are indeed incredible, perhaps none more so than in the Long Gallery, where almost its entire length of 51 metres (168 feet) and its 8-metre (26-foot) height are covered with a series of 13 Elizabethan tapestries, brought here by Bess in 1592. They have survived because her descendants, as the

Dukes of Devonshire, inherited nearby Chatsworth House as well as Hardwick. Chatsworth was remodelled and refurbished according to changing tastes, while Hardwick was rather left behind as an unloved, unfashionable sibling. That is, until the 19th century, when the 6th Duke took a shine to the place once more and filled it with Elizabethiana and other antiques. He brought in a considerable number of new tapestries from elsewhere, but there are still numerous pieces from the 16th century in the house. Some of them include even more ancient fabric in the form of medieval vestments because part of Bess's wealth derived from her second husband, Sir William Cavendish, who made his fortune as one of Henry VIII's commissioners in the Dissolution of the Monasteries (see Cartmel Priory Church, page 145).

'The needlework is a form of expression available to women at the time,' says Greig. 'I like to think of those textiles as women's writing, a display of female learning. We associate women's power with Queen Elizabeth, but there were other women who could make a strong mark on the landscape and on the cultural and political landscape too.'

Bess herself may have worked on some of the embroidery, though she took time out from that to move with the great and the good of Elizabethan society. She was generally on amenable terms with the other notable Elizabeth of her day, though she did fall out with the queen on occasion, particularly after she engineered a match between one of her daughters and Charles Stuart without royal consent. The resulting child of that marriage, Arabella Stuart, was seen as a contender for the throne after Elizabeth. Bess also quarrelled with, and separated from, her last husband. He attempted to take control of Chatsworth, but Bess challenged him in court and won. That she survived and prospered through these years of intrigue and politicking reveals her strength and intelligence.

You could spend a full day admiring the tapestries and exploring the great state rooms of Hardwick Hall, but don't forget to spare a little time for the Old Hall. This place was built by Bess between 1587 and 1596, but she appears to have decided that it wasn't grand enough, so even before she'd finished it, work had begun on the New Hall. Nevertheless, the Old Hall was clearly a mighty house in its own right until it was partly dismantled in the mid 18th century, perhaps simply to provide a romantic garden ruin within the New Hall's gardens.

To poke around in the Old Hall provides a considerable contrast to the grandeur next door. There is still enough standing for you to ascend several floors and look down into the empty shell of the place (not something I'd recommend to those who dislike heights). You can tell that this was once a grand building from the gaps where its own great windows would have been, and from the plaster friezes that linger over long-lost fireplaces, suspended in mid-air above floors that no longer exist.

With a mighty ruin and a mighty house to enjoy, there's enough here to hold your attention for some time, and that's without mentioning the lovely gardens around them. If you want to get a sense of how women were able to make an impact in what we tend to view as a man's world, a day out at Hardwick will provide just that.

Hardwick Hall
Doe Lea, Chesterfield, Derbyshire S44 5QJ
01246 850430 (New Hall); 01246 850431 (Old Hall)
www.nationaltrust.org.uk
www.english-heritage.org.uk/daysout

Rushton Triangular Lodge, Northants

Nominated by John Morrill, professor of British and Irish history, Selwyn College, University of Cambridge

'Where you can see the divide between religions old and new'

The curious three-sided lodge at Rushton is one of the oddest-looking constructions featured in this book. It was designed by the courtier and politician Sir Thomas Tresham and constructed in the last decade of the 16th century. It sits today at the side of a road in rural Northamptonshire, surrounded by trees, farmland and not much else. Across the fields and through the woods in the distance you can just about glimpse Rushton House, of which the lodge was originally an appendage. Now, however, the main house is a posh hotel and the lodge keeps its own quiet company, in the care of English Heritage. It's not a huge place, is open only on certain days, and it doesn't have much in the way of visitor facilities. That means it isn't generally thronged with people. This is a good thing, as it gives you a chance to explore the mysterious nature of the place without distraction.

The first thing you'll probably want to do is simply walk around the outside of the building. Even the most cursory inspection will quickly reveal its most obvious feature: the number three defines it. There are three sides, three floors, three-leaved trefoil windows, three triangular gables on each side, and numerous other three-related references through-out the building. If you draw nothing else from visiting, there is great pleasure to be had hunting for the threes hidden about the place.

Why the obsession with this number? Sir Thomas Tresham was making a religious point. He was a recusant, a Catholic who did not want to conform to the new Protestant faith that had been introduced in the 1530s, when Henry VIII broke the Church in England away from Rome. For his refusal to give up his Catholicism, Tresham ended up spending a lot of time in Tudor prisons, where he kept himself sane by designing extraordinary buildings, such as this one at Rushton. By modelling his lodge on the number three, he was making a rather pointed link with the Holy Trinity. It was Tresham's way of saying that he thought all good Christians who believed in the Trinity ought to be Catholics, not Protestants.

The very fact that Tresham felt inclined to go to such lengths to demonstrate his faith is clear evidence of the hold that religious differences had on Britain at the time. The divide between the followers of the old religion, Catholicism, and the new one, Protestantism, was very real and very raw. According to John Morrill, when you visit Rushton Triangular Lodge, 'You get a sense of the religious passion and the religious obsession that was to dominate the whole of the political and social life of people in Britain and Ireland over the early modern period. There's no building I can think of that tells us more of these passions during the century after the Reformation.'

The building itself did not break any laws. It was a snub certainly to the Protestants, but it was not illegal. 'Because of the way it's done, there's no idolatry in it,' notes John Morrill. 'There are no images that could be smashed down by Puritans, so it's very cunning. What the Puritans couldn't bear was any representation of the host of heaven – Jesus and the angels. It was very carefully designed to be a poke in the eye to the Protestants, but there was nothing they could do about it.'

That sums up Sir Thomas's attitude: he did not want to bring down the state – he just wanted to practise his religion without persecution, and designing buildings like this, and others such as the similarly mysterious (it has no roof, windows or floors) Lyveden New Bield, was his way of making that clear. Interestingly, his son, Francis Tresham, opted for a rather more direct course of action: he was part of the 1605 Gunpowder Plot, which aimed to blow up parliament and put a Catholic head of state back on the throne. It was perhaps the harsh treatment meted out to the father that radicalised the son.

So, for what it tells you about the charged religious times of the 16th and 17th centuries, Rushton Triangular Lodge is worth a visit. It's such a puzzling place that you'll no doubt be left scratching your head when trying to locate and understand Tresham's hidden messages. There are three Latin inscriptions that run around the façade of the building, for instance. Count the letters and you'll note that each has 33 characters. Before you climb the steps to go inside the lodge, notice the Latin text inscribed over the door, *Tres testimonium dant* (There are three that give witness) – not only a clear reference to the Trinity, but also a pun on Tresham's name. This was a man who wasn't averse to leaving a bit of wit as well as his religious message in the walls of his lodge.

Inside, you'll probably wonder about the lot of those who had to live in the building. Tresham had his warreners (rabbit keepers) reside here, and I would imagine they cursed him daily for coming up with such a palpably impractical construction. There is a reason that most of us don't have three-sided houses.

Rushton Triangular Lodge
Rushton, near Kettering, Northamptonshire NN14 1RP
01536 710761
www.english-heritage.org.uk/daysout

Hatfield House, Hertfordshire

Nominated by Pauline Croft, professor of early modern history, Royal Holloway, University of London
'Where you can appreciate the importance of the Cecil dynasty'

In the Marble Hall of Hatfield House, there are three portraits arranged in a row. The central, and by far the largest, canvas is the famous Rainbow Portrait of Queen Elizabeth I, regally resplendent and omnipotent. To her left is a portrait of William Cecil, and to her right his son, Robert. Both men served the queen as chief minister – William from her accession in 1558 to his death in 1598, then Robert until Elizabeth herself died in 1603. Robert Cecil had Hatfield House built between 1607 and 1611, while he continued in service to Elizabeth's successor, James I.

You'd be forgiven for not immediately noticing those three paintings when you step into the Marble Hall, the first great room that you come to in Hatfield House, because it is a feast of extravagantly carved oak panelling, overlain at head height by a sequence of huge tapestries, and bracketed at floor level by a chequerboard black and white marble floor. This style and opulence continues throughout, as Pauline Croft notes: 'The house is the most remarkable of all early Jacobean houses. It survives complete and unchanged, furnished in some rooms very largely as it was in the early 17th century.'

The story here actually starts with the rather less grand, but neverthe-less impressive, red-brick Old Palace, which now sits in the grounds of Hatfield House. You can poke your nose in here after you've visited the main house (and the viewing room above is a good place to look down on the Great Hall if it happens to be booked out for an event). The Old Palace was a childhood home to the young Princess Elizabeth, and it was where she held her first Privy Council meeting after she'd learnt of the death of her half-sister Queen Mary. It was here also that she confirmed William Cecil as her principal secretary. By then, Cecil had already been in royal service as a counsellor and secretary for some years, the humanistic education he'd been given at St John's College, Cambridge (see page 137), having driven into him the need to be an active public servant. Elizabeth knew him and trusted him – he had supported her when times were difficult during Mary's reign – so he was to be her leading adviser for the next four decades.

Hatfield was never William Cecil's home. His main residences were Theobalds (pronounced 'tibbalds') in Hertfordshire, and Burghley House in Lincolnshire. Theobalds has been demolished, but Burghley survives, and a very grand place it is too.

Theobalds must have been equally impressive because no less a figure than King James wanted it. After William's death, his son Robert agreed to swap Theobalds with the king in exchange for Hatfield House. Actually, says Croft, this was a good deal for the younger Cecil: 'Theobalds was a huge rambling house, very difficult to keep up, uncomfortable to live in, never warm. Instead he built himself, in effect, a modern house – compact, well designed, easy to live in, with beautiful gardens – altogether much more manageable and less expensive to run than Theobalds.'

Hatfield has been lived in ever since, and the original Jacobean style is very much in evidence. The Long Gallery, for instance, has not been divided up into individual rooms, despite such galleries falling out of favour after the Jacobean period.

As Croft says, 'There can be no doubt that each of the Cecils in turn was the most trusted minister of the two monarchs they served. Their advice was sought on every conceivable issue of importance, from foreign policy and parliamentary management to social and economic policy, so when there were successes across those two reigns, they were very strongly associated with the wisdom and guidance of the Cecils.'

The period over which the Cecils instrumented English policy was one of great and significant change, formative in the establishment of the Protestant Church of England, and the beginning of the English seaborne empire. When Robert died in 1612, he was buried in the church next door to Hatfield House. The Cecil family tomb, where subsequent generations have been lain to rest, is worth a look, particularly for Robert's skeletal memorial. Although he provided a durable family mausoleum, he was not able to groom a third generation of Cecil chief ministers, so the wise and stable government afforded by him and his father came to an end. Croft sees it as a considerable loss. 'With the death of Cecil, and James's decreasing interest in government and the decline of his capacity to govern wisely, I don't think it would be too much to say we can see the high road to civil war.'

Hatfield House
Hatfield, Hertfordshire AL9 5NQ
01707 287010
www.hatfield-house.co.uk

City Walls, Derry/Londonderry

Nominated by William Kelly, lecturer in early modern Irish and British history, University of Ulster

'Where you can see the early signs of fractures in Northern Ireland's society'

You can walk the entire length of Derry's city walls and in so doing take in one of the key stories of the history of Northern Ireland. At a brisk pace, you could probably cover the walled circuit in half an hour or so, but you'll most certainly want to stop and consider a few things along the way.

The walls were built between 1614 and 1619 to enclose and protect the Protestant colony that was established here as part of the Plantation of Ulster. The plantation scheme, implemented from 1609 onwards under King James VI and I, was devised to 'plant' Scottish and English settlers in the north of Ireland in an attempt to quell the rebellious nature of the Catholic Irish. The land for the settlers was made up of that confiscated from the Irish Earls of Tyrone and Tyrconnell and other Irish chieftains, many of whom fled Ireland in 1607, following their defeat by the English in the Nine Years' War (1594–1603).

The plantation town was not the first settlement here: in the 6th century a monastic foundation associated with St Columba, the monk who took the Irish version of Christianity to Scotland and England via Iona (page 30), was established at Derry. Following that, it was the site chosen for a short-lived Elizabethan garrison in the mid 16th century. It was with the Plantation of Ulster, however, that the city as you see it today was established.

Finance for the plantation project was provided by the wealthy companies of London, which in return received land in Ireland. This led to the existing settlement of Derry being renamed Londonderry when it was developed as a plantation town. The recent troubled history of Northern Ireland means that the city is now often referred to as Derry/Londonderry.

The thick earth and stone ramparts, complete with multi-angled bastions, are a fantastic survival from the early 17th century. It's a treat still to be able to walk along the wide battlement path. There are various points at which you can ascend to the ramparts, and regular signs along the circuit provide historical detail. A good place to start, though, is at the Tower Museum just within the walls. It gives context to the history of the city in a series of modern displays.

'The Tower Museum also includes artefacts from *La Trinidad Valencera*, one of the Spanish Armada ships that tried to make it home after 1588 by sailing around the British Isles. Many, including *La Trinidad Valencera*, were wrecked in storms,' notes William Kelly. 'The armada story is, in fact, part of the history of the walls because one of the reasons for the Plantation of Ulster was to protect the settlers from any further Irish insurgency supported by Spanish intervention. The Nine Years' War, in which Spanish troops landed at Kinsale, ended only at great cost to the English exchequer.'

If you start from the museum and head off along the walls with the Guildhall on your left, you'll soon come to a remarkable array of early cannons on the ramparts. In fact, mounted along the walls, you can see Europe's largest collection of cannons from the Elizabethan and Jacobean periods whose origins are known precisely. Military enthusiasts will also savour the wide field of fire afforded by the angled bastions.

St Columb's Cathedral, dating from 1633 and very recently renovated, was the first cathedral in the British Isles to be built after the Reformation and can be found just inside the walls. It's a fascinating place to nose about in, particularly its little museum, where you'll find the padlocks and keys of the gates from 1688, and a mortar shell of similar date. These items are indicative of perhaps the key moment in the history of the walls: the great siege of 1689.

The city was, in fact, besieged three times: in 1641 during the Irish Uprising against English rule and the plantation, in 1649 during the civil war, and most famously in 1689, in the aftermath of the events of 1688 when King James VII and II lost his crown to William and Mary (see Brixham Harbour, page 205). James, a Catholic, had fled to Ireland, via France, after the landing of William and Mary in England. The deposed king retained considerable support among his co-religionists in Ireland, and the walled city of Londonderry remained one of the few Protestant enclaves here. Supporters of James ordered that a Catholic force should replace the Protestant troops in the city, but when that army arrived at the walls, in December 1688, 13 apprentice boys inside famously slammed the gates shut. This initiated a 105-day siege, during which the population inside suffered very considerable privation, until relief arrived in July 1689.

Of the siege-related items in the cathedral, the locks and keys speak for themselves; the hollow mortar shell, containing the terms for the surrender, was apparently fired into the city. As Kelly recounts, the terms were not accepted: 'The slamming of the gates by 13 apprentice boys in the face of James II's troops was a revolutionary act, while the defence of the city played a key role in tying down Jacobite troops that might otherwise have invaded Scotland or England, thereby contributing to the ultimate success of the Glorious Revolution. Personally, though, I do not think there was much chance of this since the Jacobite forces were probably incapable of attacking either.'

If the failure of the besieging army to take the city weakened King James's position, his defeat by an army led by William himself at the Battle of the Boyne in 1690 completely undermined him. Following that, James fled Ireland and went back to France. A final defeat for his supporters in 1691 at Aughrim in County Galway spelt the end of this cause and ushered in a new Protestant government for Ireland.

The Plantation of Ulster was to leave a long and difficult legacy for Northern Ireland. The Protestant-Catholic divide that grew out of it led eventually to the violent Troubles of the 20th century (epitomised by Free Derry Corner in this very same city, page 387). To walk the walls of Derry/Londonderry is a sobering yet fascinating journey back to the very start of that process.

Derry/Londonderry Walls
www.doeni.gov.uk/niea

St Giles' Cathedral, Edinburgh
Nominated by Gillian MacIntosh, research fellow,
University of St Andrews
'Where you can see how Britain's civil wars began'

Edinburgh's Royal Mile must be home to the greatest concentration of tartan knick-knacks in all of Scotland. If you can look past the tourist shops, there's a wealth of history as well, from the mighty castle – home to Scotland's Crown Jewels – at the top of the street, down to the palace of Holyroodhouse at its foot. Between those two landmarks is a building that tells us particularly about the turbulent times in Scotland, and Britain, in the 17th century: the cathedral of St Giles.

The original fabric of the building is hidden behind later stonework, so it presents an appearance that belies its age. St Giles' is a medieval church that has been extensively altered over the years. In Georgian and Victorian times, much of its exterior was refaced, and the interior substantially remodelled. In fact, the internal alterations started back in the 16th century, under St Giles' most famous incumbent, John Knox, the Protestant reformer, who was minister here from 1560 to 1572. There is a statue of him inside. Knox needed a large, open space to preach, but the medieval layout, composed of separate chapels, did not allow for that. It was under Knox that the centre of the church was cleared and seats put in.

Knox was a key figure in the Reformation in Scotland, part of the Europe-wide reaction against the rule of the papacy. Scotland underwent its reformation at roughly the same time as England, but with a somewhat different outcome. In England, King Henry VIII created a Church that retained bishops, whereas in Scotland it led to a more radical Presbyterian structure in which bishops were replaced by a council of church leaders, the General Assembly.

The differences began to matter after the Union of the Crowns in 1603, when James VI of Scotland became also James I of England. James wanted the Scottish Church to be led by bishops, over whom he could exert control, which rankled with the Presbyterians. When his son, Charles I, came north for his Scottish coronation in 1633, he caused offence by having English chaplains in the service at St Giles'. He then ruffled feathers further still when he had the Scottish bishops publish a prayer book for Scotland that was modelled on the English service. When that was first read in St Giles' in 1637, it did not go unchallenged, as Gillian MacIntosh explains: 'A parishioner called Jenny Geddes infamously threw her stool at the preaching minister in protest at the new Book of Common Prayer and sparked a riot that led directly to the War of the Three Kingdoms – 23 years of wide-ranging conflict that did not really end until the restoration of Charles II in 1660. A memorial in the shape of a stool can be seen in the cathedral today.'

The Jenny Geddes story has been questioned by some historians, who see it as a later invention, but there's no doubt that there was a disturbance in the church, and that it had consequences. Aside from the stool, there is also a memorial to James Hannay, the dean in 1637 who was 'The first and last who read the service book in this church', and a copy of the National Covenant, the document signed in 1638 (in Greyfriars Kirk also in Edinburgh) by those opposed to Charles's attempts to remodel the Scottish church on English lines

The rioting and resistance in Scotland in 1637 and 1638 undermined not only the king's religious reform agenda but also damaged the authority of the crown itself. Charles raised an army to go north and quell the Scottish disobedience, but it was defeated in the so-called Bishops' Wars of 1639–40. The king had no standing army to impose his will and in the aftermath of the successful stand against him in Scotland, opposition to his rule elsewhere in his kingdoms was emboldened. In Ireland in 1641, a Catholic rising against the newly planted Protestant settlers (see Dunluce Castle, 165) led to considerable bloodshed. Charles had seemingly lost control, and his attempt to get it back by accusing some members of the English parliament at Westminster of treason at the start of 1642 backfired. He fled London to escape the angry crowds ranged against him, and tried to raise a force that would allow him to stamp out the resistance of the parliamentarians; thus the first conflicts of the English Civil War began that year.

The wars that raged across England, Scotland and Ireland after 1642 led eventually to the defeat and execution of the king in 1649, and continuing internal conflict after that during the Commonwealth. The roots of the clash go back to Scotland and the riots of 1637, so St Giles' is a fascinating place to visit, to see how Charles's reign began to unravel and descend into the violence that we now remember it for.

St Giles' Cathedral
Parliament Square, Edinburgh EH1 1RE
0131 225 9442
www.stgilescathedral.org.uk

York Watergate, London
Nominated by John Adamson, fellow in history, Peterhouse, University of Cambridge
'Where the army that won the civil war was planned'

You would think that a watergate would be near water. The one chosen here is over a hundred metres from the Thames, separated from it by a small public garden in Embankment Place. But before the Victorians embarked on their programme of embanking the river to better control it and reduce pollution in London, this grand gate would have stood on the lapping edge of the natural Thames, its steps ready to receive water-borne visitors to the equally grand York House just behind.

Not only is York Watergate no longer by the river, but the palace it once served is also no longer there; it was demolished in 1675. That all combines to make the place a little incongruous, entirely devoid as it is of its original context. A little imagination is therefore required to picture what once was here. As John Adamson explains: 'The watergate is one of the very few places in London where you can actually see and touch the fabric of the great 17th-century city, when the Thames was its principal thoroughfare and where its sequence of palaces lining the north bank from Whitehall all the way to the Inns of Court – all of them facing on to the river – invited contemporary comparisons with Venice. The only surviving watergate, at least of the 17th century, is the great gate of York House, which was actually built for the Duke of Buckingham.'

It's the events that occurred inside York House during the 17th century that make the place significant. The 1st Duke of Buckingham, George Villiers, was a royal favourite, who acquired York House in 1621 (the name derives from the Archbishops of York, who held the house in the 16th century). Buckingham had the watergate built in 1626 in Italianate style, and filled the house with his fabulous art collection. It was here, also in 1626, that the duke staged the York House Conference, which decided the doctrinal future of the English Church under his great patron, King Charles I. On Buckingham's assassination in 1628, the property was left to his widow, Katherine; but in the 1640s, as civil war boiled over between Charles I's Royalist supporters and the Parliamentarians,

The York Watergate now stands a considerable distance from the Thames.
As this painting by Daniel Turner shows, its steps once ran down directly to the river

it was rented to the 10th Earl of Northumberland, Algernon Percy, the Lord Admiral.

'It was in the extraordinary splendour of York House that Northumberland played host to the Committee of Both Kingdoms – the "executive arm" of the Parliamentarians' wartime government,' says Adamson. A bit of context is needed here. King Charles had decamped to Oxford in 1642 to set up his court, so throughout the war London was the headquarters of the Parliamentarians. Northumberland had sided with parliament in 1640, the highest-ranking member of Charles's government to do so. The Committee of Both Kingdoms was the body set up in 1644 to oversee the conduct of the war on the Parliamentary side, and 'Both Kingdoms' were England and Scotland, after the English parliament had negotiated a military alliance with the Scots in 1643.

What happened at these York House meetings was of particular military importance: 'One of the great turning points of the war was the creation of the New Model Army and the amalgamation of existing armies to form a single highly effective and politically controlled fighting force,' says Adamson. 'And the key meetings that produced the plan for the new army and much of the political manoeuvring to create it were actually in York House and its nearby neighbour, Derby House, of which, now, not a stone remains.'

The New Model Army, under the command of Sir Thomas Fairfax, was set up in February 1645. The aim was to create a highly disciplined professional fighting force. The newly formed and freshly trained army recorded a key victory over the Royalists at Naseby just a few short months later, in June 1645. Its further victories over the following autumn and winter led to the surrender of the king in 1646, and then to the conclusion of the first civil war (though hostilities were to recommence briefly in 1648).

As Adamson argues, things could have turned out rather differently had the York House meetings not led to the military restructuring of parliament's forces: 'If there had been no New Model Army, there would almost certainly have been no definitive victory over the king, no move towards the radicalisation of politics in the later 1640s, and a very different series of outcomes to that great decade of political and military conflict.'

Those outcomes at the end of the 1640s included the execution of the king and the abolition of the House of Lords, so it's fair to say that the eventual, and unforeseen, consequences of the committee's deliberations were far-reaching. It's hard to appreciate that from the sight of the watergate today, which, to most of the visitors to Embankment Place is probably no more than another garden ornament.

It's some garden ornament, nevertheless. Despite the weathering that it has clearly suffered (the resting lions on top seem to have fared particularly badly), you can tell that this was once quite a piece of architecture. It's festooned with the Buckingham arms and the emblems of his office as Lord Admiral. On the reverse it holds the Buckingham motto, 'The Cross is the Touchstone of Faith'. Of course, behind that would have been the house itself, and one can only wonder at the grandeur that would have confronted its waterborne visitors. Now the steps lead up to office blocks and cafés.

It's a shame that the steps are fenced off because, as Adamson notes, 'This is how they arrived – Northumberland, Fairfax, Cromwell: the grandees of civil war politics would all have been familiar with this once impressively opulent entrance.'

Those grandees would also have been familiar with the Banqueting House (page 195), once the principal Presence Chamber (or throne room) of Charles I's London palace, and the only other great surviving secular building of the period in the vicinity. It is a short walk away down the Embankment and then up into Whitehall to get there, and it would be a worthwhile excursion if you want to follow the story of the civil war. It was outside the Banqueting House that King Charles lost his head in 1649. Perhaps that would not have come to pass without the meetings that took place inside the now-vanished splendour of York House.

York Watergate
Embankment Gardens, London WC2N 6NS

St Mary's Church, Putney

Nominated by Mike Braddick, professor of history,
University of Sheffield
'Where civil war soldiers started to speak of
democracy'

Its curious concrete ceiling dates from the 1970s, while the Victorians concocted the layout of the church below in the 1830s. Yet St Mary's in Putney, on the banks of the river Thames as it follows its meandering course into the centre of London, has a particular story to tell from the 1640s. It was host to the famous Putney Debates during the English Civil Wars.

The church was quite different in the 17th century. The wholesale renovation in the 1970s and 1980s, after an arson attack in 1973, is but the most obvious of modern alterations to the fabric of this medieval foundation. In the 1640s it had no wide arcades flanking the nave (they are Victorian additions); it had no airy glass café attached to it (that has arrived only in the last few years); indeed, it didn't sit next to Putney Bridge (the current crossing dates from the 19th century) or serve such a tightly packed urban congregation. In its early days Putney was a small town surrounded by fields, with several large houses taken as summer retreats by London notables, who could get back to the city easily enough by ferry.

Despite all these changes, the heart of the church still holds the vestiges of its 1647 shape. As you stand in the nave, you're in the same place where some of the Putney Debates were held over the course of several days in October and November of that year (a nearby house was also used for the discussions). These debates took place in the aftermath of the first part of the English Civil War, which had concluded with victory for the Parliamentary forces and the capture of King Charles I in 1646. Parliament's New Model Army (see York Watergate, page 189) had been the key force in the war, securing decisive victories over the Royalists in 1645. However, with the war going their way, parliament and its army lost their solidarity. The soldiers, discontented with a variety of perceived parliamentary slights, and particularly with plans to disband the army, marched on London in June 1647 to pressure the MPs in Westminster. They set up their HQ in Putney.

Then, in October, in St Mary's Church, the rank and file of the New Model Army debated the future of the military and the country with their generals. The debates were focused around a pamphlet, 'An Agreement of the People', which had been published by Leveller agitators in the army (the Levellers were so named because they believed that all men should be equal before the law). Based on the proposals in this pamphlet, the debaters discussed such highly charged issues as who should have the right to vote, religious toleration, and whether there should be a king. Not only were the topics revolutionary, but so was the fact that the debates were conducted between leaders such as Oliver Cromwell and Thomas Fairfax and common soldiers of the army.

Nowadays, the debates are lauded for espousing principles that we now take for granted, such as universal suffrage and the sovereignty of the people. 'In some ways,' says Mike Braddick, 'it's the birthplace of the way we talk about politics,' but, as he goes on to note, the debates had limited impact at the time. 'It was a meeting of army people to decide how the army was going to try to achieve a peace. The immediate public significance wasn't great. In fact, there was a news blackout, probably because they wanted to be able to speak their minds without fear of being widely reported, as they were trying to come up with a formal and united position for the army in very fraught circumstances. So, very unusually, this significant event didn't appear in the press at the time.'

The importance of the debates perhaps wouldn't have resurfaced were it not for the discovery in 1890 of a transcript of the discussions, taken down as they occurred, but not actually published in the 17th century. With that in hand, historians have been better able to appreciate the strength of the arguments put forward, and to find contemporary resonance within them, particularly so at the end of the 19th century. 'Its significance was not emphasised until much later, and in fact it was revived in the 1890s, when franchise reform in Britain was reaching a point where it was reasonable to refer to a democracy,' notes Braddick. 'Its historical significance rose at the same time as British democracy.'

In 2006, more recent recognition of the importance of St Mary's Church as the site of the Putney Debates was delivered when it won a national contest, orchestrated by the *Guardian* newspaper, to find the most neglected monuments to British radical history. Since then, the story of the Putney Debates has become less neglected within the church through the creation of a modest but informative exhibition in a small space off the nave, with some very in-depth panels on the story of 1647, and a TV presentation that includes readings from the original transcripts.

There's also the famous quote from one of the debaters, Colonel Thomas Rainsborough, inscribed on the wall above the nave: 'For really I think that the poorest he that is in England hath a life to live, as the greatest he.' That neatly sums up some of the aspirations of those involved. If you take a moment to sit in the upper gallery, above the inscription, and look down on the nave, you can perhaps imagine the febrile atmosphere among the Roundhead soldiers crowded into the pews, ready to air their views. The action wasn't solely about political discourse, though: the men of the New Model Army were fired with religious zeal, and at least half a day in the course of the debates was given over to prayer in the hope that God would guide those involved to the correct course of action. This church, where prayer and politics were intertwined, thus merits a historical pilgrimage today.

St Mary's Church
Putney High Street, London SW15 1SN
020 8788 4414
www.putneydebates.com
www.parishofputney.co.uk

Banqueting House, London
Nominated by Jerry Brotton, professor of Renaissance studies, Queen Mary, University of London
'Where the architecture of the Renaissance arrived in England'

Plumb in the heart of London's government district, the 17th-century Banqueting House, the only surviving reminder of the great Tudor and Stuart royal palace of Whitehall, has many claims to historical fame. It was the first structure to show Londoners what Renaissance architecture was all about. It was also the place where royal banquets were held and Jacobean masques performed, and near where King Charles I lost his head. In late Victorian times it morphed into a military museum, and was packed full of display cases, with the star attraction being the skeleton of Marengo, Napoleon's horse.

Strange, then, that the Banqueting House is rather overlooked as a heritage attraction, but as Jerry Brotton notes: 'You go there and people are looking the wrong way – the tourists stand with their backs to probably the most important historical building in London.' It's easy for attention to wander to the mounted Horse Guards standing to attention on the other side of Whitehall, but both architecturally and historically, the Banqueting House deserves to be admired. Its fine white stone exterior blends easily into the other stone exteriors around it, so from the outside it doesn't look awfully remarkable. Perhaps that isn't surprising, as the place was given a uniform dressing of Portland stone in a 19th-century restoration. If imitation is the sincerest form of flattery, the Banqueting House ought to be feeling thoroughly buttered up, surrounded as it now is by buildings that mimic the style it introduced. According to Brotton, 'The Banqueting House created the architecture of power that is prevalent throughout Whitehall.'

Inigo Jones, a self-taught architect, designed the building in 1619, having returned from a trip to Italy and brought back with him the ideas of the Italian Renaissance architect Andrea Palladio. He put them into practice by creating what's essentially a Palladian villa. The style of the place would have been very foreign at the time, as virtually nobody would have travelled to Europe to see the inspiration. As Brotton comments, 'It's hard for us today to grasp just how revolutionary it was.'

At the time it was built, it sat in considerable contrast to the colourful muddle of Tudor brick and timber structures that made up the Palace of

Whitehall. In 1698 a terrible fire destroyed practically all of that old palace, bar the Banqueting House. This brought centuries of royal residence on the site to an end. The place had been a favourite of Tudor and Stuart kings, and the Banqueting House was where the monarchs entertained to impress. Elizabeth I had a great timber hall erected on the site in 1581, and that was replaced with a brick and stone structure in 1609 by her successor, the first Stuart king of England, James I (who was also King James VI of Scotland). That building in turn burnt down a decade later, and the present hall was constructed straight away.

The style of the architecture is very consciously European, and there's a reason for that. It was intended that the building should be used as a venue for the marriage of King James's son, the future Charles I. His father was trying to marry him off to a Spanish princess, but Charles bungled the match, so its original purpose was not fulfilled. The building, though, remains an ostentatious statement of the power and aspirations of the Stuart kings.

The crowning glory of the Banqueting House, the magnificent painted ceiling panels by the Flemish master-artist Peter Paul Rubens, is indeed all about the greatness of the Stuart dynasty. Commissioned by Charles I in honour of his father, and installed by 1636, the ceiling panels are an amazing statement of admiration for what he saw as the wise and peaceful reign of James I. This place, though saturated with the divine power of the Stuart monarchs, was also where one of them met his maker. In the bloody aftermath of the civil war, Charles I was declared a traitor. It was on a scaffold outside the Banqueting House that he was executed.

After that, the building was used as an audience chamber by Oliver Cromwell, before coming back into royal hands on the Restoration of

Charles II in 1660. He was greeted there with great ceremony on his return to London. James VII/II followed his brother to the throne in 1685 and was the last king to live at the Palace of Whitehall. His short reign was ended when the crown was offered to his daughter Mary and her husband, William of Orange (see Brixham Harbour, page 205), a ceremony that took place in the Banqueting House in 1689. William found the place too damp for his liking, preferring instead his new palace in Kensington, so after the fire he didn't rebuild the royal residence, but instead had the Banqueting House converted to a Chapel Royal. In 1893 it was deconsecrated and made into a military museum. Now it's one of the five historic royal palaces (the Tower of London, Hampton Court, Kensington Palace and Kew Palace being the others), and as well as being open to the public, it has also reverted to its former entertainment purpose, as it can be hired out for private functions (so do check it's not booked before you make a visit).

The main attraction is definitely the Rubens ceiling. Don't worry about tripping as you crane your head up to see the baroque glories on display – there is very little to trip over as the floor is entirely free of furniture and other impediments, bar the raised throne dais at one end. The paintings, of course, are worth spending more than a little time on, as you try to understand what the assembled choir of cherubic figures were designed to indicate about the glories of the reign of James I.

It takes some imagination to get the measure of what happened here when you're faced with such a Spartan room. I'd advise that you sit on one of the window seats and imagine what it was like when a Jacobean masque was in full swing, for Inigo Jones and his partner, the playwright Ben Jonson, staged a series of these elaborate acting and communal dancing displays here in the 1620s and 1630s. Perhaps also let your mind wander to what happened here in 1649, when Charles was led through one of the large windows (maybe the one you're sitting in) to a scaffold outside to have his head removed from his shoulders.

Once you've had your fill and stepped back outside, take a short stroll up the road towards Trafalgar Square and you'll notice an equestrian statue. Closer inspection will reveal that it's none other than Charles I, staring back down Whitehall to the Banqueting House. The statue was commissioned by his son, Charles II, after the Restoration. The regicides who were responsible for the old king's death were themselves executed on the very spot where the statue stands, their memories now perpetually trampled under the raised hoof of his angry horse.

Banqueting House
Whitehall, London SWIA 2ER
0844 482 7777
www.hrp.org.uk/banquetinghouse

Rougemont Castle, Exeter, Devon
Nominated by Mark Stoyle, professor of history,
University of Southampton
'Where English attitudes to superstition and
witchcraft began to change'

Much of Exeter was hammered by German bombers during the Second World War, then hammered again by overzealous town planners afterwards, so it's a delightful surprise to come across the remains of the old castle amid all the city's harsh modernity. Rougemont Castle doesn't have a grand keep or dramatic ramparts to draw the crowds today, so it has a quiet and secluded feel, but its red Devon stone gateway is an impressive structure, and one of the oldest castle buildings in the country, dating back to 1068 when William the Conqueror chose the site as the best place to cow the city's unruly citizens. The castle sits within the northern angle of the Roman and later city walls, on a knob of volcanic red rock overlooking the centre of Exeter.

The rest of the remains are somewhat lost among later buildings, but the walls do run through the pleasant Rougemont and Northernhay Gardens, and you can follow a path right around the outside. The castle interior had for a long time been closed to the public as it contained a set of law courts. Now, however, those courts have been moved, so, for the first time in hundreds of years, one can actually pop inside the gate. The area is now a car park, open during the week, so it's still not a great visitor attraction, but plans are being considered to turn the space over to more of a cultural centre.

If you do spend some time poking around the ruins, you'll soon come across a curious plaque fixed to a wall beside the old gatehouse, in memory of the Devon Witches. Mark Stoyle explains why it's there: 'It is the last place in England where people are known to have been sentenced to death for committing the crime of witchcraft. They held the assize (criminal) courts at the castle in Exeter, and it was at those assizes, in August 1682, that three different women – Temperance Lloyd, Mary Trembles and Susanna Edwards – all from Bideford in north Devon, were convicted and sentenced to death for committing witchcraft and were executed a few days later outside the city. Those are the last three people (in England) who can definitely be shown to have been hanged for the crime of witchcraft.'

Another Devon woman, Alice Molland, is also mentioned on the plaque. She was tried three years later, in 1685, on a charge of having consumed the bodies of three other women through magic art. Molland was also condemned to death, and although we can't be sure that she was actually executed, most scholars think it likely that she was the very last person to be executed for witchcraft in England.

There's a good deal of evidence about the 1682 trial because three pamphlets and a ballad were published about it at the time, and these documents provide a lot of detail about what the witches were said to have done and the evidence given in their confessions. The trial was clearly a major public event that aroused local passions: 'There seems to have been a great outcry against the three,' notes Stoyle. 'The justices may have been partly swayed by that. There was a huge popular desire to see the witches brought to justice.'

It seems clear that a mob mentality forced the convictions through. The assize judge, Sir Thomas Raymond, was perhaps not entirely convinced of the case against the three elderly women, but such was the pitch of local feeling that a not guilty verdict posed the risk of sparking serious public disorder and may have guided his final decision. The significance of the story is that it helps to illustrate shifting attitudes towards witch - craft during the second half of the 17th century. 'Around this time,' says Stoyle, 'we see that those at the top of society were becoming increasingly sceptical about the whole idea of witchcraft. The great English witch-hunt of 1645–7 had taken place less than 40 years before this time, and many people lower down the social scale continued to believe very fervently in witchcraft for perhaps two centuries after this. Yet the fact that no more witches appear to have been executed in England after the 1680s is a sign that the social and judicial elite were beginning to take a very different view.'

The Exeter witches would probably have been imprisoned in the old county gaol, just next to the castle, on the site of what is now a nightclub. They would certainly have been familiar with the great Norman gate tower as they were dragged in and out of the court. However, the former court buildings within the castle walls are later than those in which the trial took place. Similarly, the streets they were shoved through to get to their execution place at Heavitree, a little way across the city and outside the walls, have been much altered. One of the women had to be strapped to a horse to get there, and on arrival she and her fellow 'witches' were hanged.

Clearly, this is a dark passage in history, and the plaque on the wall of the castle gate concludes with a call for 'an end to persecution and intolerance'. Persecution and intolerance certainly didn't end in the 1680s. As Stoyle notes, 'After this time there were many instances of crowd violence against supposed witches.' In fact, they continued to be prosecuted for some years after that. The last person convicted of witchcraft in England, though not executed, was Jane Wenham in 1712. The case of Jane Yorke in 1944 is often cited as the last prosecution for witchcraft, though technically she was convicted under the Witchcraft Act of 1736, which actually expunged the crime of witchcraft from the statute books, and instead called for the prosecution of those who 'pretend to exercise or use any kind of witchcraft, sorcery, inchantment, or conjuration'. Thus by then, witchcraft, officially at least, was not a practice given credence.

Exeter Castle gives an interesting insight into the way that attitudes towards witchcraft, superstition and magic had begun to change during the 17th century.

Exeter Castle
Castle Street, Exeter, Devon EX4 3PU
07968 797135
www.exetercastle.co.uk

Brixham Harbour, Devon

Nominated by K.A.J. McLay, head of history and archaeology, University of Chester

'Where Britain's constitutional monarchy was born'

A replica of Sir Francis Drake's *Golden Hind* is moored in the harbour at Brixham. You can go on board and be taken back to 1588 and the armada, when Protestant England was delivered from the Catholic Spanish threat. One hundred years after the armada, a second Protestant deliverance came about, when the Dutch ruler William of Orange landed in 1688 at Brixham, and went on to relieve the Catholic James VII and II of the English, Irish and Scottish crowns.

William arrived by invitation, a group of English peers having written to him for help in overturning James's pro-Catholic policies. They had chosen him because he was a prominent and nearby Protestant ruler, who also had close family links to the king. William was, in fact, nephew to James, and his English wife Mary was James's daughter.

James had been on the throne for only three years in 1688. His conversion to Catholicism, however, had been public knowledge since the early 1670s, and had worried those who feared he would accede if his brother Charles II left no legitimate male heir. That, of course, is exactly what happened, and when James followed Charles in 1685, he was met with armed resistance. Although he managed to see off uprisings by the Earl of Argyll and the Duke of Monmouth, William's arrival presented a much more serious challenge. Not only did he have the backing of some senior English figures, but he also arrived with a fleet that has been estimated as four times the size of the Spanish Armada and an army of more than 15,000 professional soldiers

William would not have seen the *Golden Hind* replica when his enormous fleet docked in Brixham, of course; it's been there only since the 1960s. Nor, obviously, would he have seen the statue of his own periwigged magnificence standing just along the harbour front from the replica ship. That statue was erected to commemorate the 200th bicentenary of his landing, at a time in the late 19th century when the idea of the onward march of Protestant Britain spreading its civilising values across the globe through munificent imperialism was very much in vogue.

The landing of 1688 sits squarely alongside 1588 in the pantheon of Protestant progress (a fact reinforced by the date of the landing – 5 November – which harked back to another Protestant success story, namely the foiling of the Catholic plot to blow up parliament in 1605). William and Mary's arrival initiated what used to be widely known as the Glorious or Bloodless Revolution, reflecting the fact that King James fled England without a fight (though James himself shed quite a lot of blood as he was afflicted with incessant nosebleeds, which were part of the reason why he couldn't organise a stand against William). Historians now take a more nuanced view of events and recognise that a considerable amount of blood was spilt, particularly in Scotland and Ireland.

Despite that recasting of the story, K.A.J. McLay explains that Brixham is still a very important place in British history. 'I've chosen the harbour and the landing spot of William of Orange because it marks the initiation of the revolution of 1688. Domestically, in terms of the constitutional settlement, it was fairly radical, forcing Britain towards the modern day. I think the system we now have could be dated back quite effectively to 1688, with the establishment of a mixed constitutional system, epitomised by the constitutional doctrine of a king and queen in parliament rather than one being supreme or more sovereign than the other. In a sense, it worked against the trend in European government at the time and the trend to absolutism, which had really taken hold over most of west and central Europe. That was stopped in its tracks in Britain by William's intervention based on his landing at Brixham.'

William's landing spot was dictated more by weather than choice: the winds changed and forced his fleet further down the Channel than intended. In McLay's view, that was a good thing for this foreign invader: 'The southwest had always been uncomfortable with James's reign. Also William had a strategy of non-confrontation – he couldn't afford to be seen to be engaging James and his armies immediately in an act of conquest because the fear was that would swing the English behind the king against a foreign conqueror. His landing in this small and arguably quite obscure place was therefore useful to William.'

His men marched up from their landing point (marked by a plaque on the harbour) along the road now called Overgang (Dutch for 'passageway') to camp above Brixham. Then they went to Exeter to wait for English support to muster, which it duly did. By December, he'd marched his army without incident to London, while all support for James appeared to have slipped away. In February 1689 he and his wife were crowned joint monarchs as William and Mary, and also signed the Declaration of Rights, a document that sought to limit the power of the sovereign, and affirmed parliament's right to control taxation and legislation.

William managed to establish himself on the throne without undue difficulty, but that wasn't the last of James. The deposed king fled to France and then crossed the sea to Ireland, where he hoped to gather support for an assault to regain his kingdom. This led to the 1690 set-piece battle in Ireland, at the Boyne, when James was beaten. After that he resigned himself to a life in exile, dying in France in 1701. Supporters of the Stuart dynasty, the Jacobites, continued to stoke up resistance for the next half-century.

There is much that stems from Brixham harbour, not least the long-term development of constitutional monarchy in Britain, and the short-term Jacobite challenge to that monarchy. The understated little plaque on the harbourside that marks the spot where William landed is the start of the story, while the rather more ostentatious Victorian statue of the incoming king next to Drake's replica ship speaks of the greater significance that the episode was eventually to acquire.

Brixham Harbour
Brixham, Devon TQ5
www.torbay.gov.uk

PART 2

INDUSTRY, EMPIRE AND WAR

The second half of this book takes us from 1688 up to the 1960s. After the drama of the 1688 Revolution, many things started to change in Britain: kings and queens began to move slightly to stage left, and new themes and ideas emerged, most notably the concept of the Industrial Revolution. We see the stirrings of the latter at the place where some believe it started, at Ironbridge Gorge in Shropshire, and its spread around the country, from the copper works of Swansea to the wool market of Halifax.

Then we have industry and innovation in full swing, as at Soho House in Birmingham, the iron and coal works at Blaenavon, and then the coming of the railways at Penydarren and on the Stockton to Darlington line. Later you can see how workers came to push against a system that seemed set to force them down (the essays on Manchester Free Trade Hall and the Dorset village of Tolpuddle deal with that) and how accommodation began to be reached between workers and industrialists (as at the model town of Saltaire).

The development of industry was one of the driving forces and principal motivations of another great theme of this period – the rise of Britain as an imperial force and its surprising ascent to global superpower. Naval strength underpinned this, and you can see signs of this at the Old Naval College in Greenwich, the Cook House in Whitby, and later on board the SS *Great Britain* and HMS *Warrior*. The development of new financial systems to harness the increased wealth of the nation (as evidenced at the Bank of England), and new technologies (Porthcurno) also helped to give thrust to the imperial project.

Signal evidence of the power and bluster of the imperial motherland can be seen across Britain, as at St George's Hall in Liverpool or the People's Palace in Glasgow. The darker side of the story, the input that slavery made to Britain's imperial prosperity, can be glimpsed at Harewood House, while the fight against that business figures on Hull High Street.

Slaves were not the only people to be moved around the globe during this period. Immigration and emigration, forced or voluntary, were notable features, and there are several places across Britain where you can see this in evidence, including Bevis Marks Synagogue, Badbea Clearance Village, Albert Docks in Liverpool and the Titanic dockyard in Belfast.

Eventually, Britain could no longer maintain its imperial position, partly because of the stresses imposed by the two world wars of the 20th century (which you can see evidence of at the Cenotaph in London, the War Tunnels at Dover, Bletchley Park, and the memorials at Capel le Ferne and Spean Bridge). Britain emerged from the end of the Second World War in 1945 as a very different country, and if you visit the Royal Festival Hall in London, you'll find evidence of a nation looking for a new direction. It found that new path in the cultural revolution of the 1960s, typified by Liverpool's Cavern Club. That decade made such a clear break with what went before that it provides a natural end point for this book.

Old Royal Naval College, Greenwich, London

Nominated by Brian Lavery, curator emeritus, National Maritime Museum, Greenwich

'Where you can gaze at Britain's naval heritage'

You would expect some decent brushwork in a place going by the name of the Painted Hall. This is far more than just a lick of magnolia, though – it's a baroque feast plunging from ceiling to floor. The Painted Hall is the star attraction in what is now called the Old Royal Naval College complex, and it's part of the wider World Heritage Site that encompasses all of Maritime Greenwich along the banks of the river Thames. According to Brian Lavery, 'It's symbolic of a great deal of naval history, as well as being possibly the finest architecture in the country.'

Britain's navy has always been a key plank of the nation's success and survival. There are many sites where you can see evidence of this, mostly at ports on the coast, but perhaps the best way to get a feel for the high esteem in which the navy has been held is to come inland a little, to Greenwich, to consider the cluster of buildings that from the end of the 18th century through to the later 19th made up the Royal Naval College, and before that the Royal Hospital for Seamen.

It's a place that is curiously overlooked in the national pantheon of heritage attractions. You'll have seen it as a backdrop in films, no doubt, as it's a regular location for period dramas such as *The Madness of King George*. However, the Old Naval College isn't often mentioned as one of London's big historic attractions, let alone Britain's. Perhaps it suffers because of the wealth of riches around it. The National Maritime

Museum, the Queen's House and the Royal Observatory, all set in the grounds of Greenwich Park, are just a stone's throw away.

Maybe the college's low profile is because it's only in the last decade, after years of military use, that it has become properly accessible to the public. A new interpretation centre in the Pepys Building, just outside the college complex, should raise its presence now, though. And about time too, as there's a long historical story to be told here. There have been palatial buildings on this site since Tudor times. Henry VIII was born in Greenwich Palace, as were his daughters, Mary and Elizabeth. Henry had the place transformed into a tournament venue and held spectacular jousts here. It was also the place from which Queen Elizabeth waved off her explorers on their global voyages.

There is nothing to see of the Tudor palace today. Instead you have the powerful architecture of Sir Christopher Wren's Royal Hospital for Seamen, a series of monumental quadrangles along the banks of the Thames. Wren, the great architect who was already famous for designing St Paul's Cathedral, was called upon to build this hostel for old sailors on the site of the old palace. Brian Lavery explains what happened: 'Queen Mary in the 1690s was distressed to see poor seamen on the streets after all they'd done for the country, so, conscience-stricken, she gave them this great site, the former royal palace. Her husband William III thought it was a bit extravagant, but when Mary died, he had to carry it on. Later George II pumped more money into it.'

For the old sailors, life at Greenwich was not that far removed from their previous life aboard ship, though the replacement of hammocks with beds would have made things a little more comfortable for them. Known as 'pensioners' when they became residents of the Royal Hospital, they were originally supposed to take their meals in the Painted Hall, but once the paint was dry there, it was clearly far too posh for that. Instead, they supplemented their income by guiding respectable visitors around the hall.

The decoration of the Painted Hall took almost two decades to complete at the start of the 18th century. It's a *trompe l'oeil* masterpiece by James Thornhill, who also painted another Wren-designed London dome, the rather more famous one in St Paul's Cathedral. The story being told here is essentially the triumph of the Protestant constitutional monarchy in Britain over its Catholic absolutist counterparts on the Continent. This was a prominent matter at the time, the revolution of 1688, when the Catholic King James had been deposed by his Protestant daughter Mary and her Dutch husband William, still being a very clear and recent memory.

It's not surprising that Queen Mary features prominently in the main picture in the Lower Hall ceiling; she stands alongside the victorious William III, his foot resting on a defeated Louis XIV of France. Then, in the Upper Hall behind, you have the Hanoverian royal family, who continued Britain's Protestant monarchy into the 18th century. There is a lot going on in this fabulous artwork, which is in part an allegory of the triumph of peace and liberty over tyranny, and in part a celebration of the royal family, so you might find it useful to enquire of the friendly and knowledgeable yeoman warders about what exactly you're looking at. When you're in the Upper Hall, drag yourself back into the naval story by remembering that here was where Admiral Horatio Nelson was laid in state after his death at Trafalgar in 1805. Pop your head inside the small room off to the side of the Upper Hall, where the fallen admiral's body was prepared for the crowds of onlookers who came to pay their respects, and take a look out the window to the Nelson pediment in the courtyard outside.

You ought also to head across the road to see the chapel, or take the more entertaining, if slightly damp and musty route, to it through Ridley's underground passage. If you're lucky, you might hear singing by students from the Trinity School of Music, which is now housed in one of the old hospital buildings. The other quadrangles on the site are now home to Greenwich University, so you'll see a lot of students milling around. This is a recent development, as up until the end of the 20th century, the students here would have been naval officers at the Royal Naval College, training in the art of sea warfare, which was the function of the place from 1873 to 1998. (The hospital closed in 1869 because a lack of wars had reduced the number of needy pensioners.)

The new interpretation centre, Discover Greenwich, does a good job of explaining the story of the Old Royal Naval College, with a few nice touches, such as the re-creation of the Tudor palace and the 'cot' of a hospital pensioner. There's enough to keep you busy here for some hours, and that's without even considering going across the road to the National Maritime Museum and beyond to the Royal Observatory on the hill.

Old Royal Naval College
2 Cutty Sark Gardens, Greenwich, London SE10 9LW
020 8269 4747
www.oldroyalnavalcollege.org

Bank of England, London

Nominated by Anne Murphy, lecturer in history,
University of Hertfordshire
'Where Britain's financial stability has its roots'

It is not easy to appreciate the scale of the Bank of England, nestled as it is within its cut-stone natural habitat in the heart of London's financial district. You can walk around its monumental exterior, following the long, windowless walls and wondering what's inside, and there are a few places where you can step back and see its commanding height. You can get a good look at the colonnaded front façade, which I think could fairly be described as imposing, from the steps of the Royal Exchange opposite. But what you can't see from any angle is that the compound goes down as well as up, with a substantial area below ground level.

The bank has been on its current site in Threadneedle Street since 1734, gradually expanding over the years to become a block of buildings within buildings, with an outer wall designed to keep the money in and intruders out. Between the wars in the 20th century it was largely rebuilt, with most of the earlier building demolished.

Although you'll likely be turned away from the main doors if you don't have any particular bank business to conduct, you can get a feel of what's inside by popping around the corner and paying a visit to the Bank of England Museum. Despite the security scanners, it's a friendly place inside, with a reconstruction of an 18th-century banking hall and stock office, and some interesting displays on the history of the bank. From here you can get a sense of why the Bank of England matters in the story of Britain.

'Economic and financial stability are key to our individual wellbeing, and also to the country's economic and political wellbeing,' says Anne Murphy. 'Political strength and security go with economic strength and security. They help to establish our place in the world. The Bank of England, since it was established in 1694, has stood at the centre of that process of creating economic and financial stability.'

One of the reasons the bank was founded at the end of the 17th century, however, was not stability, but war. In 1694, England's new king, William III, had brought his nation into conflict with France, and he needed money to fund the fight. The answer came from a man called William Paterson, a Scottish merchant, who proposed the creation of a bank of credit (along the lines of an existing Dutch model, familiar to the new king) to create a fund for long-term public borrowing. There was a key difference, though, in the way the Bank of England operated compared to its Continental counterpart.

'It's uniquely British,' says Anne Murphy. 'There were public banks in various places by 1694 – the most obvious is the Wisselbank in Amsterdam. But the Bank of England was set up for a uniquely British purpose and on unique lines. It was an accident of war. If we hadn't been at war in the 1690s, the bank wouldn't have been established. The Wisselbank didn't issue notes and the Bank of England did, so that's what separated the two. Its place as the body that stands between the public lending money and the government taking it makes it uniquely British.'

After its creation, the bank was quickly able to loan the government £1.2 million. Yet, in its early years, its future was far from assured. It was given only a 12-year charter, and it wasn't until the bursting of the South Sea Bubble in 1720 that the Bank of England became more firmly established. The South Sea Company, formed in 1711, was given a monopoly on trade with South America in return for taking on and consolidating the national debt from the War of the Spanish Succession (see Blenheim Palace, opposite). In the following years, further portions of the national debt were converted into South Sea Company shares, with investors encouraged to buy them at ever higher prices on the promise of untold riches in South America. In 1720, when that promise failed to materialise, the price of the shares peaked and then plummeted, causing many people in Britain to lose their fortunes. The Bank of England took on a measure of responsibility for the national debt in the fallout of 1720. Shortly after that, it moved to its permanent premises on Threadneedle Street and became a financial fixture, and a key plank on which the nation's future success depended.

'The bank's chief job when it was set up was to lend money to the government,' says Murphy. 'It had to figure out a way to carve itself a niche, not just to be the government's pawn. This was an interesting balancing act that it had to undertake throughout the 18th century and much of the 19th as well. Without the bank's ability to raise and manage money (it managed most of the government's debt), Britain would not be the country it became in the 19th century. It wouldn't have been able to win the wars of the 18th century, all of which were dependent on being able to raise a lot of money quickly, and on sustaining that money-raising ability. Much of the money came from ordinary British citizens, and they had to trust the organisation to which they were lending money. Arguably, it's the fact that the Bank of England stood between them and the government, acting as a voice for them, as overseer of what was going on, and as a check on any government tendencies to renege on that debt, that established this trust.'

Of course, the public's faith in the banking system has been somewhat called into question in recent years. The Bank of England has shown itself quite able to respond to changing times and conditions over the last three centuries, as a visit to the museum will demonstrate, and now, more than ever, it seems like a good time to be informed on this subject. A trip to the bank and its museum is an excellent way to get to grips with the financial history of Britain, and the way it has shaped the development of the nation.

Bank of England
Threadneedle Street, London EC2R 8AH
020 7601 4444
www.bankofengland.co.uk

Blenheim Palace, Oxfordshire

Nominated by Saul David, professor of war studies, University of Buckingham
'Where you can see the moment Britain arrived as a major European power'

Winston Churchill was born at Blenheim. As he subsequently went on to lead Britain successfully through the Second World War, he's rather usurped his arguably equally illustrious forebear as the most famous resident of the palace.

The man in question, and for whom Blenheim was built, was John Churchill, 1st Duke of Marlborough. The palace was his reward from Queen Anne for his leading role in the 1704 victory over the French at the Battle of Blenheim in the War of the Spanish Succession (a Europe-wide conflict in which Britain became embroiled, over who should succeed to the Spanish throne at the start of the 18th century). You can see a lot of both Churchill and Marlborough in Blenheim today. The place is studded with portraits of the 1st Duke, and with paintings of and by Churchill (some of his landscape scenes of Blenheim adorn the walls of the palace).

According to Saul David, it's Marlborough rather than Churchill who makes Blenheim Palace important. For him, Marlborough's victory at Blenheim was the battle that gave the nation a major martial fillip, the battle that ended a three-century-long drought of military victories of any note for England on foreign soil. And it's all the more notable for the nature of the opposition. As David says, 'By the time of Marlborough, there was one absolutely dominant power in Europe, and that was the France of Louis XIV. No one saw any of the other European armies as coming close, and that's why the battle of Blenheim is so significant: not only was it a victory, it was a destruction – one of these very rare battles where you should lose, but you don't just win, you absolutely annihilate the enemy.'

If you're looking for somewhere that really demonstrates the significance of this victory, you do not have to trek over to the Bavarian village of Blindheim (where the battle was fought) to find it. Blenheim Palace is immense and stunning. Architecturally and externally, it's not much changed from how it would have looked in the early 18th century – a fine example of English baroque. To approach it is to be awed. The reason for its magnificence is because it was designed to reflect the glory of the battle and its victor. It was to be paid for by the state in recognition of the nation's gratitude to Marlborough. In fact, the state didn't fully pay up (by the final years of Queen Anne's reign, Marlborough was no longer in favour, so the finance for the construction dried up and the duke had to finish the job with his own money), but the sentiment remains plain to see in the palace today.

You have only to take in the scale of the building to feel how grateful queen and country were for Marlborough's victory. He was, at the time, a hero who inspired the nation. 'No private house will ever be built like that again,' comments Saul David, 'and it was paid for by the state. That fact reflects the extraordinary gratitude for an amazing general. Blenheim, the first major victory since Agincourt, put us on the map as a major Continental power. It was hugely significant in terms of our politics, and also in the confidence and standing it gave to the army – the sense that it could take on anyone. That feeling carried on, with ups and downs, right the way through the next 300 years. It was the moment we arrived as a major European power in modern times.'

What's interesting is that Marlborough isn't one of our national heroes today. Neither his name nor the battles he won, nor indeed the war he fought in, strike much of a chord for most Britons today. David believes it's because he had the misfortune to live in unfashionable times. 'The Duke of Marlborough still hasn't received his due and never will because he fought at a very unfashionable time. The War of the Spanish Succession has never worked well in history books or novels for that matter.'

So why don't we know more about Marlborough? Perhaps it's because schools don't tend to teach his period of history, as it's somewhat complicated with lots of belligerents involved, and yes, just a little bit foreign. Fought as it was mostly across distant fields of Europe, the War of the

Spanish Succession lacks the immediacy and impact of some other conflicts to us in Britain, plus it has the disadvantage of a distinctly unsnappy title.

Whatever our modern views on the war, the victor himself was much fêted, and you can see that most clearly when you step into Blenheim's Great Hall, which is quite a room in which to start your visit. Huge, high-ceilinged, multi-alcoved, flag-festooned and stacked with statues, it's all a bit of an overload for the eyes. But your gaze will inevitably be drawn upwards, where you'll see Marlborough painted in classical glory, kneeling to Britannia and proffering a plan of the battle of Blenheim.

Before you go on, look back through the door of the Great Hall, and you'll see across the lake and grounds to his pedestal – a column, 41 metres (135 feet) high on which Marlborough stands as a Roman general. On its base is an inscription detailing all his martial glories. You get the picture: Marlborough was very much the man.

Beyond the sheer scale and grandeur of the palace, the other clear and direct link here with the battle of Blenheim are the tapestries. Marlborough commissioned a set of them to commemorate his victories in the wars, and they are still hung throughout the building. The tapestry in the Green Writing Room is the one to stop you in your tracks. It's huge, stretching around a corner of the room. The scene it portrays is impressively detailed, and is apparently a very precise rendition of the battle. Marlborough was concerned to make sure that it was accurate, so he supplied his own battle plans to the designer. Unsurprisingly, the duke stands out from the rest of the scene, resplendent in his red jacket, as he stretches out his baton to receive the French surrender.

So, for all that, Blenheim is the place to go if you want to get a sense of the burgeoning military might of the early 18th-century nation, and to learn a little more about a man who probably deserves to be more of a central figure in Britain's story. Of course that shouldn't stop you from popping into the room where the man around whom more recent British history revolves. Churchill, a descendent of the 1st Duke and cousin to the 9th, found his own glory as Britain's wartime premier and BBC-crowned Greatest Briton. You can see the room where he was born in 1874, complete with mementoes of his life, including curls of his baby hair and one of his trademark siren suits.

Beyond that, there is much else to see here – it is a World Heritage Site after all. Both the Long Library, with its distinctly out-of-place organ, and the Saloon, with its marbled, muralled splendour, deserve honourable mention. You'd have to be very pushed for time, or have arrived on a singularly inclement day, not to want to devote some of your visit to a stroll round the grounds.

Finally, don't forget that although named a palace, Blenheim was never a royal residence; it was built to be a private home for the man who made his country great and, as David says: 'For a house reflecting an event, a major moment in our history, there's nothing to compare with it.'

Blenheim Palace
Woodstock, Oxfordshire OX20 1PP
01993 810500
www.blenheimpalace.com

Bevis Marks Synagogue, London

Nominated by Madge Dresser, reader in history,
University of the West of England
'Where you can see how far immigration has
influenced Britain'

There are many half-hidden historic gems squirrelled away behind office blocks in the heart of London. Bevis Marks Synagogue is one of them. Set back off Bevis Marks road through an arch guarded by finely decorated wrought-iron gates, you'll find a little courtyard and a handsome, though plain-fronted, brick building. It's the oldest synagogue in Britain, having celebrated its 300th anniversary in 2001.

When the synagogue was opened back in 1701, the presence of openly Jewish people in England was a recent development. In 1290 Edward I had expelled all Jews from his kingdom (anti-Semitism was rife in medieval England, and the expulsion was a populist measure made in return for the granting of a tax to alleviate Edward's heavy debts), and it wasn't until the 16th century that a few Portuguese and Spanish Jewish merchants returned to Bristol and London, keeping their faith secret. In 1655, during those kingless days after the civil wars, when Oliver Cromwell was running the country, a conference was held in London to discuss whether Jews should be readmitted. Cromwell, for one, was keen to see the Jews return because it tallied with the Puritan prophecies to which he subscribed, about the Second Coming of Christ, which required the Jews to be scattered to the four corners of the world. Although that conference ended without agreement, Jews were at least tolerated once more in England from that point on.

The Jews who came here were mostly from the community of Spanish and Portuguese exiles that had settled in Amsterdam after the Spanish Inquisition. As Madge Dresser notes, this influx of new Jewish immigrants brought more than just their religion from Amsterdam. 'The Jews who came were admitted by Cromwell partly for political and religious reasons, but also because they had a well-established trading network that brought much-needed credit into the country. As a trading community, Jews helped to foster the emerging capitalist economy. These days we tend to think of capitalism as corporate and oppressive if we're of a progressive bent, but in those days it was the harbinger of liberalism and an implicit challenge to absolutist monarchy and its claim that the state should control all aspects of people's religious and economic life. Freedom to pursue profit and freedom of conscience were intertwined, and by admitting Jews, Cromwell was in effect cocking a snook at the Spanish, saying "We're not absolutist oppressors like them".'

In the half century between the readmission of the Jews and the completion of Bevis Marks Synagogue, the government's need for credit led to the creation of the Bank of England (page 216), so it was a period of financial ideas and change. It's no great surprise that the synagogue sits within the Square Mile of London's financial district, but the building is far removed from City ostentation. Its exterior is solid but plain, and within it's not particularly showy either. It has something of a Dutch feel to it, but in its general austerity it's also not too far removed from nonconformist churches of the time. That's in part because it was designed by a Quaker called Joseph Avis. 'The Jews weren't coming in as equals,' says Dresser, 'they were coming in by permission of Cromwell and because it suited the authorities. They didn't have the right to own and bequeath property. With all that, they felt a kindred spirit with the Quaker who designed the building.'

The chapel-like feel of the place is heightened by the rows of wooden pews, which look like they could have come straight out of a London parish church, and might well have been fashioned in the same carpentry workshops that were making the seats for all the new churches that were built in London after the Great Fire of 1666. The only signs of opulence are the magnificent brass candelabra that were donated from Amsterdam's Great Synagogue back in the 17th century. What you see in Bevis Marks when you sit on those well-worn wooden pews is basically not far off what you'd have seen when it opened.

So it's a lovely historic building and a quiet place to reflect on its broader significance. For Dresser, 'It symbolises to me the beginnings of the global economy, the beginnings of religious toleration, the beginnings of a multicultural society, the beginnings of the City.'

The Spanish and Portuguese Jews were not the only immigrant communities to come to London. The Protestant Huguenots came from France in large numbers from the 1670s onwards, and other religious refugees arrived here from the Palatine in Germany in the early 18th century, often on their way to a new life in America.

Immigrants tended to gravitate towards London's East End, and from Bevis Marks you're just a few steps away from Whitechapel Road, which takes you into the heart of the immigrant area. It's a great street to walk down to understand the long-term impact of immigration in Britain. Irish, German and Jewish immigrants have all settled here in the last few centuries, though now it has an Asian or Bangladeshi feel to it.

Certainly, to visit Whitechapel today is to see multicultural Britain in all its richness. As you're taking in the bustle of the busy and very cosmopolitan road, think back to the quiet calmness of the old synagogue and German church a few streets away to remind yourself that immigration is really nothing new in this country.

Bevis Marks Synagogue
4 Heneage Lane, London EC3A 5DQ
020 7626 1274
www.bevismarks.org.uk

Old Parliament Hall, Edinburgh
Nominated by Derek Patrick, lecturer in history,
University of Dundee
'Where you can trace the story of Scotland's parliament'

The Scottish parliament meets today in its purpose-built home at the foot of the Royal Mile by Holyroodhouse in Edinburgh. It's a dramatically modern building, all timber, granite and steel, which you can visit to see the politicians in session. In 1997, a devolution referendum was held in Scotland with the outcome being that Scotland's parliament was reinstated after an almost 300-year absence. Prior to that referendum, the last time that parliament was convened in the city was in 1707. The place where that earlier Scottish parliament met, the Old Parliament Hall, still survives, further up the Royal Mile, nestling inconspicuously behind St Giles' Cathedral (page 186).

The parliament in Scotland had medieval origins, but until 1639 it had never had a permanent home (from 1563 until the 1630s it had met in the central aisle of St Giles'). The hall was constructed at the request of King Charles I (who was king of Scotland, Ireland and England) and was officially opened in 1639. You can tour the hall today, but the 17th-century fabric is easy to miss because it is encased within a later Georgian façade. The place is now part of a complex of law courts, so prepare to be scanned to get in, but the interior of the hall isn't that much different from how it would have been in the 17th century. The floor would have been stone not wood, the stained-glass window would not have been there, but the hammerbeam roof is original. The hall now throngs with lawyers and their clients rather than parliamentarians, but it's still an atmospheric place.

Charles I was executed during the civil wars, but his son Charles II was restored to the throne in 1660 and is now memorialised in a famous equestrian statue outside Parliament Hall that depicts him as a Roman emperor. His brother James succeeded him in 1685, but he was to become embroiled in another revolution in 1688, when William and Mary came to England at the invitation of Protestants who did not agree with James's pro-Catholic policies.

By the start of 1689, James had fled England (see Brixham Harbour, 205), and William and Mary had been crowned joint monarchs in London, but the Scots had yet to take a view on the matter because James had not technically fled Scotland. When the Scottish parliament met at Parliament Hall, they declared that he had in fact forfeited his crown, so they resolved to offer it to William and Mary. Derek Patrick takes up the story: 'For some reason the Scots were always viewed as reluctant to rebel in 1689. Rebellion was seen to be a largely English invention, with events in Scotland tagged on as an afterthought. But if you actually look at the records of the Scottish parliament, you'll see that's not so. The people who met at the parliament were committed to the revolution and they made some crucial decisions.'

Scotland's offer to William and Mary was not without conditions. These were expressed in a document called the Claim of Right, issued in April 1689, a statement of grievances against King James and a list of obligations for the new king and queen. The Claim of Right, says Patrick, helped set in train the move towards the union of the two nations of England and Scotland in 1707.

'It was really a constitutional document with a constitutional flavour. It set the tone between parliament and monarch from then until union. It became much more difficult for King William and later Queen Anne to manage the parliament effectively. They became much more dependent on officers of state. It grew really difficult for the king to control Scotland, and that's one of the reasons why he began to look towards union. This was all played out against the backdrop of Edinburgh and the Parliament Hall. It became crucial. Certainly, on the way to union, parliament became volatile and the focus of attention.'

The union of 1707, under William and Mary's successor Queen Anne, brought an end to the role of the hall in Edinburgh for parliamentary business. The last meeting of the independent Scottish parliament took place in the Old Parliament Hall on 28 April 1707, before it was transferred to Westminster. It's a contentious point in history, remembered in some quarters as the moment, when, in the much-quoted words of the poet Robert Burns, the Scots were 'bought and sold for English gold'. Historians continue to debate whether the union was forced on, or actually welcomed by, the Scottish people. Certainly, it did not bring an end to the previous century's disputes, as there were still many who felt aggrieved at the removal of King James back in 1689: they were to press their Jacobite cause in the years ahead (see Fort George, 238), and create continuing problems for those intent on pushing England and Scotland together in a new British project. In the long run, the Jacobite cause faltered and the project was to become imperial and global in reach through the course of the 18th and 19th centuries.

Now that Scotland's parliament is back up and running after its three-century hiatus, it's all the more timely to take a long look at the origins of the institution at the Old Parliament Hall, and of course to combine the visit with a look at its new home at the foot of Edinburgh's Royal Mile.

Old Parliament Hall
Parliament Square, Edinburgh EH1 1EW
0131 348 5200
www.scottish.parliament.uk

Ironbridge Gorge, Shropshire
Nominated by Dominic Sandbrook, historian, writer and columnist
'Where the Industrial Revolution began (symbolically at least)'

The Ironbridge Gorge in Shropshire is often tagged as the 'Birthplace of Industry'. The reason why it holds that grand title, or at least one of the reasons, is for what went on in a blast furnace that is now housed under a protective glass pyramid in front of the Coalbrookdale Museum of Iron. It's an old furnace, but not any old furnace: here, in 1709, Abraham Darby perfected the process of smelting iron using coke.

Iron-making had been going on in these parts for some time before 1709. Darby, who had a brass-making business in Bristol before coming to Shropshire, would presumably have known that Coalbrookdale had a long history of coal-mining and iron-working going back to the mid 16th century, when Sir Robert Brooke took over the estate from the recently dissolved Wenlock Priory and began exploiting its mineral wealth. Indeed, Darby didn't build the furnace in 1709; it was already half a century old when he took it over and renovated it. What he did do, critically, was to work out how to use coke (part-burnt coal) rather than charcoal (part-burnt wood) in the smelting process. The reliance on charcoal up to this point had been a severe impediment to the development of iron-making on an industrial scale; there simply wasn't enough wood available to turn into charcoal to allow for large-scale iron-making in one place. Darby solved the problem with coke, and it's a moment that is often cited as the catalyst for the Industrial Revolution.

Dominic Sandbrook is in no doubt as to its significance. 'The Ironbridge Gorge is not merely one of the most beautiful corners of the English countryside, it's also the single most important historical site anywhere on these islands, and probably in Europe. It is true that the Industrial Revolution – the revolution that marks the transition to the modern era – did not really begin in any one place. But as the site where Abraham Darby first perfected the technique of smelting iron with coke, Ironbridge well deserves its symbolic reputation as the birthplace of industry.'

Darby's furnace is now handsomely preserved and displayed, and it affords the visitor a great opportunity to get very close to this notable industrial monument. You can climb the stairs to the charging ramp, and look down into the mouth of the furnace, through which the iron ore and coke would have been poured back in 1709. Then you can walk around the base and see where the molten iron would have been tapped out. The tent of glass over the whole affair lends the surviving brickwork a calm and stately nature, which is perhaps rather out of keeping with its original purpose, yet feels appropriate enough today.

Once you've explored the remains of this notable piece of industrial heritage, you'd be well advised to spend an hour or so in the adjacent Coalbrookdale Museum of Iron, which gives chapter and verse on the story of iron-making here and its impact on the development of the Industrial Revolution. Then you'll be ready to see the rest of Ironbridge Gorge, which is now one expansive World Heritage Site. It's full of historical attractions, none more obvious than the famous Iron Bridge, the first of its kind in the world, which was built by Darby's grandson.

'The spectacular Iron Bridge itself, soaring across the river Severn to Broseley, is still one of the wonders of the modern world,' comments Sandbrook. 'Nowhere in Britain do you get a better sense of the sweat and enterprise wrapped up in the Industrial Revolution, or of its dramatic impact on the rural landscape. Indeed, what makes Ironbridge so spectacular is that the great Iron Bridge rises so unexpectedly out of an otherwise pastoral landscape. Coming from the little medieval town of Much Wenlock, just a few minutes away, you feel that you are jumping forward centuries in time – which is exactly how the people of Shropshire must have felt when the bridge first went up in the summer of 1779.'

The bridge is a must-see. You can walk across it, drive past it, and get quite a nice view of it from the Museum of the Gorge just beneath. The problem, notes Sandbrook, is that you won't be able to linger too long in respectful admiration if you're going to take in the rest of the history of the place. 'I've been dozens of times to Ironbridge and I still haven't seen all the historical sites. By one estimate, there are 35, from chapels to workshops, all packed into a tiny cliffside village. Nothing beats walking over the bridge across the river Severn and marvelling at our ancestors' ingenuity, although a trip to the Coalport Tar Tunnel, where the bitumen literally oozes through the walls, is right up there. There's even an excellent Victorian pub, the Horse and Jockey, which serves the best steak and kidney pies in England, and there you should raise a pint of the local ale to the town's favourite son, the Wolves captain Billy Wright, the first footballer in history to win a hundred caps for his country.'

If you're visiting just for the day, you would be hard pressed to do all of the above *and* fit in a visit to Blists Hill Victorian Town, a recreated 19th-century settlement a little further along the valley. It would be a shame to miss it as it gives a great feel for the sort of society that the changes wrought by the Industrial Revolution gave to Britain. To get to Blists Hill from Darby's furnace, it's a short drive that will take you past the Iron Bridge, and on via the remains of the Bedlam Furnaces, built in the 1750s specifically for coke-smelting of iron. They feature in the darkly satanic painting *Coalbrookdale by Night* by Philippe de Loutherbourg, which has come to typify the polluted and smoke-soured complexion of the Industrial Revolution that we tend to think of today.

With that in mind, you've got an interesting chronological journey to make, starting with Darby's furnace, which kick-started Britain's move into the Industrial Revolution, along to one of its crowning glories, the Iron Bridge itself, then on past the Bedlam Furnaces, inspiration for the painting that's gifted us with the abiding impression of the fire and fury of the age, finally ending at a re-creation of the Victorian society that emerged out of this period of enormous change and development.

Ironbridge Gorge

Coalbrookdale Museum of Iron, Coalbrookdale, Telford, Shropshire TF8 7DQ

01952 884391

www.ironbridge.org.uk

Captain Cook Memorial Museum, Whitby, North Yorkshire

Nominated by Glyn Williams, emeritus professor of history, Queen Mary, University of London
'Where you can understand what drove Captain Cook on his global explorations'

Up under the rafters of a large 17th-century house on the edge of Whitby harbour is the attic room in which lodged the apprentices of the Quaker sea captain and shipowner John Walker. One of those apprentices, from 1746 to 1749, was the teenaged James Cook, later to be Captain Cook, perhaps the most famous explorer in history.

The house is now the Captain Cook Memorial Museum, open to the public, so you can go up into that attic and get a feel of where the man spent three of his most formative years. Appropriately enough, some of the rafters exposed in the roof void were originally ships' timbers. The attic is now a temporary exhibition space, so it's not dressed up with

While living in this house James Cook developed many of the
characteristics that made him a great explorer

hammocks or divided into smaller rooms as it might have been in Cook's
day (there would have been several apprentices to Walker at any one time,
though some of the time they would have been out at sea, of course). It's
nothing that a bit of imagination can't resolve, though, to picture a serious
young man studying his books, perhaps occasionally looking out to the
beckoning sea, readying himself for what lay ahead.

Says Glyn Williams, 'Not only did he live there, he had to accept the
lifestyle of a Quaker household. If you look at his later career and the characteristics that define him – his sobriety, his single-mindedness and his
humility – I think there's a very strong case for arguing that those
characteristics were at least strengthened and confirmed by those years
with the Walkers.'

The ground floor of the house today has been restored to the Quaker look that it would have had when Cook was there, so you can see the austere, picture-free rooms that would have welcomed him. He would probably have appreciated the opportunity for quiet and reflection in the house after the bustle of activity outside. Whitby at the time was the sixth busiest port in England, and the hub of the collier and whaling trades, so it would no doubt have been quite a shock for the young lad from the country. Cook had grown up in the inland calm of Marton village in Cleveland, not far from Whitby in distance, but a world away in character. You can visit a birthplace museum for Cook in Marton too (and a school-room museum in Great Ayton, a monument on Easby Moor, a heritage centre in the small fishing village of Staithes, and a replica of one of his ships, the *Endeavour*, in Stockton), but perhaps Whitby, with all its seafaring bustle, is where the man was made.

Captain Cook is a name known the world over, and that's partly because his travels were so extensive. The upper three floors of the house are devoted to Cook's life and voyages, and you get a great sense of how far he went by looking at the large world map in the Voyages Room, where three coloured lines snake around the globe, tracking the course of the three expeditions he made (in 1768–71, 1772–5 and 1776–9), from deep south in the Pacific to far north in the Arctic.

Apart from the breadth of his expeditions, it's the manner in which he carried them out that makes him a household name, says Williams: 'In the second half of the 18th century, the Pacific, one-third of the Earth's surface, was more or less unknown. Thanks to Cook's efforts, by the time he died, the map of the Pacific, in outline at least, was very much as it is today. He showed new methods and motives of exploration, which at the time were often contrasted to the excesses of early European explorers. He was humane and fascinated by the peoples of the Pacific.'

It wasn't just his humanity that won him high regard: the scientific work carried out in the course of his voyages earned him global respect. One of the rooms in the museum is devoted to the science (botany, astronomy, ethnology) carried out under his sails. As one of the exhibits in the room points out, the importance of Cook's expeditions was recognised at the time; even the belligerents in the American War of Independence, in full flow when Cook was at sea, agreed not to attack his ships.

Cook remained on good terms with his mentor and former master John Walker, and there are several pieces of original correspondence between the two men on display in the house. To read them drives home the point that Cook's time in Whitby was pivotal in the development of his character, long after he'd left the port and the coal-shipping trade far behind for a life in the Royal Navy. Perhaps just as important is the familiarity he gleaned here as an apprentice with sturdy Whitby colliers; his expeditions were carried out in those very ships, converted for longer journeys of course.

The significance, and tourism potential, of the Cook association is not lost on the people of Whitby today. Aside from the Captain Cook Memorial Museum, you can enjoy a trip in a replica of the bark *Endeavour* from the harbour, and see a statue of the man himself overlooking Whitby Sands. You can also follow a signposted car route from here to the various birthplace attractions and monuments to the north. All told, aside from heading out to the Pacific, Whitby is as good a place as anywhere to get a feel for the man who put much of the world on the map, for British eyes at least.

Captain Cook Memorial Museum

Grape Lane, Whitby, North Yorkshire YO22 4BA

01947 601900

www.cookmuseumwhitby.co.uk

Fort George, near Inverness

Nominated by Chris Whatley, professor of Scottish history, University of Dundee

'Where you can see how the British state responded to the threat of internal rebellion'

The thing to do at Fort George is to walk along the great, grassy ramparts and bastions that surround and defend it. Built of earth and faced with sloping stone walls, they were designed to absorb the impact of artillery shells. When the place was built, in the mid 18th century, these fat earthy banks were at the sharp end of military engineering. And they needed to be, because this part of Scotland was at the sharp end of military activity; when construction started in 1748, memories of the Battle of Culloden, the famous victory of the Hanoverian army of King George II over the Jacobites under Bonnie Prince Charlie, fought just a few miles away in 1746, would have been very fresh indeed.

The roots of the story go back to 1689 and the accession of William and Mary to the thrones of Scotland and England in place of James VII and II (see Brixham harbour, page 205). In 1707, England and Scotland were joined in union by act of parliament (see Old Parliament Hall, page 227), then in 1714 the crown of the new united nation passed to George I, the German-speaking Elector of Hanover. At that point, the Jacobites, supporters of the exiled son of King James, took the opportunity to rise up against George in a bid to get their own man back on the throne. They failed, but agitation continued into the reign of King George's son, George II, with James VII and II's grandson, Charles Edward Stuart (Bonnie Prince Charlie) as the figurehead for the resistance, which was particularly strong among the Highland Scottish clans. Matters came to a head at Culloden, when the Hanoverian king's troops defeated Bonnie Prince Charlie's Jacobites, destroying the cream of the Highland clans' warriors in the process.

The site of the battle at Culloden is certainly worth visiting – not just to walk over the boggy ground where so many died, but also to visit the 360-degree battlefield immersion room in the smart new visitor centre, which is quite an experience. But perhaps the more enduring memorial is Fort George, which was the Hanoverian state's response to the threat of the rebellious Scottish Highlands.

The ramparts of Fort George today are a tremendous place on which to stroll, with lovely views out over the Moray Firth (a good place for dolphin spotting) and the hills around Inverness. They also offer the perfect vantage point from which to take in the size of the fort within, a point that Chris Whatley stresses: 'It is stunning in its scale. It's the largest artillery fort in Britain, possibly the largest in Europe. It cost about £200,000, which is about a billion now, so in scale and cost, it exemplifies the extent to which the Hanoverians were concerned about the Jacobite threat, even after Culloden. It represents the power of the Hanoverian state, but it also reflects their concern at the threat of the Highlanders associated with the Jacobite cause.'

It's obvious from the moment you pass under the gatehouse, with the arms of George II prominently and magnificently displayed above, that the awesome size of the place was designed to cow anyone who harboured further thoughts of revolution after Culloden. The enormous parade ground immediately inside the gate emphasises the troop strength within. In a sense, says Whatley, 'this is the Glorious Revolution still being acted out, the ongoing civil British war, probably the most impressive material remnant of that period.'

Some 1600 men would have been housed in the fort, but, as it turned out, they were never called into action to quell another revolt. Culloden was the last battle fought on British soil, and, perhaps surprisingly, within just a few short decades, those Highland troops were at the heart of the British imperial war machine, as Whatley reminds us. 'While in the 1740s and 1750s the Highlanders were viewed as disloyal, understandably so, that changed in the second part of the 18th century as so many of these soldiers were recruited into the British army and gave sterling service on the part of Britain, as in the American wars of independence, for example. So by the end of the century, Highland warriors were celebrated.' (See Spean Bridge, page 378.)

That military tradition continues to this day, as Fort George is still an active military base. You'll see soldiers in uniform about the place, and, if you're lucky, you might hear the bagpipes of a military band rehearsing inside. In fact, most of the solid stone buildings inside the fort are off-limits to the visitor because they are still used for army purposes. Some parts have been made up as 18th-century barracks and guardrooms, while the Grand Magazine, with its gunpowder barrels, and the old prison cell, the Black Hole, are open to the public. Frankly, even if all the doors of the barrack blocks were firmly closed, there would still be enough to see from the ramparts to merit a visit.

As Fort George was never called upon to defend against a renewed Jacobite assault, the military engineering of these defences quickly became outdated. By the end of the 18th century, it probably wouldn't have been able to withstand an attack from the latest artillery weaponry. However, in the 19th century, the fear of French invasion prolonged the fort's life, as it was rearmed to face the possibility of a naval assault up the Firth. It's worth remembering as you tour the ramparts that it was not a foreign force that the fort was first designed to deal with. Whatley notes: 'While it's on a peninsula, the threat it was designed to repel was not external – it was within Scotland itself. A lot of people stand on the ramparts and imagine it was designed to defend against French invaders, but in fact the defences are turned primarily inland.' Fort George stands, therefore, in testimony to the early days of the British project, when the strength of the bonds of union between England and Scotland were being tested.

Fort George
Inverness IV2 7TD
01667 460232
www.historic-scotland.gov.uk

Queen Square, the Circus and Royal Crescent, Bath

Nominated by Peter Borsay, professor of history, Aberystwyth University

'Where you can see the status game of Georgian high society'

Some cities are a little bit ostentatious, and then there's Bath. Here the entire place is about status and showing off, or at least it was when some of its most characteristic architecture was laid out and put up. Take a stroll around the city and you're back in the 18th century, among the high-society townhouses of the Georgian elite.

Even if you disregard the remains of Roman and medieval Bath (though that would be a foolish move), there's still a fearful glut of heritage to take in. Peter Borsay's suggested trio of seminal sites – Queen Square, the Circus and the Royal Crescent – is a good place to get started. What you get here is a father and son act: 'This sequence wasn't the outcome of a planning blueprint,' says Borsay. 'In many ways it was accidental because it was constructed between 1728 and the 1770s – a huge span. John Wood, who designed Queen Square and the Circus, actually died laying the foundation stone of the latter, so his son, also John, completed it and then went on to design the Royal Crescent, so there are two architects involved.'

If you start with Queen Square as the earliest part of the sequence, what's immediately striking is its north side with its palatial front. That aspect, thinks Peter Borsay, 'is really the first of its kind in terms of squares in Britain. That idea of putting a lot of houses together around a country-house front is pioneered by Wood in Queen Square and goes on to be very widely used'.

The ambience of the square isn't quite what it could be with traffic rumbling constantly around, but a spot for quieter contemplation of that uniform northern façade does exist in the central green around the obelisk. Once you've taken it in, head up Gay Street to the Circus, which as the name suggests, is a circle of fine houses, again around a green centre.

John Wood senior, the architect of the Circus, had some eccentric views on the foundation story of Bath, which he held to be the creation of the mythical prince Bladud. So although the Circus has long been thought of as a sort of inside-out version of Rome's Colosseum (and when you're there, you can see why someone might reach that opinion), another view is that perhaps Wood was endeavouring to recreate a Druidical city associated with Blandford. Certainly the acorns on the parapets of the buildings here are an allusion to part of the Bladud story where, having been banished after being afflicted by leprosy, the prince was cured by following the lead of some acorn-eating pigs that he saw rolling in a pool of healing water.

Whatever the architect's underlying intentions, there's no denying that the Circus was somewhere to see and be seen: 'A lot of people refer to the architecture as being theatrical, and in many ways I think it is,' says Borsay. 'If you go to the Circus, it is like standing in a theatre. The window design is reminiscent of theatre boxes: people would be pulling back their curtains and looking at who was getting in and out of their carriages, and who'd arrived in Bath.'

The final part of the sequence, the Royal Crescent, is not far away, but as you take leave of the Circus, you might feel as if you're leaving the city.

You are not, but you are falling prey to John Wood Junior's vision here, which was to create a space that drew in the countryside. Overlooking the green expanse of Victoria Park below it, the Royal Crescent maintains a spectacular bucolic view. Built between 1767 and 1775, the crescent is perhaps the most spectacular of the three sites for its scale and verdant setting.

Aside from being a very pleasant trip through the heart of Georgian Bath, a tour of the three suggested sites tells you a lot about what was happening with the elite of the 18th century, says Borsay. 'With the north side of Queen Square, the idea of putting a lot of houses under one grand façade was all about status, which was at the heart of the Georgian psyche. What appealed to them was the idea of subsuming their individual interest within this grand idea and acquiring the status that went with it. They could live in a country house in the middle of a town. These were enormously prestigious buildings. All the Georgian elite came to Bath, and many of them stayed in these buildings.'

Bath was, after all, the site of the marriage market depicted in Jane Austen's novels, where people were on display and looking for potential partners of the right status. This was where the upper classes came to seal the deals, and the external architecture and city layout reflects that. If you want to see what these houses were like on the inside, number one on the Royal Crescent is open to the public through the good offices of the Bath Preservation Trust, who have renovated it and taken it back to its Georgian best.

The reason why Bath continues to draw so many visitors, and why it's been added to the World Heritage list, is that the plan of the town and the architectural integrity of the buildings has remained broadly intact from the 18th century. There have been some modifications but it's mostly how it was two centuries ago. The Georgian status game influenced urban architecture and also led to the creation of many of the great houses and gardens that now dot the British countryside. Bath is a perfect place to come to appreciate the culture that underpinned all that.

Bath Preservation Trust

1 Royal Crescent, Bath BA1 2LR

01225 338727

www.bath-preservation-trust.org.uk

Bath Tourist Information Centre

Abbey Chambers, Abbey Churchyard, Bath BA1 1LY

0906 711 2000

www.visitbath.co.uk

Covent Garden, London

Nominated by Vic Gatrell, former professor of history, University of Essex, now a life fellow, Gonville and Caius College, University of Oxford
'Where you can summon up the creative underbelly of Georgian England'

There are signs admonishing you to guard against pickpockets on every corner of Covent Garden. This is sage advice, particularly, I would imagine, for those whose attention is diverted by the street performers in the piazza. The pickpockets and performers of today perhaps offer a little inkling of the character of the place two centuries ago, when Vic Gatrell thinks the area was at its most fascinating: 'Covent Garden has become a tourist trap with a commercial market now. That same location 200 years ago was sleazy, mucky, boozy, dangerous and sexy, but also very creative.'

For Gatrell, 'Covent Garden is where you can see 18th-century culture coming to life. If, at the time, you wanted a place in Britain that was generating everything we call culture – theatre, art, literature – it was around Covent Garden that you would have to go.'

In the 1630s the area was laid out for the elite and the aristocratic after the Bedford family acquired the land and employed Inigo Jones to create a 'piazza' that would attract moneyed folk of London. Jones duly did, but of his square, only the western side survives – in the form of St Paul's Church (though that is itself a later restoration of the original, which was damaged in a fire in 1795). The grand houses and arcades that made the other three sides of the square are now all gone, replaced by mostly Victorian buildings. The original high-class inhabitants deserted the area for the newly fashionable West End towards the end of the 17th century. In their stead came an influx of creativity, as artists, dancers, writers and actors moved in. In the early 1730s the painter William Hogarth, for example, lived in the piazza with his father-in-law, Sir James Thornhill, who painted the dome of St Paul's Cathedral and the Painted Hall at the Old Royal Naval College in Greenwich (page 210).

Part of Covent Garden's character lay in its geography, says Gatrell: 'To the north you've got St Giles, which was the impoverished Irish slum that supplied Covent Garden with its cheap workforce and market people, along with prostitutes, thieves and vagrants. To the south you've got the Strand, then the most fashionable shopping street in London. And in between was a space occupied by artisans, artists, coffee shops and taverns.' The territory was the sexiest in London, as well as the most creative. As the poet John Dryden put it three centuries ago: 'This town two bargains has not worth one farthing, / A Smithfield horse, and wife of Covent Garden.'

Inigo Jones's church makes for a good starting point to a stroll around the historic area. For one thing, it lets you catch your breath. As soon as you step into its pleasant garden precinct, you've escaped the hullaballoo in the piazza. Inside the Actors' Church, as it is also known because of its long association with the acting community, is an interesting place to mooch around and see various memorials to film and theatre greats of the past.

You do need to go back out into the mêlée of Covent Garden to get a sense of the vitality, past and present. There's perhaps not that much to glean from the piazza itself (the market building in the centre is much later than our 18th-century period), so you'd be advised to dive off into one of the side streets. Walk down to Maiden Lane, just to the south of the piazza, and you're into the heart of the old world of Covent Garden. The French writer Voltaire lived there, at number 10, while in exile in London. And in 1775 the artist J.M.W. Turner was born in number 21, his father's hairdressing and wig shop.

'The Bedford Tavern, or a version of it, still stands in Maiden Lane,' notes Gatrell. 'I don't think you'd find anyone among the big names in 18th-century literature who didn't go there.'

If you head out of Maiden Lane and back towards the piazza via Southampton Street, you'll pass David Garrick's house. Garrick was the foremost actor-manager of the Georgian period, and 27 Southampton Street was his city home for 23 years from 1749. When he moved in, Covent Garden was already established as a theatrical area, which becomes apparent if you nip around the east of the piazza to Bow Street (passing the bookshop on Russell Street where Boswell and Johnson first met; it's now a coffee bar). At the top of Bow Street is the Royal Opera House. This began life as the Covent Garden Theatre in the 1730s, when it was one of the grandest buildings in London.

On the way up Bow Street, you'd have passed the site of Will's coffee house, where Johnson and other literary luminaries, such as Samuel Pepys, John Dryden, Jonathan Swift and Alexander Pope, would have lingered in their times. Thus, this street alone demonstrates both the theatrical and literary preoccupations of Georgian Covent Garden.

At the top of Bow Street, however, is evidence of the seedier side of the area. There you can see the site of the former Bow Street Magistrate's Court, where the first police station in London once stood. It's a reminder of the fact that Georgian Covent Garden was a place of crime as well as creativity: 'There was sleaze, sex, violence, courtesans, tarts and so forth. It was light years away from the polite culture that we tend to associate the 18th century with today,' explains Gatrell.

Covent Garden therefore provides a very different expression of 18th-century life from what you'd find, for example, in Bath (though there was a fair deal of scurrilous intrigue behind the polite veneer of the upper classes who went there for the season). If you want to get a sense of a society that wasn't as straitjacketed as we tend to think, Covent Garden is the place to head for.

Covent Garden
London WC2E 8RF
0870 780 5001
www.coventgardenlondonuk.com

White Rock Copper Works, Swansea

Nominated by Chris Evans, professor of history,
University of Glamorgan
'Where you can see an early stage of the Industrial
Revolution'

Sandwiched between the centre of Swansea and the city's Liberty sports stadium is a little haven of greenery. A couple of centuries ago it was more hive than haven, and more smoke and industry than green space. It's the former site of the White Rock Copper Works, where, says Chris Evans, 'You'll find one of the few visible remains of an aspect of early British industrialisation. The copper and brass industries really emerge in the late 17th century, a hundred years or so before what we conventionally think of as the Industrial Revolution in Britain.'

The rise of the copper industry in Swansea was an astonishingly rapid one. 'Britain moved from being on the absolute margins of this industrial sector in a European perspective to being its most dynamic centre within the space of just a generation,' notes Evans, and it was all about Swansea. 'Wales as a whole by 1820 accounted for over 50 per cent of the world output of smelted copper, and the Swansea district accounted for pretty much all of that.'

Why Swansea? It was all about geography and geology, and specifically about the development of coal power, over wood fuel, to smelt the copper ore. Coal-smelting technology was in its infancy in the 17th and 18th centuries, and the process demanded coal and ore in the ratio of three to one. It therefore made sense for the smelting process to be nearer the coal than the ore. There was a lot of coal in the Swansea–Neath district, and there was a lot of copper ore in Cornwall. In between the two was open sea, which happily afforded the easiest way of transporting goods at the time. So the copper was shipped from the Cornish mines to Swansea, the coal was brought from nearby pits, and the smelting furnaces were set up along the banks of the river Tawe, in the most accessible site to receive both products.

From the 1770s through to the mid 19th century, Swansea was 'Copperopolis'. It went from being a small seaside town with a little porcelain production to a sprawling centre of industry, where the farmers lodged court cases against the owners of the works for ruining their once-fertile soil. As geography was the key factor in deciding the location of smelting furnaces, all the copper works were hemmed into a tightly confined area. You could have walked across this globally important industrial area in a day, reckons Evans, and you can do the same now, though you have to use your imagination a little to conjure up what was once there.

You should start your visit at Swansea's newly built Waterfront Museum on the quayside. Pop in for a look around and you can get a bit of background on the Industrial Revolution in Wales (don't miss the replica of the world's first engine, originally built at nearby Penydarren by Richard Trevithick). While you're in the museum, see if you can spot a print of the painting of the White Rock Copper Works by Henri Gastineau (c.1830), which gives you a taste of the what the landscape you're about to stroll into once looked like. Then set off alongside the river, heading north towards the city; cross over at the Sail Bridge and walk a little way along the side of the Tawe on cycle route 43. It's a pleasant woody stroll that will shortly take you to the remains of the White Rock works. Now be warned: although the place has been designated an

Industrial Heritage Park by Swansea Council, there is precious little in the way of signage or interpretation boards. If you get to the car park by the roundabout with the Liberty Stadium looming up in front of you, turn around – you've just missed it. There are plans afoot to make more of an effort to let people know what's left here, but for now you're free to wander around and see what you can make of the place.

Evans explains what you can see: 'There are the ruined wharves, which pretty much date back to the foundation of the works, and there are old abandoned kilns and storage works. There's also a massive ramp that used to carry the slag up to Kilvey Hill. If you gaze up Kilvey Hill and run your eye across the contours, you can see patches of slag where it's still recovering from the very toxic nature of copper smelting.'

The works closed in 1929 because by then it was more economic to smelt the ore where it was mined, but the waste tips were not cleared away until 1967. Now it is a pleasant place for a historical mooch around – grassy, quiet and with a view down the Tawe. Perhaps the most atmospheric site is the old dock on the river, where it doesn't take much imagination to picture the copper barges bringing in the ore and shipping away the finished copper products. You might be wondering what the finished copper was used for. It was ubiquitous in a domestic context in Britain, in terms of pots and pans and suchlike, but it also had a darker side. 'You could buy human beings with copper,' says Evans. 'Copper and brass articles were important as trade goods on the Guinea coast of Africa, either in the form of copper rods, wire or ingots, or as ready-made semi-decorative items, such as manillas (bracelets), that eventually acted as an African currency.'

The White Rock works were started by a Bristol company in 1737, and the leading figure was Thomas Coster, an MP, a mine adventurer, and a dealer in copper and brass. Bristol was, at the time, the main focus of copper production in the country (some evidence remains along the banks of the Avon in east Bristol), but it was also Britain's premier slaving port. The Coster family were partners in the 1730s with some of the leading slaving houses in Bristol, and they were interested in expanding their production of copper because it was such an important commodity in the slave trade. The White Rock works, from the very outset, were fully integrated into this. Says Evans, 'The first-known print of the works, from 1744, clearly identifies one of the structures as the Manilla House, where these objects for the slave trade were produced or stored. It takes Welsh industrialisation from a parochial setting into a hemispheric one.'

White Rock was but one of the smelting works along the Tawe, and you can see further evidence of the industry by continuing a little further north along the river, crossing over just before the stadium and doubling back to the Hafod Copper Works buildings. At the moment, all these remains of Swansea's industrial past are perhaps a little unloved, but that's all the more reason to pay them a visit and spread the word about this early stage in Britain's industrial history.

National Waterfront Museum
Oystermouth Road, Maritime Quarter,
Swansea SA1 3RD
01792 638950
www.museumwales.ac.uk/en/swansea

Dr Johnson's House, London

Nominated by David Dabydeen, professor, Centre for Translation and Comparative Cultural Studies, University of Warwick

'Where a masterpiece of the English language was constructed'

Samuel Johnson lived in many houses (17 in fact) across London. Money troubles in the early part of his career obliged him to move around regularly. His other lodgings don't survive, so it's not necessary to tire yourself of the city trying to find them. The property at 17 Gough Square is by far his most important residence, and where he was most settled, and it has been preserved as a museum to the life and career of this hero of dictionaries. The survival of the house was a close call as it was almost destroyed on three occasions during the Second World War, and the roof and attic were burnt out in 1941.

It was here, in this fine four-storey brick house among the courtyards and alleyways off Fleet Street in central London, that Dr Johnson lived from 1748 to 1759, and where he composed his most famous work, *A Dictionary of the English Language*. He started work on it in 1746 and took nine years to complete the task. When it was published in 1755, it made the name of the 46-year-old lexicographer, whose writing and editing career up to that point had been productive but a struggle.

Dr Johnson's volume was not the first dictionary to be produced, but it immediately became the unquestioned reference source for questions of the English language. His use of quotations from across the whole canon of literature to illustrate usage was innovative at the time, while his sharp and witty definitions have given the dictionary enduring appeal ever since. It is surely one of the most important books ever published, and it was composed in the garret attic of 17 Gough Square.

Take yourself up the wooden staircase to the top of the house and you'll now find a large, plain, bare room. In Johnson's day, according to his famous biographer James Boswell, it was set up like a 'counting house'. There were tall desks at which his six assistants could stand and copy out quotes and definitions, and the walls were lined with bookcases. It would have been a busy place.

There are numerous diverting items of Johnsonalia scattered around the place, but most interesting is the collection of portraits that adorn the walls. They are all of people with whom Johnson had an acquaintance, so it gives a good idea of the wide social circle in which he moved. You'll find likenesses of people ranging from the Corsican patriot Pasquale Paoli, through the East India Company governor Warren Hastings, to the blue-stocking Elizabeth Montagu, and many more besides. Perhaps most noteworthy, though, is a portrait you'll find in the ground-floor parlour, which is thought to be of Francis Barber. Strikingly, for this was a time before the abolition of slavery, he is black.

Barber was born a slave on a sugar plantation in Jamaica in the 1730s. He was then brought to England by one Richard Bathurst, father of a friend of Johnson, and subsequently freed before being placed in the service of the doctor in 1752. The timing was important: Barber entered his service just after the death of Johnson's wife, a loss that had plunged the author into depression (he was prone to melancholy throughout his life). Barber was to become a significant figure in the writer's life, as David Dabydeen explains: 'Johnson's wife died and a couple of weeks later

Barber was given to him as a present. Johnson became very fond of him, regarding him as a son rather than a servant. Indeed, Dr Johnson took up some very strong anti-slavery positions, probably because of his affection for Barber.'

Black people were not uncommon on the streets of London in the 18th century, and there are numerous instances of them in the art of the time – William Hogarth and Thomas Gainsborough painted them, for example. With the slave trade at its height and millions of black Africans in forced servitude on the plantations, the position of black people in England was a difficult and ambiguous one. Plantation owners brought back slaves from the Americas, and some were treated as status symbols; others, such as Barber, enjoyed good relationships with their masters. Those who took the opportunity to run away to escape the possibility of being returned to the plantations could find themselves recaptured and forced back across the Atlantic. It was not until the celebrated Somerset case of 1772 that this was ruled to be against the law, though of course it wasn't until the 19th century that the abolition of the slave trade, and then the abolition of slavery itself, were passed by parliament.

In London it was through the actions and writings of former black slaves, such as Ignatius Sancho and Olaudah Equiano, and of white anti-slavery activists, such as Granville Sharpe, Thomas Clarkson and William Wilberforce (see Wilberforce House, page 285), that the campaign to end the horror of the slave trade began to gather pace in the later years of the 18th century.

So in 17 Gough Street you can not only see a memorial to the work of Dr Johnson as a great lexicographer, but also get an insight into the very conflicting values of the time in which he lived. Although racism must have been ingrained in some parts of society, it cannot have extended to the likes of Dr Johnson. Indeed, he made Francis Barber his heir, leaving him an annuity of £70 on his death in 1784 and advising him to leave London for Lichfield (where Johnson was born) to escape the temptations of the capital. Barber did so, and although he didn't particularly prosper, his descendants continue to live in the Potteries to this day – a personal legacy of Dr Johnson's to match his great literary one, the *Dictionary of the English Language*.

Dr Johnson's House
17 Gough Square, London EC4A 3DE
020 7353 3745
www.drjohnsonshouse.org

Halifax Piece Hall, West Yorkshire
Nominated by Pat Hudson, professor emeritus of history, Cardiff University
'Where you can see how an early stage of the Industrial Revolution was played out'

Halifax has a fairly ordinary centre for a British provincial town – that is until you step inside the Piece Hall. You can't really make out the treat within from the outside because the place is hemmed in by other, more recent buildings that prevent you from surveying the scale of the structure. So, for the unwary visitor, there's quite a surprise in store. If you enter via the South Gate, passing through an arched gateway flanked by enormous and ornate iron gates that date from 1871, you'll perhaps get an inkling that you're not wandering into just any old shopping precinct.

Once through the gates, you'll find yourself looking at a large, open-air courtyard surrounded by a stone-built quadrangular arcade of two and three storeys in what, for all the world, feels like a Mediterranean market square (bar the weather). Behind the colonnades are rooms (315 in total) that were once the sale rooms of the local cloth manufacturers.

The Piece Hall was opened in 1779 and is a classic example of Georgian architecture, the only one of the northern wool markets to survive intact and in such a good state of preservation. 'Piece' refers to the pieces of cloth that were woven on handlooms in homes and workshops throughout the region. Each piece represented about a week's part-time work by a clothier and his family. The hand textile industry in this part of Yorkshire has roots going back to the 1300s, but it developed into a very considerable business with a lot of wool being woven by small-scale producers – so much so that by the mid 18th century, Halifax's existing cloth market (dating back to 1572) was no longer sufficient, and plans for the Piece Hall were put into motion.

According to Pat Hudson, 'It is a fitting icon of the early stages of industrialisation in Britain. It's a monument to wool textiles rather than cotton, and that is important because although the Industrial Revolution was to a large degree energised by the rise of cotton, England's textile wealth for many centuries before, and particularly during her rise to prominence in international trade through the 18th century, was founded on wool. It is also a monument to domestic and workshop manufacturing, artisan skills, ingenuity and enterprise rather than to the factory. It represents the final stages, perhaps the culmination, of an early Industrial Revolution, when innovation was abroad, when industrial employment opportunities for men, women and children were expanding, and when most workers felt themselves to be, to a large degree, in control of their work routines, their skills and their capital. And it is, ultimately, a monument to the key relationship between manufacturers and merchants, which generated a high degree of success for British textiles in international markets in the 18th century.'

Halifax was at the heart of this activity. Every Saturday the Piece Hall was home to a regulated market for the sale of woven wool. The manufacturers would bring their produce by packhorse from places within a radius of about 25 km (15 miles) of the town, and they would have a couple of hours to sell their wares to the assembled merchants. Those who didn't have the finances to subscribe to one of the rooms showcased their cloth in the courtyard itself. It would have been a busy place.

What is particularly noteworthy about the Piece Hall is that it was funded by subscriptions from these local, small-scale cloth workers, yet the building is far from humble: 'In no sense is this a plain or merely functional building,' notes Hudson. 'Its size, style and grandeur are clearly designed to reflect the pride of the manufacturers and of the town and locality in the products of labour and in the successful expansion of industry and international trading that had brought increasing prosperity to the region.'

Curiously, though, this fine place, with its Doric columns and handsome arcades, had a short-lived existence for its intended purpose. That's because it was built just before the next stage in the economic development of the nation, as industrialisation led to the mechanisation of the textile

With its colonnaded arcades, Halifax's Piece Hall lends
a Mediterranean feel to this Yorkshire town

trade and soon wiped out the place of the cottage handloom weaver. The factory culture of the Industrial Revolution in the 19th century essentially made the Piece Hall redundant as a cloth market because traders looked instead to do business directly with the large-scale manufacturers.

After that, the Piece Hall had a varied existence as a meeting place, a venue for religious singing festivals in the later 19th century, and as a wholesale fish and fruit market. In the 1970s it was very nearly the victim of a town centre redevelopment scheme, which would have pulled it down and replaced it with a modern shopping centre. But, happily such a travesty was averted – by just one council vote – and it is now a pleasant, if a little neglected, haven of shops and cafés. Calderdale Council has grand plans to give the place another makeover and turn it into a rejuvenated town square for Halifax.

For now, you're still free to walk around the covered arcades and peer into the rooms. In so doing, you'll get a very good feel of what the place was like back in the 18th century as it's not (currently) much changed at all. There's a friendly visitor centre on the second floor with a small exhibition space about the history of the hall, along with a diverting art gallery. If you want to see the Industrial Revolution before the dark satanic mills clouded the picture, this is a good place to come.

The Piece Hall
Halifax, West Yorkshire HX1 1RE
01422 321002
www.thepiecehall.co.uk

Badbea Clearance Village, Highland

Nominated by Annie Tindley, lecturer in history,
Glasgow Caledonian University
'Where you can understand the impact of the
Highland Clearances'

With the advantages of modern technology, and with the romanticism of the modern mind towards wild places, you might well be drawn to thinking that Badbea, on the ferny cliffs overlooking the North Sea, would be a marvellous place to have a house. Perhaps you'd be tempted by its remoteness (it's a couple of hours' drive from Inverness on the northeast coast of Scotland) and the drama of the setting (the cliffs plunge away steeply to the sea far below). Neither of those factors would have been particularly alluring to the people who did live here once; indeed, the last residents left a century ago. Badbea then was not an attractive place for a home.

Now those people are remembered by a monumental obelisk on the site of their village, along with the stone foundations of some of the long-houses that they lived in. These, along with the flattened patches of ground that represent the remains of their gardens, are all that's left of more than a hundred years of occupation here. Today there is a car park for visitors clearly signposted on the side of the A9, and there are several information panels that explain the story to you. There is a moderately demanding walk to get from the car park to the village site.

The ruins that you'll see are the result of one of the most emotive episodes in British history: the Highland Clearances. This was the process by which, from the late 18th century onwards, thousands of Highlanders left their homes inland, many of them settling instead in places on the coast, such as Badbea. Others went further afield, either south to the Lowlands, or across the sea to new lives abroad. The contentious element of the story stems from the fact that the relocation tended to be driven by landlords, who saw more profit to be had from populating the hills with sheep than from taking rents from their often impoverished tenant farmers. Some of these landlords employed brutal force to clear the people and make way for the sheep, though some Highlanders did not have to be pushed to seek better lives elsewhere.

'What's interesting about Badbea is that rather than being the village they were cleared from, it's the village they were cleared to,' says Annie Tindley. 'You can see the kind of conditions that people were living under from the late 18th century onwards. And as Badbea wasn't abandoned until 1911, you can actually see the buildings pretty clearly. Unlike a lot of clearance villages, which are little more than lumps under the heather, you can actually see it pretty well.'

Perhaps the most striking feature of the living conditions at Badbea is that the houses sit on a very steep slope running sharply down to the high cliffs. The signs warn you today to watch your step, and tradition has it that the villagers had to tether both their livestock and their children to keep them from straying into danger. The people were pushed this close to the edge so that as much of the fertile land back from the coast could be reserved for those money-making sheep. In fact, the people were hemmed in (or kept out) by a great stone wall that held back the sheep and protected them from the perilous cliffs beyond.

'The landowner who cleared the villagers to this site was John Sinclair of Ulbster. He was a famous improving landowner who had all the rhetoric of clearance. He was keen on introducing new breeds of sheep and farm leases and suchlike, so Badbea encapsulates all those things,' says Tindley.

The villagers began to arrive in the late 18th century and early 19th. They were given plots of land, but they had to clear them and build their homes with whatever stone was at hand. At first they were able to make a living – the men from herring fishing, the women by weaving. At one point 12 families were able to support themselves in this windy spot, but from the middle years of the 19th century, the population declined as residents left to find better lives elsewhere. Indeed, the imposing memorial, which stands on the site of one of the longhouses, was erected by one David Sutherland of New Zealand, the son of Robert Sutherland, who was born in Badbea in 1806, but left for the other side of the world in 1839.

Badbea is typical of the Clearance experience, with people being swiftly moved from the Highlands to the coasts in the late 18th and early 19th centuries, and then many moving on again from there. Evocative ruins such as these clearly demonstrate the impact that this would have had on individual people. Yet the fact is that the Clearances were part of a bigger process of agricultural reform that had been going on across Europe since the 17th century. The Highland Clearances are unique in that the process of change was squeezed into a much shorter period than elsewhere, their start being delayed because of the general impoverishment of the region and because of the complexities of the clan system in the Highlands. It was the speed with which the Clearances took place, and the fact that they were often imposed by rich people on the poor, that has given the story such an emotional charge.

Many of the places established on the coast for the uprooted High-landers, such as Helmsdale, 8 km (5 miles) down the river, did go on to become villages, but Badbea's peculiar precariousness was always going to make that an unlikely possibility for the settlement on the cliffs. Helmsdale lies at the end of a river valley and has an altogether more amenable location for habitation. It was designated as a fishing village for some of the cleared people, and a harbour was built here in 1818. The money spent on the place ensured that it would have a longer life than Badbea, and now it's a pleasant place to stop on your way to the deserted village. It boasts a bronze statue to those who emigrated from Scotland, and a Heritage Centre, Timespan, that explores the story of the Clearances.

Badbea Clearance Village
Badbea, Highland
Grid reference: ND084204

Soho House, Birmingham
Nominated by Malcolm Dick, director, Centre for West Midlands History, University of Birmingham
'Where you can get a feel for the 18th century's silicon valley'

The dining room should be the first place you make for if you visit this fine Georgian house, which today hides in a quiet side street off Birmingham's busy Soho Road. The dining room is fairly large and far from plain, with a shallow vaulted ceiling, some marble-effect pillars, a full bay window with hand-painted curtains to match the pillars, and an extending mahogany table on top of a complicated and colourful carpet. The effect

The ramparts of Fort George are wide and deep, a show of strength for any Jacobites thinking of rebellion, and a great place for a walk today

HMS *Warrior* was for a time Britain's greatest maritime deterrent. Soon made obsolete, she now resides permanently at Portsmouth's Historic Dockyard

The rusting remains of the mine buildings at Blaenavon's Big Pit are an evocative reminder of the days when coal was king in South Wales

John Dobbin's splendid painting of the opening of the Stockton and Darlington Railway graces the wall of Darlington's Head of Steam museum

Coalbrookdale by Night by Philip James de Loutherbourg: the painting was based on the furnaces at Bedlam in the Ironbridge Gorge

The Bank of England in the heart of London: where financial innovation helped drive the increasing wealth of the nation

The brick warehouses of Liverpool's Albert Dock are now filled with shops, galleries and museums. In the 19th century, they were stocked with the global wealth of an empire

Part of St George's Hall in Liverpool, where the confidence of an imperial city was expressed through its grand architecture

The Round Reading Room at the British Museum: here great thinkers have found time to pause and hone revolutionary ideas

Titus Salt's mill was the heart of the village, Saltaire, that he laid out in the mid 19th century in an effort to give his workers a life worth living

A lone RAF pilot looks out over the English Channel from the memorial at Capel-le-Ferne. In 1940, during the Battle of Britain, this was Hellfire Corner where dogfights raged overhead

The commando memorial at Spean Bridge: reflective of the way that the once rebellious Highlands have been incorporated into the British state

was the height of style when it was created in 1792, and in the recent renovation of Soho House, great pains have been taken to return the room to that late-18th-century look.

It's not for the decor that you should linger here, though; rather for what happened around the table. Soho House was the home from 1766 to 1809 of the manufacturer and entrepreneur Matthew Boulton, and it was in his dining room that a remarkable group of men, the Lunar Society, often convened. The name derived from the fact that they met on full-moon nights so that they had light to ride home in afterwards.

Along with Boulton, the society included his business partner, the inventor and engineer James Watt, the physician and poet Erasmus Darwin, chemist and polymath Joseph Priestly, and Josiah Wedgwood, master potter. These men, and several more, began meeting in the mid 1760s in their homes around the West Midlands to discuss and demonstrate the latest developments in science, engineering and industry. With the Industrial Revolution gathering pace, it was a time of many such developments, and the members of the Lunar Society were in the vanguard of the action. Matthew Boulton was a leading light in a very bright group, says Malcolm Dick.

'He was one of the key figures in this group of intellectuals, industrialists and writers, which stimulated a high-tech version of industrialisation at the end of the 18th century. I would make a claim that the West Midlands was the equivalent of Silicon Valley at the time, not just because of the significance of Birmingham, but because of a whole range of areas connected with it – the Black Country, the Potteries and Ironbridge Gorge at Coalbrookdale. Boulton was central to the development of the area – as an industrialist and a promoter of the canals that provided the transport network linking Birmingham and the Black Country with the rest of Britain and enabled local goods to be transported to the rest of the world. He also spent a lot of his time in the public sphere, lobbying parliament, advertising his products to the rich and famous, and entertaining influential visitors at Soho.'

As you peer into this industrious man's dining room, it's fascinating to think of the chairs being occupied by those great minds of the Lunar Society and of the seminal discussions that would have taken place across the table. There are no longer many houses of the society's members that you can visit, so this room holds a particular significance in the industrial development of Britain. Boulton was a lot more than just a member of a society, though. He was an innovator and entrepreneur, and throughout his house there are signs of that. Take the glazing bars in the bay window of the dining room, for instance. Although hard to see from behind the rope at the back of the room (and probably hard to see up close too, I imagine), they are made from an alloy called Eldorado, which was quite new in 1792, having been developed by Boulton's friend and fellow Lunar Society member James Keir.

'The house was in many ways a pioneering piece of technology itself,' says Dick. 'It had an underfloor heating system, which was very unusual for the time. It had a bathroom with a hot water system. It used the new Eldorado metal for the fanlights. So in many ways it was a showcase for new domestic technologies.'

You can see evidence of these innovations as you wander around Boulton's home, and also learn a lot more about the man and his various enterprises. The house, a fine Georgian, three-storey affair, was but a small part of Boulton's industrial empire in the area. His nearby manufactory was where his workers produced a range of metal products, from buckles and buttons to fashionable ormolu (gilded) decorative objects of desire. It was a pioneering place, where Boulton introduced a whole series of developments, such as the division of labour and, most notably, the use of steam power in the industrial process. The manufactory was the centre of his business, and people came from far and wide to see what he was doing in these showcase industrial premises. It's now been demolished, but you can see many examples of the sort of products that came out of it in Soho House.

'The house itself contains a number of items that were manufactured by Boulton's firm or in partnership with other individuals, including a remarkable sidereal clock,' notes Dick. 'There are a number of luxury goods that Boulton produced, and he also went into the mass-production of coins using steam-powered presses. There's even an early example of a copying machine that he and Watt manufactured.'

Boulton's partnership with James Watt is probably what he is best remembered for now. It came about in 1774, when, having spotted the potential of the Scottish engineer's work on steam engines, he persuaded him to move down to Birmingham and join him in business. With Boulton's entrepreneurial instincts and energy, the partnership led to the widespread dissemination of steam-powered engines for various industrial tasks across many countries.

Although the business of Boulton and Watt was certainly significant, it was just one of many enterprises in which Matthew Boulton was involved. A visit to his home will enlighten you on the other interests he held, and his wider importance in the development of industry in Birmingham and across the world. More generally, it will tell you something about the febrile atmosphere that must have existed amongst people of inquisitive mind as the 18th century progressed and scientific develop-ments began to feature ever more in daily life.

Soho House

Soho Avenue (off Soho Road), Handsworth, Birmingham B18 5LB

0121 554 9122

www.bmag.org.uk/soho-house

Harewood House, Leeds

Nominated by James Walvin, professor of history emeritus, University of York

'Where you can see an example of Britain's link with the enslaved Atlantic'

Britain has many fine stately homes. It was an 18th-century tradition to build the home that demonstrated your wealth and standing, but the money had to come from somewhere to pay for such displays. In the case of Harewood House, just outside Leeds, it came, at least in part, from the slave trade.

The house was built in the mid 18th century by Edwin Lascelles with money from his father, Henry, who had profited from the West Indian sugar trade in the early part of that century. This was part of the infamous triangular trade, where European goods were shipped to West Africa and exchanged for human beings, who were enslaved and shipped to the plan-tations in the West Indies to produce the sugar and cocoa that were in turn exported back to Europe. From its mid-17th-century origins to the early part of the 19th century, this trade was very big business indeed for Britain.

Harewood was built on a grand scale between 1759 and 1771, with Robert Adam adding an architectural flourish to the design of John Carr, while Capability Brown and Thomas Chippendale saw to the grounds and furnishings respectively. In 1787 the family of Edwin Lascelles had a stake in 47 plantations and owned thousands of slaves. It's clear where the money to pay for the opulent house came from.

This is not a uniquely dark story. Many people in Britain were involved in the slave trade at the time. It wasn't until the latter part of the 18th century that people began to agitate seriously against the practice, and even then, campaigners and slaves had to wait until 1807 before Britain's Slave Trade Abolition Bill was passed. Britain, as a principal partner in the trade, was sucking in so much wealth from slaving and associated businesses that there are many places across the land that were built off the back of it. Bristol is a case in point, with many fine buildings benefiting from its place as the home of the sugar importing and processing business (the raw material was the product of plantation slave labour).

For James Walvin, Harewood shows how far the money from the slave trade infiltrated British society. 'The Lascelles family built this fantastic house, having moved in the space of a century from modest farming stock to being part of the elite. It has the finest collection of Chippendale that was made on the spot, a fantastic gallery, which they built up over the centuries, gardens that are some of the finest in northern England, and all of it based on money-lending and plantations in the Caribbean.'

You can get a sense of how much wealth was sloshing around in the ships of the sugar trade when you tour the state floor at Harewood, an architecturally splendid suite of rooms that drip with paintings, fine furniture and expensive china. The porticoed front elevation of this grand house will surely grab your attention as you pass it en route to the car park, and after you've been around the rooms you will be left in no doubt that considerable money has been spent on the interior too. You will also have learnt about where that money originally came from, as there is an introductory panel on the sugar trade and the Lascelles family in the library. Although the current owner, the 7th Earl of Harewood, can trace his descent directly back to family members involved in the slave trade, he is open about this aspect of their past, although, not surprisingly, it isn't a huge aspect of the visitor experience.

What's particularly sobering and thought-provoking is to take yourself around the 'Below Stairs' exhibition at Harewood. Far removed from the opulence above, this is the former servants' area. It has everything you might expect: a big kitchen, a scullery, cupboards full of pots and pans. Clearly, there would have been a lot of people beavering away here to meet every need of the grand folk above. It's an interesting slice of social history, and one that tells you something about how far the slave trade money had filtered through British society. The servants would have been paid with money that came from the sugar and slave trade, or investments made in it. As Walvin says, 'Harewood tells the story of Britain's link to the enslaved Atlantic,' and if you go below stairs you can see just how deep that story goes. It's not just the rich and the mighty who benefited from Britain's part in the slave trade. That tainted money went far and wide.

Harewood House: a grand place with links to a dark trade

It's no longer just the rich and the mighty who can enjoy Harewood today. As a heritage attraction, it has a lot going for it. Palpably, the house is worth a look, and the gardens are also a rewarding place to take a stroll, while the café in the old stable block offers an excellent place to rest your legs halfway round.

Harewood House

Harewood, Leeds LS17 9LG

0113 218 1010

www.harewood.org

Edward Jenner Museum, Berkeley, Gloucestershire

Nominated by Michael Worboys, professor specialising in medical history, University of Manchester

'Where humanity scored a notable victory against disease'

The small town of Berkeley in Gloucestershire, standing above the course of the widening river Severn as it flows out towards the Bristol Channel, can boast two particular historical distinctions. First, it has an impressive Norman castle, within which it's reputed that the English King Edward II was murdered in 1327 (though this is now disputed). Second, it's where a country doctor injected a young boy with cowpox in 1796. The latter event is our story.

Edward Jenner was born in Berkeley in 1749. He returned in 1772, having trained as a doctor, and set up in practice. After a time he bought the large house known as Chantry Cottage, next to the parish church, where he lived with his wife and their children. He died in the house and was buried in the church in 1823. His former home is now a museum dedicated to his life and work, and his role in the defeat of smallpox.

During the 18th century, smallpox was a terrifying killing machine. Victims could expect to suffer a horrible rash of blistered pustular pimples over their skin, followed by a good chance of death, blindness or disfigurement. It spread particularly easily in urban centres, and affected all levels of society. The pockmarked faces of survivors would have been a common sight, and perhaps led to the fashion among ladies for applying beauty spots to disguise the blemishes.

People were not completely defenceless against the disease, however. In 1721, Lady Mary Wortley Montagu, the wife of the British ambassador in Constantinople, introduced the concept of variolation to England, having seen it practised in Turkey. The technique basically involved deliberately infecting patients with a mild form of smallpox in the hope that they would then become immune to the more lethal strain. This was effective for some, but there was still an unhealthy risk of death, and the process itself was an unpleasant one. Jenner himself was variolated as a boy, and seems to have found it a particularly traumatic experience.

In his work as a doctor, Jenner travelled around rural Gloucestershire, where he encountered some cases of people, mostly milkmaids, who had caught a mild disease known as cowpox. Local lore had it that such victims would then be immune to smallpox. The doctor recognised the similarity between the two poxes and spent some years carrying out observations to see if there were any truth in this folk tradition. He came to the conclusion that there *was* a link worth investigating, so determined to carry out an experiment. Needing someone who could not have come into contact with either cowpox or smallpox led him to his gardener's eight-year-old son, one James Phipps. The boy was first injected with cowpox, and subsequently with smallpox. Happily, he did not contract the latter disease.

As Michael Worboys notes, this was a monumental moment in medicine: 'It's where modern vaccination originated, and vaccination has probably been the greatest public health benefit of any medical innovation in the last 200 years.'

Jenner went on to publish his results, and, despite some initial scepticism, the concept of vaccination caught on quickly. It did indeed prove to be an effective defence against smallpox. Jenner became something of a celebrity, was afforded audiences with royalty, and was honoured by academic societies and institutions the world over. After his death, there was a backlash against vaccination, particularly after it was made compulsory in 1853. However, in the 1880s the French chemist Louis Pasteur worked out the science behind Jenner's vaccine, establishing that injecting a weakened infectious agent of a disease could provide immunity against it.

'The significance is that when Pasteur started to develop protective substances in his laboratory in Paris, he chose the word "vaccination", which means literally "inoculation with cowpox", for all protective inoculations,' says Worboys. 'Pasteur's success there created modern medical research.'

The last outbreak of smallpox in Britain was as recently as 1962 in Bradford, but a century after Pasteur, the fight against smallpox was concluded when, following a targeted campaign of isolation and vaccination in areas where the disease persisted, smallpox was declared eradicated in 1980 by the World Health Organisation. Jenner's work from his house in Berkeley helped set in motion the process by which this notable victory was achieved. The house has been renovated to resemble how it might have looked in Jenner's day, though most rooms are turned over to museum displays and information boards.

There are two places that are particularly worth looking at: first, the attic. You might have to ask the curators if they will take you up there as it's not always open, but it's worth enquiring because it's quite an experience. The rooms have been taken back to their Georgian state, so it's all bare timber and dusty rafters, with the aim of recreating the sort of trauma the young Edward Jenner might have had in quarantine from the outside world when he was being variolated. If you see a ghost up there, you're not the first – a photograph taken in 2010 with a shady outline on it went around the Internet in double-quick time.

Your other point of call should be the garden. In the far corner, next to the churchyard wall, is a curious structure with a thatched roof, stone walls and a doorway constructed of gnarled sections of tree trunk. This 'Temple of Vaccinia' was where Jenner, following his discovery, vaccinated the poor of Berkeley against smallpox for free. If you go that far into the garden, you're almost at the church, so you could pop through the gate and take a look at Jenner's memorial inside.

There have been many notable medical breakthroughs and advances made in Britain, but Jenner's achievement deserves particular mention for the millions of lives that were saved as an end result, not only in the fight against smallpox, but indirectly against all manner of infectious diseases that can now be vaccinated against. Given that the house in which he lived played an active part in the discovery, it's well worth taking a look.

Edward Jenner Museum
The Chantry, Church Lane, Berkeley, Gloucestershire GL13 9BN
01453 810631
www.jennermuseum.com

Blaenavon, Torfaen

Nominated by Bill Jones, reader in Welsh history,
School of History, Archaeology and Religion at
Cardiff University, and co-director, Cardiff Centre
for Welsh-American Studies
'Where you can see how iron and coal powered the
Industrial Revolution in South Wales'

You need to go underground to fully appreciate this story. The first port of call on a visit to historic Blaenavon should be the Big Pit, where the ex-miners will equip you with a hard hat, a battery belt and a head torch, then escort you 90 metres (300 ft) down in a lift to the coal mine below.

As the Big Pit, which dates from 19th and 20th centuries, is now part of the National Coal Museum, this tour is free. After an hour or so of the head-smacking, back-bending walk underground, you'll have a very rough idea of what it must have been like for the men, women and children who for generations worked this mine, and many more like it, across the valleys of South Wales. You'll have seen the working conditions for the miners, the stables for the pit ponies that lived underground, the tracks of the underground railways and the engines that powered them, and you'll have heard stories of rats, explosions and unending hard, dark, hot labour. From the second half of the 19th century through to the middle years of the 20th, it was King Coal around which life revolved here, and which made the area one of the key industrial zones of Britain, if not the world.

Coal is really the second part of the industrial story of Blaenavon. It was iron that brought people here initially. Down the road from the Big Pit are the Blaenavon ironworks. Started in 1789, they are a tremendous reminder of an earlier phase of the Industrial Revolution, dating from the time when iron-smelting technology was developing. Between the 1750s and the 1830s, ironworks appeared across South Wales, harnessing the new smelting technology based on the power of coke (coal that had been part-burnt to remove impurities) to heat the furnaces where the metal was released from the raw ore. The area, with its ready mineral reserves of coal, iron ore and limestone, was well suited for the new enterprise.

Blaenavon's ironworks were neither the earliest nor the biggest (in the 1790s that honour went to the works in neighbouring Merthyr Tydfil), but they are very well geared up for the visitor today. According to Bill Jones, 'It's hard to pinpoint industrial growth to a particular place. Blaenavon offers very easy access to places where visitors can get an appreciation through interpretation. It's not that Blaenavon is any more important than anywhere else; it's just where a visitor can immediately get an impact of those profound changes that are at the root of Victorian and Edwardian prosperity in Britain.'

With the blast furnaces, heating kilns, a huge water lift, tramlines, and the houses of the ironworkers all preserved, it's a fascinating place to poke around the old order of industrial activity. The site survives in such detail because it was superseded by a later ironworks, Forgeside, on the other side of Blaenavon, where technology for the conversion of iron to steel was introduced in the 1870s. The old ironworks, happily enough, continued to be useful as a maintenance depot for Forgeside, so its buildings were not demolished when it ceased to be operational at the start of the 20th century. A campaign against demolition in the 1960s and 1970s was successful, and the ironworks are now at the centre of the World Heritage Site in and around Blaenavon.

The water lift structure, hugely imposing and grandly built (too grandly, in fact – the man behind it was criticised for spending too much money on its stone facing), is the one that draws the eye at the ironworks, then leads you to look at the upland beyond. The lift, with two balanced cages propelled upwards and downwards by means of alternately filled and emptied water boxes, was the mechanism by which pig iron was raised. It went by tram road to a forge on Blorenge Mountain behind the town, then down the other side to barges waiting on the new canal.

The World Heritage Site inscription for Blaenavon stresses that it's for the whole industrial landscape in and around the town. From the ironworks, you can drive or walk up Blorenge and see the ponds where they held back water to drive the forges. You also get a view of the limestone quarries, tunnels, slag heaps and even the coal itself in parts; then down on the far side are the wharves and canal that took the metal away to its markets. It's a very instructive experience, and well worth spending some time to explore.

Eventually, the iron industry declined and the coal industry blossomed. In fact, coal came into its own in the later years of the 19th century, says Jones, as the major fuel for the world until the First World War. 'It was the fuel of empire because coal exports from Wales were driving the world economy. There were many coalfields in Britain, but the largest producer in the immediate First World War period was South Wales. It was probably the best known overseas because two-thirds of its output was exported. The Admiralty exclusively used Welsh coal. Britain's empire was based on sea power, and in the 19th century that power came from Welsh coal.'

And that takes us back to the Big Pit, one of the many collieries that would have been dotted across the valleys. The earliest part of the mine dates back to 1812, but it was in 1860 that the main shaft was sunk (deepened in 1880). That's the way that visitors have descended since the place morphed from mine to museum in the early 1980s.

Now, after decades of decline, coal-mining is an almost vanished industry. However, the Big Pit presents with great skill the story of coal mining and its crucial importance to the development of both the area and the world. With the rusting metal remains of past endeavour still littering the site, it's undeniably evocative of an age now lost. The renovated pit-head baths are unmissable, giving you a sense of the social history of the industry. Housed in a 1930s' modernist building, they were built even as the industry was tailing off, but they take you into the lives of the men who actually worked the mines. The preserved showers and long lines of lockers are fascinating to view, as is the exhibition on the stories of the men who used these facilities.

Of course, if you want to know how industry, and coal in particular, dominated the social fabric of life, you need do nothing more than head back into Blaenavon and take a stroll around the place that now brands itself a 'Heritage Town', but is in reality an archetypal coal town: 'In Blaenavon, one doesn't just get a colliery,' says Jones, 'you also have the trappings of the coalfield society, the very distinctive cultural social grouping that grew up around these industrial enterprises.'

You can see it in the terraced streets, the public houses, the tremendously grand Workers' Institute, and in the old schoolhouse, now home to the World Heritage Site Interpretation Centre. There you can view an illuminating exhibition on the story of the town, and enjoy a pleasant rest in the café while you think about Jones's concluding comments: 'It's one of those areas today that can give us an insight into the tremendous changes that happened in Wales during the Industrial Revolution through the iron and coal industries. They made South Wales one of the key sectors in the British industrial economy.'

Blaenavon

World Heritage Centre, Church Road, Pontypool, Torfaen NP4 9AS

01495 742333

www.world-heritage-blaenavon.org.uk

Penydarren Tramway, Merthyr Tydfil
Nominated by Helen Nicholson, reader in history, Cardiff University
'Where the steam age was ushered in'

Iron made Merthyr Tydfil. Well, coal had a part to play too, but it's iron that this South Wales valley town is best known for. Dubbed 'the iron capital of the world', by the end of the 18th century it was home to four great ironworks, each of them belting out great quantities of iron. The place was blessed with ready supplies of iron ore, and plenty of coal with which to power the furnaces to smelt it.

Once it had started producing these industrial quantities of iron, Merthyr faced one not inconsiderable problem – how to move the stuff out of the valley and away to its global markets. In attempting to solve this logistical issue, the town played a key role in the history of mechanised transport. As Helen Nicholson says, 'It was the site of the first example of steam traction on rails in the world.'

In the 1790s the Glamorganshire canal was dug from Merthyr Tydfil to Cardiff. Three of the town's ironworks clubbed together to create a tramway to link them to the canal. This enabled horse-drawn carriages to cart iron down to waiting barges and away. Such an arrangement was not unusual: 'At the end of the 18th century,' says Nicholson, 'Britain was becoming covered in little tramways that ran from industrial works and collieries down to a canal so that they could take their loads to the nearest port. Production had become so great that the traditional backpacks on mules were no longer enough.'

It is what happened next that was so unusual. The owner of the Penydarren Ironworks engaged a Cornish engineer by the name of Richard Trevithick to do something revolutionary: namely, to replace the horse power on this tramway with steam power. Trevithick had already demonstrated his prowess in this regard with his work on steam pumps for Cornish mines. He'd followed this up in 1801 by creating a steam locomotive that did actually move and carry some passengers around the Cornish town of Camborne, before irreparably blowing up. Word of this must have reached the Penydarren iron master Samuel Homfray, who presumably saw the potential.

By 1804, Trevithick had built a steam locomotive for the tramway. The story goes that Homfray and the master of a rival Merthyr ironworks, Richard Crawshay, had a wager on the likely success of this venture. On 21 February, therefore, Trevithick's machine was put through a trial to see if it could haul 10 tonnes of bar iron and 70 passengers 15 km (9½ miles) down the tramway to reach the canal at Navigation Basin in Abercynon. The contraption reached its destination, travelling at a breakneck 8 kph (5 mph). However, the tramway didn't fare so well; its rails broke under the weight, so the locomotive couldn't get back again. Crawshay seized on the engine's failure to return as an excuse not to pay up, so Homfray didn't collect on his wager.

Although this episode was not the start of the Industrial Revolution (that was already well under way), it was, says Nicholson, 'the ushering in of the steam age. It was another step in Wales becoming the world's first industrial nation.' The tramway locomotive's career wasn't one of garlands and glory, though. The rails could not be sufficiently strengthened, so Trevithick's 'Iron Horse' spent the rest of its working life as a stationary engine. It was left to the engineers of northern England to pick up the steam locomotion baton a decade later (see Stockton and Darlington Railway, page 296).

Nevertheless, the Penydarren demonstration did prove the potential of steam locomotion. How is this very significant episode commemorated in Merthyr Tydfil today? Principally through the Trevithick Trail, which follows the line of the tramway from Penydarren, where a small model of the engine sits atop a pedestal at the side of the road, through the centre of Merthyr and down through the pleasant surrounds of the Taff Vale to Abercynon. The tramway actually continued to run until the early 20th century, but there isn't that much left to see – the trail is essentially a pleasant, fairly flat path now pounded by walkers and cyclists. However, there are still some diverting sights, notably the Trevithick Tunnel (arguably the oldest railway tunnel in the world), which now has a mosaic at its entrance commemorating the first locomotive journey through it. Your imagination is encouraged to conjure up the groundbreaking journey that took place along the line of the trail through various bits of artwork and inscriptions. You might want to download the map from the Trevithick

Trail website before you leave home as it's not as well signposted in Merthyr as it might be.

The Trevithick Trail was created in celebration of the 2004 bicentenary. Although Merthyr Tydfil has seen a sharp post-industrial decline since the centenary back in 1904, the town is now actively trading on its cultural heritage. Perhaps the trail itself isn't the most visually exciting heritage attraction you'll ever visit, but it's a good stab at using what little is left of this key early moment in locomotion history. You can also learn about Trevithick's achievement and the rest of Merthyr's story at the town's Cyfarthfa Castle Museum (housed inside the ostentatious home of Richard Crawshay's son William – we don't know if either of them ever settled the 1804 bet). The Ynysfach Engine House, also in town, will give you an idea of what went on in the ironworks. If the small model of the engine on the pedestal in Penydarren doesn't give you quite enough on what the machine was like, you'll want to make a visit to Swansea's new National Waterfront Museum, where they have a full-size replica.

Neither Trevithick nor his steam locomotive get quite the credit they deserve, overshadowed as they are by Robert Stephenson and his 1829 locomotive *Rocket*, so do your bit to redress the balance by taking a stroll down the line of the tramway that heralded a transport revolution.

Penydarren Tramway

Tourist Information Centre, 14a Glebeland Street, Merthyr Tydfil CF47 2AB

01685 727474

www.trevithicktrail.co.uk

www.visitmerthyr.co.uk

Wilberforce House and High Street, Hull

Nominated by David J. Starkey, director, Maritime Historical Studies Centre, University of Hull

'Where you can see Britain's maritime past in microcosm'

Wilberforce House is just one of several grand brick buildings with a frontage on to the narrow cobbled High Street in Hull. These were the homes of the great maritime trading families that made Hull a major port city in the 17th and 18th centuries. The merchants lived here to be close to the wharves and warehouses on the river Hull, which runs parallel to the High Street. Their ships loaded and discharged goods bound for, and conveyed from, the Baltic and northwest Europe.

The High Street is no longer the business heart of the city; things have moved on, and it's now home to Hull's Museum Quarter. That means it's a calm and pleasant place where you can amble between museums and historic houses, and peer down the shoulder-width streets, known as 'staithes', which provided the link to the wharves on the river.

As David J. Starkey observes, 'Hull's rich history – itself a microcosm of Britain's highly significant maritime past – can be glimpsed in these houses, in the dry docks where the *Bounty* and many other ships were built, and in the Streetlife, Wilberforce and archaeological museums, all of which are situated along the High Street.'

Hull can certainly lay claim to an impressive pedigree when it comes to maritime history. Some of the earliest seagoing craft yet discovered, three Bronze Age sewn-plank boats, were found at Ferriby, a few miles west of Hull. Later Iron Age log boats have also been excavated in the waterlogged muds of the area, and you can see one example, the Hasholme boat, in the Hull and East Riding Museum, which is one of the attractions on Hull's High Street. Quite feasibly, that craft could have worked the waters of the Humber estuary in the 4th century BC. At the other end of the timescale, and at the other end of the staithe that leads from the museum to the river bank, you can take a tour of the *Arctic Corsair*, which was built in the 1950s and is now the last surviving sidewinder trawler – a reminder of the days when Hull was one of the greatest fishing ports in the world.

As well as the museums, there are the grand merchants' houses on the High Street. 'A number of these merchants' houses have survived,' notes Starkey, 'including Blaydes House, home of the builders of Bligh's *Bounty*, and Wilberforce House, where William Wilberforce, the MP who championed the abolition of the slave trade, was born.'

Quite apart from the place's general maritime resonance, Wilberforce House offers reason enough for a visit to Hull's High Street. It was built in the 1660s, and in 1732 it was bought by William Wilberforce's grandfather, a merchant in the Baltic trade. The abolitionist was born in the house in 1759. He grew up in Hull and would have been quite familiar with the ships arriving with their goods from northern Europe, and a bustling High Street busy with traders and sailors. Hull did not engage in the slave trade, so it was not an obvious starting point for one of the key figures in the drive to abolish slavery. Nevertheless, Wilberforce took the cause to heart in the 1780s and then devoted his political career to ending the nefarious business. This was achieved in increments and against considerable opposition for there was much money being made across Britain from the trade (see Harewood House, page 268, for example). Yet the tide turned towards the abolitionists in 1807, when the British slave trade was abolished, and in 1833 with the abolition of slavery itself.

Although recent scholarship has identified the role played by the slaves themselves in gaining their freedom, Wilberforce has long been seen as one of the key figures in this process. He was elected MP for Hull in 1780, and spent much of his political career pressing for parliamentary action on slavery. When the Abolition of the Slave Trade bill was passed in 1807, he was the hero of the evening in the Commons. Following that, he came to be seen as the nation's moral conscience, as, despite worsening health, he continued to press for full abolition of slavery. Wilberforce died just days after the passing of that final act in 1833.

For his achievements in the fight against slavery, Wilberforce was widely lauded in his lifetime, and he was taken to heart as one of Hull's most famous sons. He was given a state funeral, and very soon after his death a towering column atop which his statue stands was erected in his home town, paid for by public subscription. In 1906 the house in which he was born was turned over to a museum devoted to the history of slavery and its abolition.

The Wilberforce House Museum retains that role today, with interesting and disturbing displays on slavery past and present, and information about Wilberforce's role in its demise. Behind the display panels you can get an inkling of the merchant's house in which he was brought up. The grandeur of the great staircase and the quality of the wooden panels gives a little taste of the money that was to be made in maritime commerce in Georgian Britain. Wilberforce was able to pursue his political career partly because he was born into mercantile wealth.

And that takes us back to the broader maritime story. Although the slave trade is ably documented in Wilberforce's one-time home, Hull was not a slaving port but an entrepôt chiefly involved in the shipment of manufactured goods, coal, grain, timber and passengers across the North Sea, and (from the 1850s to the 1970s) a trawling port. The High Street, with its empathetic buildings and range of museums, is an excellent place to visit to understand how that story unfolded.

Wilberforce House
23–25 High Street, Hull, East Yorkshire HU1 1NQ
01482 300300
www.hullcc.gov.uk

Free Trade Hall, Manchester

Nominated by Malcolm Chase, professor of social history, University of Leeds

'Where the fight for democratic rights was built on the blood of peaceful protestors'

A luxury hotel might seem an odd place for a memorial to one of the most famous events in the history of political protest in Britain. Yet the Radisson Edwardian on Peter Street in the centre of Manchester is where you need to go for physical expression of the Peterloo Massacre. The red plaque on its outer wall is succinct. It reads: 'St Peter's Fields. The Peterloo Massacre. On 16 August 1819 a peaceful rally of 60,000 pro-democracy reformers, men, women and children, was attacked by armed cavalry resulting in 15 deaths and over 600 injuries.'

When this event took place, the hotel was not here, nor indeed were most of the streets around it. Although Manchester, at the heart of the Industrial Revolution, was expanding at an electric pace in the early 19th century, there was still open ground near the centre of the city. This area was known as St Peter's Fields, after St Peter's Church, which was a short distance away. The church was demolished in 1907, and its site is now occupied by the Cenotaph and Memorial Gardens in St Peter's Square, while building has encroached on the rest of the open ground.

So what were those 60,000 people doing here in 1819? They had come to demonstrate for a more inclusive electoral system, to challenge the fact that only a very small minority of the population had the right to vote. The backdrop was the aftermath of the Napoleonic Wars, which although concluded with British victory in 1815, had led to terrible unemployment and famine. This situation was not helped by the government's introduction of the Corn Laws, which blocked the introduction of cheap foreign corn in order to keep up the price of British-grown corn. While this policy protected the incomes of landowners and farmers, it made it even more difficult for anyone else to afford to eat.

The rally was to be addressed by the well-known orator Henry Hunt. Although Hunt had demanded that the demonstrators come to the meeting unarmed, the local magistrates ordered the yeomanry to break up the meeting and arrest him. They charged the crowd on horseback and in so doing killed 15 (or thereabouts – the figure is not clear) of the protestors, and injured hundreds more. The massacre soon came to be known as Peterloo, in ironic reference to the last Napoleonic battle at Waterloo four years previously. This assault by British troops on unarmed British civilians had huge repercussions, explains Malcolm Chase.

'In British domestic history it had the same kind of pivotal importance that Waterloo did in European history. It was one of the defining moments of the 19th century in the sense that it was seen as an unprecedented act of violence by the authorities on ordinary defenceless people, many of them women, who were gathering to make a legitimate peaceful political protest. It was seen as a mark beyond which the British state should never again step. At the time, it was also considered unprecedented, but that's not quite true: in Hexham in 1761 there was an anti-militia riot that led to 51 people dying. But essentially, in the popular memory, Peterloo is one of the worst instances of violence by the authorities in putting down political protest. So it's a benchmark to which all subsequent political movements, not just the left, refer to.'

Despite the public outcry after Peterloo, there was no change in suffrage until the Great Reform Act of 1832 (and that was limited in its extent), and no change in the Corn Laws until 1846. That the latter were eventually repealed was due in large part to the campaigning of the Anti-Corn Law League, an organisation that was founded in Manchester in 1838 to bring an end to the protectionist laws. In 1839 they held a large meeting in one of the last remaining undeveloped plots of land in St Peter's Field, where in fact much of the blood in the 1819 massacre had been spilt. The campaigners built a pavilion on the site, followed a few years later by a more substantial building, and finally a much grander affair still, with a handsome colonnaded façade, was opened in 1856, with the name of the Free Trade Hall. It was used for concerts and public meetings – including the Liberal party meeting of 1905 that was disrupted by suffragettes (see Pankhurst Centre, page 359). That building was destroyed during the Second World War, but such was the affection in which it was held by the people of Manchester that it was rebuilt in 1951. Eventually, it fell out of use and was demolished, bar the Victorian frontage, and converted into the hotel that now stands on its site.

The red plaque now displayed on the hotel is itself an interesting piece of history, as until 2007 there was a differently worded blue plaque here. It referred only to the dispersal of the crowd by the military, and made no mention of the casualties. This was seen was an insult to the memory of those who died at Peterloo, so a campaign was started (www.peter-loomassacre.org) not only to have the plaque altered (which has now been achieved with its red replacement), but also to press for a more fitting memorial to the massacre, as aside from the plaque, there is currently very little to commemorate the events of 1819. Agreement has now been reached to erect a more substantial tribute to the sacrifice. Until that comes to pass, there is a memorial of sorts in the form of the People's History Museum just a short walk away, where you'll find an excellent exhibition on the subject, and on the longer battle for suffrage and demo-cratic rights.

'For the Chartists [who called for a raft of democratic rights] in the 1830s and 1840s, Peterloo was one of the central events of the recent past,' says Chase. 'It's referred to again in the reform movement in the 1860s. Working-class radicals contested with middle-class liberals over who owned Peterloo. For example, the Manchester Free Trade Hall was intended by its middle class, largely mill-owning Liberal promoters to be a cenotaph raised on the shame of the victims of Peterloo. But at the same time the Chartists said this was purely an act of middle-class authority trying to close down working-class radical expression. It's frequently invoked by the Labour movement in the 20th century.'

The Peterloo debate continues to this day with the discussions over how best to memorialise it, and that is all the more reason for paying the site of the massacre a visit.

Free Trade Hall
Radisson Edwardian Hotel, Peter Street, Manchester M2 5GP
http://peterloomassacre.org

People's History Museum
Left Bank, Spinningfields, Manchester M3 3ER
0161 838 9190
www.phm.org.uk

Apsley House, London
Nominated by Gary Sheffield, professor of history,
University of Birmingham
'Where you can get the measure of a man who held
sway over Britain for the first half of the 19th century'

Gaze out of the windows from the upper floor of Apsley House at Hyde Park Corner and not only do you have a grand view over such notable London landmarks as Hyde Park and the Wellington Arch, but you're also afforded the opportunity for an interesting historical reflection. Back in the 1830s, these very windows were the target of protestors angry about the obstructive attitude to parliamentary reform of the man inside. That man was Arthur Wellesley, 1st Duke of Wellington, victor at Waterloo and vanquisher of Napoleon.

Apsley House, Wellington's London residence at the end of his active military life, gives an excellent insight into the character and long career of this soldier-turned-politician. That's the fascination for Gary Sheffield: 'It's almost like a shrine to the man himself. He lived there and it came to embody him. There are portraits of his military career, plus a fantastic dinner service given by the Spanish, but it's also symbolic because one version of how he got his nickname of the 'Iron Duke' relates to the iron shutters he had to put on his windows to stop them being broken when he was a politician and hugely unpopular. The house reflected the political class under siege and marked the man as both hero and villain.'

Wellington is most closely associated with warfare. His military career spanned more than two decades and took in much of the central action of the Napoleonic Wars. His victory at the battle of Waterloo in 1815 finally spelt the end of Napoleon's European domination. However, throughout that time Wellington also pursued a political career, serving as an MP and, for a time, as chief secretary for Ireland. After Waterloo he moved more deeply into politics, eventually becoming prime minister in 1828.

What's interesting in his long career is that it encompasses a period of fundamental change, including not only the upheavals of the Napoleonic Wars, but also the enormous changes of the Industrial Revolution and the subsequent challenges to the established order through demands for reform of the political system. As Sheffield says, 'He was a politician in an era edging towards democracy.' Wellington, born into the established order, proved out of step politically in that march to democracy. His resistance to calls for a fairer political system and for more people to have a vote saw him move from a popular hero to a popular villain.

Opulent dining was the order of the day in Wellington's Apsley House

If you can picture that fall from grace within the iron shutters, you can certainly see the hero worship that preceded it here too. Outside the windows are the monumental arch and statues dedicated to Wellington, while inside the house, the adulation continues. He was granted £700,000 from a grateful nation to create a Waterloo Palace after his victory in 1815. Instead of using the money to build the 19th-century equivalent of Blenheim Palace at his Hampshire estate of Stratfield Saye, Wellington opted instead to embark on the less ambitious project of renovating and remodelling Apsley House. This resulted in the sumptuous Waterloo Gallery, where the annual Waterloo Banquet was held to commemorate the battle. It's quite a place, but perhaps even more impressive now is the State Dining Room on the other side of the house, which was where the banquet was held in the years before the completion of work on the Waterloo Gallery. Here, for today's visitor, the table has been laid with the astonishing Portuguese centrepiece that was given to Wellington after the battle, in 1816. This 1000-piece extravaganza of golden dancing nymphs is no average table decoration.

Before you go upstairs to the dining rooms take a look at the large painting in the entrance hall depicting one of the Waterloo banquets. On your way to the first floor, you'll probably be sidetracked by a large statue of a nude Napoleon in the stairwell. Commissioned by Napoleon himself, this work by the Italian sculptor Canova was bought by the British government in 1816 and presented as a gift to Wellington. The duke wasn't gloating when he had it installed in his house, though: Wellington genuinely admired his erstwhile enemy, who, by coincidence, was born in the same year as him, 1769.

That sculpture isn't the only work of art in the house; the place is packed with paintings, many of them masterpieces originally in the Spanish Royal Collection, but discovered abandoned in the baggage train of the retreating enemy after Wellington's victory at the battle of Vitoria in 1813. There are also many portraits of Wellington's military comrades, plus a large panorama of the battle of Waterloo itself, hanging in the Striped Drawing Room. It all adds up to something of a visual feast, though the overall effect pales in comparison to Blenheim Palace (page 217), the home of another victorious general, the 1st Duke of Marlborough.

Wellington's decision not to saddle his descendants with the upkeep of a Waterloo Palace along the lines of Blenheim was probably a wise one, though Sheffield doesn't think it should be seen as downplaying the duke's achievements. He differs with Saul David on who has been the key figure in Britain's military story: 'I think Wellington rather than Marlborough is the man who put Britain on the map militarily. The defeat of Napoleon and all the rest of it makes him genuinely a world figure.'

On that assessment, Apsley House, or Number One London, as it was otherwise known (due to its being the first place you'd come to in the city as you approached from the west), circled outside by the monuments to his martial prowess, and crammed inside with memorials on a similar theme, remains a fitting tribute to the victor of Waterloo. It has been a shrine to the man almost since the day he moved in, back in 1817, and don't forget that despite the hiccups in his political career, he was firmly back in the public's affection when he died in 1852. Perhaps a million and a half people turned out to watch his funeral procession to St Paul's Cathedral. His historic house provides a good opportunity to get the measure of a man who held such sway over the nation in the 19th century.

Apsley House
London W1J 7NT
020 7499 5676
www.english-heritage.org.uk/daysout

Stockton and Darlington Railway, County Durham

Nominated by Emma Griffin, senior lecturer in history, University of East Anglia

'Where the power of steam locomotion was demonstrated'

You don't have to be a steam buff to find *Locomotion Number One* an alluring piece of engineering. The machine is all varnished wood and dark metal, with its working parts on display over a barrel cylinder, and a tall, fat chimney rising up at the front. It would perhaps have a toy-like quality if it weren't a full-size steam engine.

This particular train stands motionless today at the Head of Steam Museum in Darlington. In 1825, in a crucial moment in British transport history, it pulled some carriages along the track near to where it now resides. On 27 September that year, the ceremonial opening day of the Stockton and Darlington Railway, it was the first time a steam locomotive had been used to transport passengers on a public railway.

This was a notable first. Of course, it wasn't the first time a steam loco-motive had been used. Richard Trevithick had done that 20 years earlier (see Penydarren, page 280). It wasn't even the first time a steam locomo-tive had been used commercially (that was in 1812 at Middleton Colliery in Leeds). It certainly wasn't the first railway, says Emma Griffin.

'Tracks had been around for a long time: carriages were put on them and horses pulled them along. Engines too had been around for quite a long time. But not until they built the Stockton and Darlington Railway had anyone been able to put the two things together and make passenger transport as we now know it.'

So this was a very important milestone that transformed Britain in many ways, not only in terms of transport, but with knock-on effects such as the development of the postal system and the start of the tourist industry.

The Head of Steam Museum not only has the steam engine that did the work on the day, but it also sits along the route of that original journey. This makes it a great place for historical exploration into the Stockton and Darlington Railway story. Even better, it's a fabulous place to visit. Housed in mid-19th-century railway buildings and featuring exhibits of several other early steam engines, it also provides a wealth of information about the Victorian railway (ticket offices, toilets and passenger carriages are all faithfully recreated here), and particularly focuses on the events of 1825.

A couple of things are definitely worth inspecting. First is the tremen-dous painting by John Dobbin of the famous journey, with the crowds watching *Locomotion Number One* pulling its train of carriages (including the covered Experiment coach for dignitaries) over the Skerne Bridge in Darlington. Second is the model of the route of the first railway, showing the terrain it passed through and the key landmarks along the way. The main thing that's demonstrated by the model is that although it was called the Stockton and Darlington Railway, the track actually went beyond Stockton to a place called Shildon, because its original purpose was to get coal from the Durham coalfields to the river Tees (at Stockton). From there it could be more easily shipped elsewhere. That at least was the initial ambition of Edward Pease, the founder of the railway, whose original plan was to use horse-drawn carriages. George Stephenson, by this time an accomplished engineer, persuaded Pease that it would be better to harness steam power rather than horse power, and so it was that Stephenson, with his son Robert, built *Locomotion Number One* and the track it ran along.

The decision by Pease to go with steam was the key one, according to Griffin. 'Until this time, everyone was moving around on foot or by horse power. That limited how fast you could go and also how many people could travel because for every horse, you needed to set aside quite a lot of land to feed it. You couldn't set aside all your land just to feed horses, so there was a limit to capacity. Once you started laying tracks and using coal, you had a vastly increased capacity, and that marked the beginning of the modern transport age.'

Funnily enough, Stephenson's steam engine wasn't used to pull the passenger carriages along the tracks for the first few years of its operation; that task was left to horses so that the locomotive could get on with the work of hauling the coal. Nevertheless, the seed was sown, and the next notable milestone in the history of steam locomotion came just a few years later with the Rainhill Trials to decide which machine would be used for the new Liverpool and Manchester Railway. Famously, George and Robert Stephenson's *Rocket* won that contest, and intercity steam train transport began.

Incidentally, a replica of another engine that contested those Rainhill Trials, the *Sans Pareil*, can be seen just up the road from Darlington, at Shildon's Locomotion Railway Museum. This is a sprawling place with a substantial collection of trains in a vast shed, but also some interesting relics of its early days at the head of the Stockton and Darlington line. After 1825, the company established its workshops here under the leadership of another engineer, Timothy Hackworth, who designed the *Sans Pareil*. You can visit his house within the boundaries of the Locomotion Museum, along with some other early evidence of the railway's story.

Curiously, at the other end of the line, in Stockton, there isn't that much to see, aside from a few plaques commemorating the events of 1825. One thing they do have is a replica of Captain Cook's ship *Endeavour*, a Whitby collier converted for expeditionary use (see Captain Cook Museum, page 234), which, if nothing else, highlights the fact that the pressing need for efficient coal transport was nothing new in 1825.

The reason why they wanted to move the coal is worth emphasising. When Abraham Darby perfected the use of coked coal in the iron-smelting process in 1709 (see Ironbridge Gorge, page 230), coal became the catalyst for the Industrial Revolution. It remained a key fuel throughout the process of moving from an agricultural to an industrial nation.

'One of the big things that happened during the Industrial Revolution is that industrialists moved away from using organic resources, such as wood, wool and leather, towards using inorganic resources, above all coal and iron. Exploiting the great reserves of natural resources that lay beneath the soil opened up the possibilities of much greater economic growth,' concludes Griffin. 'If you try to get everything from the land, you're never going to have a rich industrial nation.'

Stockton and Darlington Railway

Head of Steam Museum – Darlington Railway Museum, North Road Station,

Darlington, North Yorkshire DL3 6ST

01325 460532

www.darlington.gov.uk/culture

Tolpuddle, Dorset
Nominated by Keith Snell, professor of rural and cultural history, Centre for English Local History, University of Leicester
'Where workers made a collective stand for a better life'

The Dorset village of Tolpuddle stretches out along one main road, a pretty mix of thatched cottages mingling among later brick and tile houses, with the river Piddle burbling behind at the foot of the valley. It doesn't have the feel of somewhere that would have instigated a national agricultural labourers' movement, but if you make for the sycamore tree on the small village green, next to the parish church of St John, you'll be at its revolutionary heart.

It was under this tree in the early 1830s that a group of agricultural labourers met to discuss the idea of banding together to give themselves a collective chance of improving their lot in the world. That lot at the time was a very poor one, and the already extremely low wages were at threat of falling further, while unemployment was rising and new technology endangered what work they could get. The situation was not unique, and at the start of the 1830s unrest at this state of affairs boiled over across southern England in the form of the Captain Swing Riots, during which gangs of labourers smashed threshing machinery and demanded better pay from the farmers and landowners. Direct physical action was the only way they felt they could make their voices heard in a political situation that overwhelmingly favoured the interests of the landed and moneyed.

In Tolpuddle in 1830 the workers' weekly wage had been nine shillings. By 1834 it had been reduced to seven, with a threat that it could fall further, to six. The Tolpuddle men who gathered on the village green looked to the Grand National Consolidated Trades Union (GNCTU) for help. Since the repeal, in 1824, of laws that banned collective action by labourers (the Combination Acts of 1799 and 1800), unions had sprung up in the newly industrialising cities. The GNCTU was one of a number of general unions that had developed with the purpose of improving society across the board. Two of its delegates came to Tolpuddle in 1833 and, under the leadership of a local Methodist preacher, George Loveless, helped the men to set up their Friendly Society of Agricultural Labourers, whose aim was to push peacefully for better pay.

In the light of the Swing Riots, the relationship between farmers and labourers was tense and recriminatory. The government was keen to stop further agricultural unrest, so, with guidance from the home secretary, Lord Melbourne, the local squire, James Frampton, moved to stamp out the Tolpuddle action. Consequently, six men were arrested on 24 February 1834 and marched in chains to Dorchester, where they were imprisoned and tried in March. As collective action was not illegal, the case against them was cooked up on something of a technicality, as Keith Snell explains: 'They were not convicted for being members of a friendly society or a trade union, but rather because of an oath they swore. Most of these societies included the swearing of oaths on the Bible, and the Tolpuddle men were convicted under an older act which prohibited the use of such oaths.'

The Tolpuddle six – George Loveless and his brother James, Thomas Standfield and his son John, James Brine and James Hammett – were all found guilty and sentenced to transportation to Australia for seven years. This sort of punishment was not unusual for criminals, but as Snell notes, 'These six men were fairly respectable working people, so the reaction of the authorities was a massive overkill. There was a colossal, particularly urban, backlash, and huge agitation against the local landowner, James Frampton. It is a good example of one Justice of the Peace overreaching his powers. Trade unions throughout the country backed the men's case. As a consequence, they were reprieved and brought back to great national acclaim.'

When the Tolpuddle Martyrs, as they came to be known, got home from Australia in 1838 and 1839, great meetings were held in their honour. So much money for their families had been raised in their absence that they were able to take on tenant farms in Essex. All but James Hammett, who returned to Tolpuddle and died there in 1891, left for Canada on the expiry of their Essex leases, and lived out their lives without further notable excitement. Their brief moment of celebrity was well in advance of the main bout of rural trade unionism in the 1870s, but their story has continued to resonate.

'The Tolpuddle Martyrs feature in a very iconic way in the history of the Labour movement. They were religious, righteous individuals who weren't breaking conventional laws, but trying to insist on a working wage in a notoriously low-waged region,' notes Snell. 'Right through to today, union activists go back to the touchstone of Tolpuddle. The great injustice that was done in 1834 is constantly used to justify labour organisations and protests in the countryside.'

On the centenary of the trial of the martyrs, the Trades Union Congress raised enough cash to build six cottages and a meeting room on the outskirts of Tolpuddle to house retired agricultural labourers and remember what happened in 1834. The row of cottages, each house bearing the name of one of the martyrs, still stands, and the meeting room is now a small but informative museum of their story. In the centre of the village you can see James Hammett's headstone in the churchyard, and you can consider the sycamore tree, where the martyrs met, from the cover of the memorial shelter next to it. Further along the road, a plaque marks out John Standfield's cottage, where the men held meetings, and towards the edge of the village, the Methodist chapel, where George Loveless preached, can be visited. To get to it, you go through a memorial arch that was erected in 1912 and opened by the Labour politician Arthur Henderson.

In short, there is much to remind the passer-by of the significance of the Tolpuddle Martyrs' story. Thousands of people still descend on the village for an annual commemorative festival in July, so if you want to experience the full force of the martyrs' continuing power, go then, but if you want to have the history to yourself, choose another weekend for your trip.

Tolpuddle

Tolpuddle Martyrs' Museum and Memorial Cottages, Tolpuddle, Dorset DT2 7EH

01305 848237

www.tolpuddlemartyrs.org.uk

Albert Dock, Liverpool

*Nominated by Tony Lane, emeritus professor of
social science and former director of the Seafarers
International Research Centre, Cardiff University*
**'Where you can see a principal gateway to
Britain's empire'**

Britain's empire encompassed a large part of the globe in the 19th century.
Goods and products had to be moved around that empire, and the best
way to do this, considering the vast distances involved, was by ship. Many
of the materials being transported were destined for, or passing through,
Britain itself, so the port cities prospered and grew. Liverpool was one
such port, and the Albert Dock on the banks of the river Mersey, is the
place to go to witness the scale and nature of the enterprise.

The first thing that will strike you on reaching Albert Dock is the
workmanlike feel of the place. Everything here is brick and iron; this
industrial, functional appearance is as it should be because there would
have been a lot of labour going on here. Built in the mid 1840s, Albert
Dock was the latest, bang-up-to-date addition to an already heavily
busy dockside on the banks of the river. The city's population rocketed
from a modest 80,000 at the start of the 19th century to some 685,000
at its close, and you can put most of that huge rise down to the success of
the docks during that time.

The ever-increasing volume of traffic here put pressure on Liverpool's
facilities. The multi-storeyed brick warehouses that enclose the rectangle
of water in Albert Dock were designed to alleviate the problem of ships
unloading on the riverbank and then shifting their cargo to warehouses

throughout the city. Until the dockside warehouses were built, fire, theft and customs evasion had been significant problems. The dock surveyor Jesse Hartley used brick, iron, and stone to make the buildings fireproof, and incoming ships could unload directly from the quay, cutting back the opportunities for thieves and making it easier for customs officials to keep an eye on what came in. Hartley even came up with a hydraulic lifting system to improve the unloading process.

In the mid 19th century, goods were coming into Liverpool from all over the world, particularly from places in the British Empire. For Tony Hall, Albert Dock is symbolic of the extraordinary global reach of the shipping operation here. 'Not to mention the outstanding commercial architecture and the museums and galleries of the city, all of whose collections are products of what was once known as the "gateway of empire".'

After years of decline, as the dock's once ultra-modern facilities were superseded, the place was finally renovated and reinvented as a visitor attraction in the 1980s. So Albert Dock today is home to cafés, bars and restaurants, plus the museums and galleries to which Hall refers. As well as the modern art gallery Tate Liverpool, there is also the excellent Maritime Museum and International Slavery Museum, both contained within one of the former warehouses. They are worth a visit, the Slavery Museum providing a singularly thought-provoking experience.

Albert Dock was constructed after the official end of British involvement in slavery (the slave trade was abolished in 1807, slavery itself in most of the British Empire in 1833), but Liverpool had deep roots in the business. Although it came slightly later to it than other British ports, notably Bristol and London, Liverpool by the 1740s was the principal route for ships involved in the triangular trade (goods shipped from

Europe to West Africa, slaves from Africa to the Americas, cotton and tobacco from there back to Europe). In the 18th and early 19th centuries a great many ships left the docks here for Africa, packed with cargo with which to buy slaves. Look out of the museum windows to the north and you'll be staring down on the dry docks, where these slave ships would have been repaired and fitted out.

There are many more reminders of Liverpool's role in the slave trade, but the place where the ships of the day would have berthed is now occupied by the Pierhead with its famous trio of early 20th-century buildings. Liverpool's 'Three Graces' – the Royal Liver, the Cunard and the Port of Liverpool buildings – are monuments more associated with another kind of human traffic: the emigration business. From 1830 to 1930 it's estimated that some 40 million souls left Europe for new lives in the New World, and that almost a quarter of those departed from Liverpool. They came from across Europe to use Liverpool as their jumping-off point. Some were fleeing dire circumstances, like the many thousands of Irish who left their famine-stricken homeland in the 1840s for America. The one shared experience was that they all travelled in ships, at first sail and then steam. Fortunes were made by the companies that transported them, and Cunard's towering building was home to just one of the many shipping firms that headquartered in the city. It's hard not to look out over the Mersey here and mull on how many people departed for new lands, willingly or forced, and the great impact their journeys were to have on global history.

The Cunard Building and its famous neighbours were actually built as Liverpool's fortunes were about to go into reverse. The peak year for emigration from here to America was 1907, and it declined from then, further exacerbated by the onset of the First World War in 1914. The new

Museum of Liverpool between the Pierhead and Albert Dock, will allow you to review the whole story of this great city. It's the latest stage in the redevelopment and reinvention of the area from empire gateway to heritage mecca.

Albert Dock
Albert Dock, Liverpool L3 4AA
0151 708 7334
www.albertdock.com

Derby Arboretum, Derby

Nominated by Paul Elliott, lecturer in modern history, University of Derby

'Where interest was sparked in the idea of the urban public park'

In the first half of the 19th century, some towns and cities burst their boundaries to keep up with the pace of the Industrial Revolution. One of the consequences of this was that traditionally common open spaces were swallowed up by urban expansion. The workers who flocked to the factories and foundries were therefore increasingly surrounded by mills rather than green and pleasant land.

It was in Derby, a place dominated by the textile and engineering industries in the 19th century, that this trend began to be arrested. Close to the city centre today, hemmed in by Victorian terraces on all sides, you'll find the handsomely moulded landscape of Derby Arboretum. What since the 1850s has been the main entrance, at the end of Arboretum Street, is an ostentatious Italianate affair, with arches, an ornamental clock and an orangery behind. Inside there are 4.5 hectares (11 acres) of greenery peppered with mature trees, and a network of paths that converge at a modern café building in the centre, next to a popular children's play area.

In 1840, when the place was opened, it was something of a revelation. As Paul Elliott explains, although there had been various forms of public gardens before it (Glasgow Green, for instance, has a long history as an urban public open space), Derby Arboretum was a transitional institution: 'It would be wrong to call it the first public park. You had Georgian pleasure gardens and other forms of subscription garden, which made their money as commercial businesses through paid entry. Also there was public access to common lands. But no one had suggested a garden or a park in its own right. In fact, there's a debate about what is the first Victorian park. Derby has a claim to be the first public municipal Victorian park, and that's one part of its importance. It became widely publicised and served as a model for the establishment of other Victorian public parks.'

A man called Joseph Strutt was behind the project (his statue stands at the summit of the Arboretum Street entrance). He was a local textile magnate and philanthropist who wanted to give something back to the community that had made his family rich. He bequeathed the land to the town and instructed the landscape gardener and horticultural writer John Claudius Loudon to design the gardens. The result was a planted manifestation of Loudon's eight-volume *Arboretum Britannicum* (1838), the most significant study of the science and culture of trees in British history. The idea was to give the citizens of Derby a landscaped place to walk through, with many beautiful and interesting trees and shrubs planted upon distinctive mounds. The most important part of the newly designed arboretum consisted of single examples of each species so that visitors could clearly see the differences between each tree and taxonomy or classification of plants. Visitors were encouraged to walk around the park surveying the trees, perusing the guidebook and reading the labels printed with English and Latin names and dates of introduction. You can still see the mounds and some of the 19th-century trees, although all the original labels or tallies have disappeared, and later additions have meant that the single species rule is no longer adhered to.

The arboretum's opening ceremony was quite an event, with three days of celebrations, processions and even hot-air balloons. It wasn't just the people of Derby who were impressed. 'The way it was endowed generated a great deal of interest,' notes Elliott, 'because it was down to a local industrialist, Joseph Strutt, whose wealth came from the cotton and textile industries. Such benefaction solved a problem for the Victorians because it was very difficult to fund things like public gardens on the rates. A wealthy benefactor coming forward and endowing an institution was an attractive notion. The idea of a public park captured the attention of the country, and led to the creation of other parks, such as Joseph Paxton's at Birkenhead. But I think it was the Derby one that really set the ball rolling.'

From the 1840s onwards, public parks began to spring up in towns and cities across the country. It was part of the 19th-century movement for rational recreation, whereby moneyed Victorian patriarchs, such as Strutt, attempted to direct the leisure time of the labouring poor into brisk and purposeful activity. The park model of Derby Arboretum fitted the bill exactly. Of course the labouring poor, as the description suggests, did not have much in the way of either time or money to spend on such activities, so from the start, the park was free at the times they were most likely to be able to visit – Wednesday afternoon (early closing for shops) and Sundays. Beyond that, it was open to subscribers and those who bought tickets, and it was only in 1882 that universal free entry was established.

Towards the end of the 19th century the Derby Arboretum was no longer maintained as a botanically significant collection, and between the 1960s and 1980s it declined as a public park, but its fortunes have improved of late, says Elliott: 'They've recently had several million pounds of Heritage Lottery Fund money to restore the park and give more sense of how it would have been around 1840, when it opened.'

Happily, it's once more a place where locals and visitors can come to stretch their legs and enjoy a bit of greenery. Its history has not been forgotten, as there are information plaques at every entrance, the Victorian gates have been restored, and there's a small exhibition on Loudon, Strutt and the events of 1840 in one of the former park entrance buildings, Grove Street Lodge.

The arboretum occupies an important place in the development of the concept of leisure in Britain – and even abroad, as it seems to have attracted attention from America and inspired urban park creation there too. It also encouraged interest in botany and landscape design, so its historical significance makes it worth a visit. Plus, of course, as originally intended, it remains a pleasant place for a walk.

Derby Arboretum
Arboretum Square, Derby DE23 8FZ
01332 292612
www.derbyarboretum.co.uk

Rochdale Pioneers Museum, Rochdale
Nominated by Frank Trentmann, professor of history,
Birkbeck College, University of London
'Where working people banded together to help
themselves'

The 18th-century former warehouse that houses the Rochdale Pioneers
Museum is perhaps a little lonely these days. Although it sits in a conservation area, most of the busy street – Toad Lane – that it was once part of
is now under a modern shopping centre, while a nearby dual carriageway
completes the encroachment of the 20th century.

The building has survived, while those around it have not, because it
was the original store, in 1844, of the Rochdale Pioneers, a group credited
with bringing the idea of co-operation to the world. Its significance was
recognised in 1931 when it was converted to a museum, and that's what
it has been ever since. Inside is a re-creation of the Pioneers' storefront
and a wealth of artefacts relating to their story.

The museum reveals how 28 local working men set up a co-operative
society, with the aim of offering a fair trading service for its members,
along with educational and social facilities. Calling themselves the
Rochdale Society of Equitable Pioneers, they raised enough money
through subscriptions to take out a year's rent on the lower floor of 31
Toad Lane, and on 21 December they opened their shop for the first time.
The Pioneers did not have a wide range of stock to sell that day – just
butter, sugar, flour and oatmeal – but it was a start. The front room of
the museum is set up to resemble the way the shop might have looked in
those early days.

The Rochdale Pioneers were certainly not the first people to flirt with the idea of a co-operative (the social reformer Robert Owen popularised the idea in the early 19th century), but they were the first to make it really work. Frank Trentmann explains: 'In the 1780s there were some associations among artisans that were mini co-operative enterprises, where people paid in and got a share of the proceeds. There were also co-operative credit groups in early medieval Japan. So some elements of a co-operative society existed previously, but the Rochdale Pioneers combined them under one roof and created a viable enterprise.'

The Pioneers set down the principles by which they aimed to run their society. Chief among these were voluntary and open membership, democratic control, and the dividend, whereby members got a share of any trading surplus in proportion to their purchases. In a time of considerable hardship for workers across Britain and social upheaval across Europe, this proved to be a compelling model of co-operation for mutual protection and gain. The Rochdale Principles, as they have become known, formed the basis for co-operative societies around the world.

Guided by these principles, the Pioneers prospered and the society was soon able to expand its product range and rent out the upper two floors of the old warehouse. It also started offering library facilities and education classes for members (you can still see where these classes were once held). By 1867, the Pioneers had outgrown Toad Lane and moved to new premises in Rochdale. Their success was already attracting admirers.

'These were not just ordinary co-operators,' says Trentmann. 'They signalled where future societies might find social harmony, peace and welfare. The store became a model of a better world. Very few places have that ambition. You can see the store as a microcosm of peaceful co-operation between individuals and different social groups. The attraction of the Rochdale model was that after the failures of the big social revolutions, particularly of 1848, it offered an alternative, showing that you could have social peace and raise the standard of living for working people through co-operation. You didn't have to go on the barricades – you could buy from the co-operative shop and thus help everyone else who was a member. The concept of co-operation was an idea in which Britain led the world. The Rochdale Pioneers were international stars of radical politics. They were admired in Germany and Scandinavia, Russia and Japan. The Rochdale shop attracted social investigators and reformers interested in creating a better society.'

By the 1900s, the co-operative had become a larger social movement than the trade unions, with something like 4 million members by 1914. Today it is huge and global, with more than 800 million members in over 100 countries around the world. In Japan you can find a slightly larger than life replica of the Toad Lane building, while Venezuela once issued stamps featuring the image of one of the Rochdale Pioneers. The movement owes its lasting popularity in part to the Pioneers who succeeded the first generation and created a cult of their forebears, highlighting the significance of what happened at Rochdale in the story of social reform.

The somewhat isolated museum building still manages to attract a regular stream of international visitors looking to pay homage to the roots of the co-operative movement. For a site with such a global legacy, 31 Toad Lane is a low-key attraction, but pay a visit and you'll be left in no doubt that the ideas once generated here transcend its humble location.

Rochdale Pioneers Museum

31 Toad Lane, Rochdale, Lancashire OL12 0NU

01706 524920

www.co-op.ac.uk/our-heritage/rochdale-pioneers-museum

NOTE: The museum is closed for refurbishment throughout 2011, and due to reopen in 2012.

St George's Hall, Liverpool

Nominated by John Belchem, professor of history, University of Liverpool

'Where you can see the confidence of an imperial city in its pomp'

St George's Hall is not somewhere that's easily overlooked in Liverpool. That's particularly the case if you arrive by train at Lime Street Station because its grand, colonnaded elevation rather fills your view. The hall was opened in 1854 and generally has two words applied to it: 'Neoclassical masterpiece'. It sits in the middle of St George's Plateau, an open space dotted with statues and memorials and edged by other huge Victorian edifices, most notably Lime Street Station, the Walker Art Gallery and Liverpool's World Museum.

On the outside, St George's Hall is straight out of ancient Greece, complete with portico and friezes. On the inside, it's somewhat more modern, boasting the latest in Victorian technology (it had the world's first air conditioning system when it was constructed).

Although the hall is a working venue, you can explore its interior via the Heritage Centre at the south end of the building and following a trail around some of its sights. Be ready for a surprise, as the first thing you're met with is a set of prison cells. If that doesn't seem in keeping with the majesty of the building, it makes sense when you learn that when it was built, it was designed to combine the functions of courtroom and concert hall, both of which were lacking in Liverpool at the time. The character-istically gloomy Victorian cells were used to house those awaiting trial in the courtroom above. The place was a working court from 1854 to 1984, and can still be visited today.

Less unexpected is the vast and magnificent vaulted main concert hall next door to the courtroom, which you can look down on from a gallery above. It's a huge open area, with a notable tile floor, great bronze gates, a very grand organ, and niches around its edge in which stand statues of various Victorian notables. It's a tremendously impressive space, but, says John Belchem, something deeper underpins this place than the need for a good music venue. 'St George's Plateau was set up as the area that would establish Liverpool as Liverpolis – an independent city state with rich cultural facilities. It's an absolutely classic statement that Liverpool saw itself as a city republic. The message was, "This is no provincial place: this is the great city of commerce, civilisation and culture".'

It's not just the hall that's designed to give this impression. The range of buildings on the northern edge of the plateau, from the World Museum to the Walker Gallery, are of similar style and date. The statues on the plateau to the east and in St John's Gardens to the west of St George's

Hall depict great Victorian heroes and commemorate service and sacrifice on a national scale. You could be mistaken for thinking you were in the capital city of the country to whom these great men owed their allegiance. In fact, the similarity to London's major commemorative space, Trafalgar Square, is perfectly obvious when you note that there is even a 19th-century warrior-hero on a column (Wellington, rather than Trafalgar's Nelson) and four lions residing on plinths beneath.

'Have a look at the lions,' advises Belchem. 'Are they a match for Landseer's in London? Here's an indication that the city fathers thought Liverpool second only to London, or was it the other way round?'

Like Glasgow (see People's Palace, page 353), Liverpool in the 19th century could well claim to be the second city of empire, or even to mount a challenge to London's position. The monumentality of the buildings in and around St George's Plateau was a not terribly subtle message to that effect. Liverpool could afford all this bluster because it had grown rich, very rich, on the fruits of the dues that were paid by all the imperial traffic that was passing through its docks on the banks of the river Mersey (see Albert Dock, 301).

Despite this wealth, it's worth noting that 19th-century Liverpool was a place of extremes. Throughout the city you'll find elaborate and grand Georgian and Victorian buildings (it has more Georgian architecture than Bath or Edinburgh), which were funded by the mercantile elite. However, there was also extreme poverty and dreadful slums. Indeed, the construction of St George's Hall itself was not without controversy as its critics decried the enormous amounts being invested in the place, at a time when money was so clearly and urgently required for public health reform and improvements for the living standards across the city.

Nevertheless, St George's Hall was built and Liverpool was able to present itself as the great city of empire that its merchant princes called for. If you want to see evidence of a time when Britain was globally dominant, and knew it, then this very grand building and the plateau that surrounds it will certainly not disappoint.

St George's Hall
St George's Place, Liverpool LI IJJ
0151 225 6909
www.stgeorgesliverpool.co.uk

Lincoln Castle, Lincolnshire
Nominated by Alyson Brown, reader in history,
Edge Hill University
'Where you can see the long story of British justice and punishment'

Think of castles and the mind tends to be drawn to medieval knights, arrow slits and hot oil down murder holes. But Lincoln Castle shows that castles had purposes that went far beyond sword fights and siege towers. Within the well-preserved circuit of its castle walls, there are two buildings that highlight how these places tended to be centres of justice and punishment.

First, there is a Georgian magistrates court, and second, a Georgian and Victorian prison building. These two structures dominate the centre space of the castle. The prison, or at least part of it, is open to the public, and it's the place to visit if you want to learn about attitudes to crime and punishment in that era.

The cells of the women's prison are enlightening, but the most illuminating yet disturbing aspect of a tour of the castle has to be the prison chapel. It's a little bit like an old-style lecture hall, with a pulpit from where the preacher would have spoken, but rather than desks and seats, there is a half-circle of wooden cubicles, each one separated from the next by high timber partitions. The prisoners would each occupy a cubicle and, once inside, would be able to see only directly ahead to the person delivering the sermon. They would be contained by an ingenious central locking system and would have no contact whatsoever with their fellow inmates during the course of the service. It's the most striking example of the Separate System, a prison regime imported from America in the early 19th century that demanded the isolation of every inmate. The idea was to force prisoners to reflect on their sins and thus progress towards reformation and redemption.

Alyson Brown explains the significance of Lincoln Castle's chapel: 'For me, the single most important aspect of the site is the complete Separate System chapel, which may well be the last surviving in the world. It's extremely evocative, with a very subdued, pensive, reflective atmosphere, but also with a hint of menace, control and submission. In short, this one room is imbued with the philosophy and practice behind the disciplinary system that was established in most prisons in Britain during the mid 19th century.'

The prison went out of use in the 1870s as attitudes towards detention shifted from redemption to deterrent. The prison and chapel survived because the site was basically used for storage. That was a lucky break for

Prisoners wrestled with their consciences in isolation in the chapel in Lincoln Castle

posterity because its existence today really helps us to understand what Victorians thought of criminals and how to deal with them.

'Currently, it's just the women's prison that's open to the public,' notes Brown, 'but there are future plans to open the men's prison too. Even as it stands, it's impressive and really reflects Victorian values and ideas about how to achieve reformation of individuals.'

Some felons, however, were deemed beyond redemption, and Lincoln Castle was also the site of executions in the first half of the 19th century. Hangings were initially conducted outside the castle walls, but from 1815 they were carried out from the roof of the 13th-century tower called Cobb Hall, where crowds below could more readily bear witness. Some 37 people were hanged there between 1817 and 1859. You can ascend to the top of Cobb Hall today, where its past history affords an opportunity for sober reflection as you lean on the battlements and look out across the city. You can also descend to the lower level of Cobb Hall, which was a medieval dungeon, where prisoners were chained to iron rings on the walls, and scratched graffiti into the stones, which you can still see today: another place to consider the bleak prison experience of the past.

Many of those executed at Cobb Hall were buried in the Lucy Tower on the opposite side of the castle. After a steep hike up its mound, you can view the rather pitiful grave markers they were allocated. And then, between the two towers, you've got the Georgian courthouse in which justice was dispensed. All told, then, you walk through a short history of justice and punishment on one site.

As an interesting aside, the castle also has an exhibition devoted to the Magna Carta, the charter agreed between King John and the barons in 1215 (see Runnymede, page 88). An original copy of the charter is owned by Lincoln Cathedral and is on show as part of the castle exhibition in a suitably dark and reverent room. Uniquely, alongside it is a copy of the other, less famous document that goes with it, the Charter of the Forest. One of the provisions in the Magna Carta was the right to a fair trial for all free men, the basic idea behind this justice and punishment story.

All these fascinating sights sit within the bounds of an extremely well-preserved medieval castle. Although you can't currently walk the length of the walls, plans are in place to make that a reality, and to open up the courthouse to visitors once it is no longer in active use. As it is, you can progress around some portions of the ramparts and reward yourself with excellent views over a historic city. If you do so, you'll struggle to miss the heavenward-pointing spires of the great medieval cathedral, just a few paces away from the castle walls, which of course you'd be remiss not to include in your visit to Lincoln.

Lincoln Castle
Castle Hill, Lincoln LN1 3AA
01522 511068
www.lincolnshire.gov.uk

Down House, Kent

Nominated by Stephen Halliday, lecturer in history,
Institute of Continuing Education, University of
Cambridge
'Where Darwin conceived his big ideas'

'Charles Darwin,' according to Stephen Halliday 'was a very unsatisfactory student who spent his time at Cambridge University collecting beetles when he should have been studying theology with a view to become a clergyman. He was the despair of tutors and his father.'

It was, however, as a result of his collecting beetles that he got the job as a naturalist on the expeditionary vessel the *Beagle*. This came about through the agency of John Henslow, the professor of botany at Cambridge who had managed to capture the interest of the young man with his lectures on natural history. So it was that Darwin left in 1831 for the famous journey around the world that he himself said 'determined my whole career' and set his mind thinking about evolution.

On his return to England in 1836, he spent a few years in Cambridge and London before moving in 1842 to Downe in Kent (by which time he was both a husband and father). As Halliday notes, 'It was at Down House that he wrote *On the Origin of Species*, *The Descent of Man* and a treatise on earthworms, and had what Richard Dawkins has described as possibly the most important idea that anyone has ever had.'

That idea was, of course, the concept of evolution through natural selection. As befits such a pivotal place in the history of science, Down House is now a heritage attraction, restored to the look and feel of Darwin's day. The undeniable highlight is his study, which is where he wrote *On the Origin of Species*. You glean an enormous amount about the character of the man by just standing and looking, albeit from behind ropes, at the mostly original furniture and effects. Most imposing is his high-backed armchair, with its iron frame and wheels. He wasn't one to write on a desk, so he had a wooden board – a bit like a TV dinner tray – that rested on the arms of his chair. With his feet on a cushion, he would compose his books in what must have been reasonable comfort.

Continuing the wheeled furniture theme is Darwin's microscope stool, which the scientist's children (of which there were a considerable number by the time he published *On the Origin of Species* in 1859) used to requisition to punt themselves around the floor. Particularly telling is the large tin bowl in the far corner of the room, slightly obscured by a screen. This was Darwin's 'privy', a feature that enabled him to remain in his study while attending to bodily functions (a boon, no doubt, for a man blighted by illness; he suffered from stomach problems, flatulence and vomiting throughout middle age).

Even though Darwin had been all around the world on the *Beagle* voyage, his declining health meant that he never again travelled far from Downe. Naturally, he was selective about where he wanted to live, so he chose the place for its rural calm coupled with its proximity to the metropolis, yet even though Downe is but 25 km (15 miles) or so south of London, he rarely made the journey to the capital, instead relying on the Royal Mail to service his prolific letter-writing habit.

Today the ground floor of the house is set up as it was in Darwin's time, with many original fixtures and fittings. You're guided around the rooms with an audio tour voiced by none other than Sir David Attenborough, whose soothing tones are a perfect and informative accompaniment. Don't miss the cupboard under the stairs, which is now full of tennis rackets and Victorian garden apparel, but where in 1844, says Halliday,

'Darwin left the manuscript of *The Origin of Species* and told his wife that should he die, she was to publish it. He seems to have been terribly worried about the fuss it would cause. He had the idea of evolution many years before he published his theories about it. He kept postponing, but was finally prompted into print when the naturalist Alfred Russel Wallace wrote to him and proposed the same idea.'

Upstairs is an exhibition space about Darwin's life, times and discoveries, which is well structured and educational, but if time is tight, don't linger too long and miss the chance for a good look at the grounds, which are splendid and reflective of Darwin the botanist. He would no doubt appreciate the well-stocked kitchen garden and the orchids in the greenhouse. The vegetables are all named with tags if you're interested in the origin of each species. Make sure you continue to the end of the garden and out through the door to the famous Sandwalk, the path through a copse of woodland where he used to take a stroll every day to clear his busy mind. 'Every time he completed a turn,' says Halliday, 'he'd kick aside a stone to see how many times he'd walked round.'

Inside and out, Down House makes for a great visit, where you'll get the measure of the man who, some would say, has done the most to form and inform the modern world view. Incidentally, should you not be able to visit, the English Heritage website has an excellent interactive tour of the house, which allows you to scan panoramic photographs of the entire ground floor and click on various objects of interest for more information.

Down House
Luxted Road, Downe, Kent BR6 7JT
01689 859119
www.english-heritage.org.uk/daysout

Houses of Parliament, London

Nominated by Pat Thane, emeritus professor, Centre for Contemporary British History, King's College London
'Where you can see the story of British democracy'

For a place that boasts almost a thousand years of history, the Houses of Parliament, or the New Palace of Westminster as they should properly be known, are terribly Victorian. That's because in 1834 an almighty conflagration almost completely destroyed the Old Palace of Westminster. The new Houses of Parliament were opened by Queen Victoria in 1852.

Although the building remains a working parliament, you don't have to be a politician to have a look around. If you live in the UK, you can request a tour at any time of the year, even when parliament is sitting, by contacting your MP. Anyone, British or otherwise, can pay to take the same tour during the summer recess, when the politicians are away from Westminster. The tour follows a prescribed route, starting in Westminster Hall (the oldest part of the palace, thankfully not a victim of the fire), then through St Stephen's Hall, into the Central Lobby, on to the House of Lords, followed by a quick turn around the Royal Gallery and Queen's Robing Room, before the grand finale of the House of Commons itself. Clearly, the tours are held outside parliamentary sessions, which is why you don't see lines of tourists shuffling past the Despatch Boxes during Prime Minister's Questions.

Don't expect to be alone on this tour. You'll be one of several groups, each with a guide competing to be heard in the chambers. And don't anticipate nipping off to have a wander on your own. Understandably, there are guards everywhere (woe betide anyone who sits down in the House) and you'll have to submit to an airport-style security check to get in.

Given its much-referenced position as 'the mother of all parliaments', with all the pivotal moments in the story of democracy that have occurred here, there are many reasons to visit. When you stand in Westminster Hall, under the rigid timbers of Richard II's 14th-century hammerbeam roof, you can think of the medieval origins of parliament, from Simon de Montfort's summoning of bishops, peers, knights and town burgesses in 1265, through Edward I's Model Parliament of 1295, and on to Edward III's Good Parliament of 1376. Those parliaments would not have met in this mighty hall at that time, but it's the closest you'll get to the medieval fabric of the old palace.

The first-known use of the term 'parliament' dates to 1236. Prior to that, English kings ruled with the aid of a small council of nobles and advisers, but in the early 13th century, during the reign of King John, the barons became increasingly dissatisfied with arbitrary royal rule. In 1215 at Runnymede (page 88), John was forced to agree to take greater account of their views. His successor, Henry III, continued to struggle to find an accommodation with the barons. This came to a head at Westminster in 1258, when they tried to force him to call regular meetings of parliament. Henry refused, so the barons, under Simon de Montfort, rebelled and beat the king in 1264, thus leading to the parliament of 1265 that is seen as a forerunner of today's parliament. Henry's son Edward I called parliament reasonably regularly in order to gain approval for the taxes he needed for the various military campaigns he took on. His Model Parliament of 1295 was so called because two knights from each county and two burgesses from each town were called to attend, setting the pattern for the future composition of parliaments.

Parliament became increasingly potent through the 14th century, so much so that by Edward III's reign, during the Good Parliament of

1376, several of the king's corrupt ministers were impeached by the Commons. Richard II, who succeeded Edward III, regularly clashed with parliament and, indeed, was eventually deposed by a parliamentary assembly of 1399. As you look up at Richard's mighty roof in Westminster Hall, you can dwell on the fact that his demise helped cement the rising authority of the Commons.

Once you've progressed up to St Stephen's Hall, you're on the site where the House of Commons sat from 1547 through to the 1834 fire (you're standing in the Victorian reincarnation of the chamber). Consider the fact that in 1909 a group of suffragettes chained themselves to the statues that line the walls here, and had to be removed with bolt cutters by the police (Viscount Falkland was slightly damaged). Then, when you proceed into the House of Commons, you should think on the various great Acts passed here and the many examples of high oratory that have occurred. And, of course, aside from the business of parliament itself, there are moments of drama that could divert you too: the foiling of the 1605 Gunpowder Plot, the successful Fenian bomb attack of 1885, and the shooting of Prime Minister Spencer Perceval in the Member's Lobby in 1812 spring to mind.

For all that drama and democracy, though, what might well strike you even more forcefully is the very Victorian strangeness of the place. The fire ripped through the old palace just two years after the passing of the 1832 Great Reform Act, which extended the right to vote (though it would take many years before we got anywhere near universal suffrage). You might have thought that parliament would have taken the fire as a chance to create a new and dynamic building to reflect the changing nature of politics. Yet what was chosen, after a public competition, was the Victorian Gothic behemoth designed by Charles Barry and Augustus Pugin, in which every effort appears to have been made to hark back to the medieval predecessor.

There was discussion at the time of a neoclassical design, similar to the White House in Washington, which would have reflected the fashion of the day, but that was rejected for having too republican a feel. It would not have sat at all well with the regal splendour of the Royal Processional Route, along which Queen Victoria advanced to open the new building in 1852. It was glass and iron that ruled in the construction of the Crystal Palace for the Great Exhibition of 1851, yet stone and dark wood panelling were the order of the day for parliament's home.

The deliberate decision to look back rather than forward seems curious when you consider that this was the time that Britain's imperial and technological future must have appeared to hold so much promise. But it is a very confident memorial to Britain's national history; both inside and out, the visitor is left in no doubt as to the power of the country that paid for this building. The historical theme is particularly apparent inside, with a sequence of grand paintings and murals depicting great moments in the national pantheon: Waterloo and Trafalgar, for example, appear on huge panels in the Royal Gallery. Recently, the Armada Paintings, replacements for fire-consumed 16th-century tapestries depicting the Elizabethan naval triumph, have at last been installed in an antechamber to the House of Lords, 160 years after Prince Albert commissioned them (he died before they were completed and the money ran out).

In the view of Pat Thane, it's all quite strange for the modern visitor. 'Walking around the halls and the lobbies, you're struck by how peculiar it is. It's that large echoing lobby, and the corridors and the people who shout at you when you take a wrong turning. The chamber of the House of Lords has an amazingly over-the-top gilt throne from which Her Majesty opens parliament.'

When a bomb fell on the Commons chamber and annihilated it during the Second World War, parliament again had a chance to adopt a more modern design. Winston Churchill argued against the building of a semi-circular chamber, insisting that the rectangular approach, which forced the opposition parties to face each other in adversarial combat, was at the heart of the way democracy works here. The rebuilt chamber was also kept small (far too small to seat all the members of parliament, in fact) in order to maintain the intimate atmosphere.

The archaic peculiarities of the building reflect the way politics are played out in Westminster, where historical traditions and practices continue to dictate everyday business. The best way to appreciate that is to visit the place itself.

Houses of Parliament
London SW1A 0AA
www.parliament.uk

British Museum Round Reading Room, London

Nominated by James Gregory, lecturer in modern British history, Bradford University

'Where you can track several centuries of the pursuit of knowledge'

When you walk into the Great Court at the heart of the British Museum, you're met with the shining vision of the brilliant white, rounded walls of the Reading Room, snug beneath the glorious glass and steel canopy. It was not always thus. The Great Court was revealed to the public only ten years ago. Prior to that, the light, airy, echoey space that surrounds the Reading Room today was a forest of bookshelves. The change came about when the British Library left the crowded confines of the British Museum for its new, purpose-built premises near St Pancras.

The Reading Room has taken on a new life since then. Although it still has its original mahogany desks, of late it's been turned over to high-profile exhibitions, with the likes of China's Terracotta Warriors and the Aztec treasures of Moctezuma on display under its dome. Whether exhibition space or library, the theme of knowledge pervades the building, says James Gregory. 'For over 200 years it's been used as a reading and research room, but now it's a place associated with blockbuster exhibitions. In that it has continued its function in the sense of intellectual enquiry and the study of the past.'

To understand the Reading Room's significance, we need to go back to the early days of the British Museum. In 1753 Sir Hans Sloane offered his great collection of artefacts to the nation, and the museum was founded by act of parliament, with Sloane's bequest at its heart. The objects were displayed in the 17th-century mansion of Montagu House, which stood on the site of the current museum. Then, in 1823, King George IV gifted his father's library to his people, and to accommodate the 60,000 books, the quadrangular building that houses the modern museum was built, with one wing given over to the King's Library.

The central court was originally to be an open area, but the collection quickly outgrew the available space because the gift of the King's Library also brought with it the right to a copy of almost every work published in the United Kingdom. By 1857, therefore, the Reading Room had been constructed inside the central court, surrounded by 5 km (3 miles) of shelves for the ever-increasing quantity of books. That was the situation until 1997, when the library was moved to St Pancras, the bookshelves around the Reading Room dismantled and the domed building itself carefully restored for its grand reopening in the year 2000.

For James Gregory, it's the association of the place with knowledge and the dissemination of learning that makes it important: 'It's part of the mythology of academic life, not just in history, but in intellectual enquiry in this country and worldwide. It has seeped into international consciousness. Many globally renowned people came to do research in the Reading Room – people like Karl Marx and Mahatma Gandhi. Rather than a place that's associated with royalty or battles, it's all about knowledge.'

In the Victorian period, the library in the British Museum was indeed internationally renowned, attracting the cream of the intelligentsia from across Europe, some of them perhaps just looking for a warm place to sit, but others, notably Karl Marx, working on ideas that would fundamentally change the world. Other notable names from Britain and beyond who received a reader's ticket to work in the library include Mark Twain, George Orwell, Virginia Woolf and Nicolai Lenin. In short, a galaxy of genius has been assembled under this dome in the last century and a half. If you can get inside the building and sit down at one of those desks, you won't perhaps be standing on the shoulders of those intellectual giants, but you will at least be occupying their seats.

The influence of the Reading Room has stretched beyond academia, notes Gregory: 'It has impinged on our consciousness in cinema too. It features in the 1929 Alfred Hitchcock film *Blackmail*, when the black-mailer is pursued over the roof of the dome and falls through it. It also tends to crop up in novels, so it's associated with the metropolis and impe-rial capital.'

Now the visitor can more readily appreciate the magnificent domed building that was planned by the Italian émigré librarian Anthony Panizzi, who was the key figure in the development of the library in the mid 19th century. When it reverts to being a library rather than an exhibition space, you'll be able to go inside once more, and marvel at the beautiful blue, cream and gold papier mâché dome. More importantly, you'll be able to see and perhaps sit at the handsome old desks, arranged in 'spokes' around the central hub that was the librarian's domain.

Now the Reading Room, with its new role as the centrepiece of the great open space at the heart of the museum, has become part of public consciousness in a different way. If you're interested in the history of knowledge production and dissemination, you shouldn't miss the rest of the British Museum that surrounds the Great Court. It's a treasure house of global knowledge (and certainly a controversial one, with regular calls for the return of artefacts, most famously the Elgin Marbles, to their

The Victorian Reading Room, with its wonderful dome and spokes of desks

homelands), and one that you could spend several days in before making any serious inroads into its collections. Knowledge is everywhere here, inescapable and global in its reach. There is no better place to appreciate the Victorian spirit of academic enquiry.

As a final note, the new British Library near St Pancras is also well worth a visit. It's the next phase in the history of knowledge creation in this nation, and will no doubt create its own share of intellectual heavyweights to talk about in years to come.

British Museum Round Reading Room
Great Russell Street, London WC1B 3DG
020 7323 8299
www.britishmuseum.org

Old Course, St Andrews

Nominated by Gerard De Groot, professor of history, University of St Andrews

'Where you can sense the contribution of sport to British culture'

There are a good number of nicely groomed lawns in this book's collection of significant historic sites, but they are mostly attached to large stately homes. The grass in question here has a presence in its own right, given that it's the playing surface of the most famous golf course in the world. Although the first tee of the Old Course is overlooked by several substantial buildings, including the clubhouse of the Royal and Ancient

Golf Club, none of them can lay claim to ownership of the greens and fairways; it's a public course over common land.

The Old Course is one of the more spectacular sporting venues you could hope to visit. Starting at the foot of the medieval town of St Andrews, it stretches out across the undulating ground just behind the town's long white beaches and the North Sea. Golf has been played here for 600 years or so, and today the Old Course regularly hosts one of the four major golfing championships, the Open. Despite that, members of the public can still walk around the course, particularly on Sundays when golf is banned so that the people of St Andrews can enjoy their common land unchallenged by low-flying balls. You can take a guided tour and walk the first and last fairway with an informative local, who'll give you a bit of the history of the place.

Sport is often given scant attention by historians, but for Gerard De Groot, that is an oversight: 'Sport is such a big part of our culture, and within that whole sporting firmament, golf is one of the top three or four sports in this country.'

Certainly, sport matters to a lot of people today, but in historical terms, it also sums up some cultural values that Britons have long aspired to: 'It is hugely important in the sense that it's not just seen as a leisure pursuit,' continues De Groot. 'It's a package of cultural values that have been exported along with the other elements of civilisation that the British feel they have given to the rest of the world. Sports have been seen not just as a way to exercise and have fun, but also as a way to convey the cultural values of fair play, decency and honesty. It's interesting that golf embodies that better than most because it is based on the fundamental honesty between the people playing it.'

If sport does embody British cultural values, the Old Course, for its long history, is the place to go to feel that, and to see how those values have been exported, because you're sure to see a lot of foreign visitors here, waiting for their turn to tee off. Look down the first fairway and you're surveying a piece of sporting heritage. Even if you don't hold the slightest interest in the sport, you'll sense the reverence others have for the place.

For those who want to know a little more about the history of the game, the British Golf Museum is just over the road from the Old Course. It will tell you how golf originated and that the first written reference to it was in 1457, when Scotland's King James II banned it, and football, in favour of archery practice. It will also tell you how, in the mid 16th century, the Archbishop of St Andrews acknowledged the right of the locals to play golf; how in the mid 18th century the Society of St Andrews Golfers was formed; and how in 1836 it received patronage from the king and changed its name to the Royal and Ancient Golf Club of St Andrews.

It was not until 1854 that the Royal and Ancient clubhouse was built at the head of the Old Course. Although the R & A does not own the course its clubhouse overlooks, it is the organisation that administers the laws of the game across the world (apart from the USA). Significantly, its position was formalised in the second half of the 19th century, at the same time that the laws of Association Football were written down, the Rugby Football Union established, and international cricket matches began. In short, it's the Victorians who set down the British sporting culture that was then adopted around the world.

As De Groot notes, 'The whole idea of the gentlemanly ethic of sport is a Victorian concept. Golf was probably already that way, but the ethic was grafted on to it because the two harmonised so well.'

Of course, the Old Course itself predates the Victorian era by some margin. It was never designed, but just evolved over the centuries, with the grass kept short by the grazing sheep, and the sandy bunkers perhaps originating from collapsed rabbit warrens. The famous bridge over the Swilcan Burn, the stream that meanders across the 1st and 18th fairways, is probably older still. It's thought to have its origins eight or nine centuries ago, when it was built for monks to get to service at St Andrews Cathedral up on the hill behind the course.

You should make time to follow in the monks' footsteps and pay a visit to the cathedral while you're in town. During the medieval period it was the premier Christian site in Scotland, and though now a ruin (since the Scottish Reformation), it is still a magnificent site. Make sure you have a wander around the extensive graveyard, as you'll no doubt come across some of the golfing memorials that have been erected. That's one example of how far golf has permeated life for the people of St Andrews, and perhaps not especially surprising as residents do get to play their world-famous course for a fraction of the price that a visiting golfer would have to pay.

Old Course
Bruce Embankment, St Andrews, Fife KY16 9XL
01334 466666 (head office)
www.standrews.org.uk
(The Royal and Ancient Golf Club has its clubhouse at the start of the Old Course.)

SS *Great Britain*, Bristol

*Nominated by Mark Horton, reader in archaeology,
University of Bristol*

'Where you can see a revolutionary ship that made
the world a smaller place'

It's the bow of this lovely old ship that Mark Horton would suggest you
make a beeline for when you visit: 'Go and stand on the platform and
look out over the unconserved part at the front, and take in the sheer
scale of the ship.' You do get a fantastic sense of the size of the SS *Great
Britain* from this standpoint, peering into a land of girders and rivets in
her dark metallic cavity.

Her size is one of the reasons why she was such an innovatory vessel.
When launched in 1843, the SS *Great Britain* was the first large iron ship,
and the first large screw-propelled ship. The man who designed her is, if
anything, more famous than the ship itself, for it was of course Isambard
Kingdom Brunel, 'One of our great engineers who changed the face of
industrial Britain with his railways, bridges and ships,' says Horton.

By the 1830s Brunel had already designed Bristol's iconic suspension
bridge and started work on the construction of the Great Western Railway
linking London to Bristol. Not content with that, he'd also designed a
ship, the SS *Great Western*, to meet the train passengers arriving from
London and convey them on their way across the Atlantic to the USA.
The SS *Great Western* was itself revolutionary; the idea of a steam-
powered, paddle-wheeled, wooden-hulled ship that could cross the
Atlantic without running out of fuel halfway across was considered a
highly unlikely proposition by the great minds of the time. Brunel proved

them wrong, and then set out about designing the even more revolutionary SS *Great Britain.*

There were already iron-hulled ships, and there were already screw-propelled ships, but the concepts had never before been combined in a craft of the scale of the *Great Britain.* 'It was the prototype not just of ocean liners, but of everything that came to epitomise modern shipping. It also has a claim to be the prototype of early iron military vessels.'

Horton believes that Brunel's vision for the SS *Great Britain* represents a great moment in globalisation, 'harnessing mechanical power to cross the oceans of the world'. It was a vision that very nearly came a cropper in 1846 when she became grounded en route to New York at Dundrum Bay on the northeast coast of Ireland. Stranded there for a year, she brought in no revenue and the expense of freeing her bankrupted the Great Western Steamship Company. And yet, thinks Horton, 'If it had been a wooden ship, it would just have got smashed up. The fact that she survived the winter storms on an Irish beach for a whole year, something publicised by the *Illustrated London News* and suchlike, convinced people that iron ships were the way forward.'

On release from her enforced Irish sojourn, the *Great Britain* spent several further years plying her trade as an Atlantic passenger ship. What you see today when you visit her in Bristol is a re-creation of how she would have looked in the 1840s. It presents an extremely evocative image of Victorian voyaging: from the uncomfortably short sleeping cots to the handsomely decorated dining saloon, it conjures up a very different travel experience from the one we have today. While exploring the passenger cabins, the steerage hold and the various saloons, it's hard not to let your mind wander to imagining bearded, frock-coated Victorian gentlemen stepping the same boards as you with imperialist commercial missions on their minds.

Frankly, it's amazing that the ship survives to offer this excellent family heritage day out. Converted in 1852 to an emigration ship, the *Great Britain* was put to hard work over the next quarter of a century, making 32 voyages to Australia, transporting expectant souls ready to make their fortune in the Gold Rush down under. Then, as technology overtook her, she was converted to a sail-powered coal barge in the 1880s, before fetching up in the Falkland Islands, where she continued as a port hulk. Eventually, during the 1930s, she was left to rot on a South Atlantic beach, until plans were drawn up in the 1960s to bring her home. Her final journey up the Avon and under Brunel's suspension bridge in 1970 was greeted with much pomp.

The renovation work that has saved her is incredible, and the glass seal that controls humidity around the hull to prevent it from corroding further also allows for a tremendous 'underwater' perspective for the visitor. What's particularly pertinent is that her final resting place is the very same dry dock where she was built. It's lucky indeed that she is still with us (Brunel's other two ships, the SS *Great Western* and *Great Eastern*, were both scrapped in the 19th century) and even luckier that she has made her way back to her home port.

Two ships invite comparison: first, the *Matthew*, a replica of the Tudor sailing ship that took John Cabot to America in the 15th century. When not out on sailing trips, she now tends to sit moored up adjacent to the *Great Britain*, and appears ludicrously small in comparison. Second, there's HMS *Warrior* (page 342) in Portsmouth, another very fortuitous survival of a pivotal early iron ship. Longer, leaner and a little bit later than the *Great Britain*, she took iron-hulled technology a step further, into the military sphere. Taken together, these craft are twin pillars of the industrial age at sea, and both are well worth a visit.

SS *Great Britain*

Great Western Dock, Gas Ferry Road, Bristol BS1 6TY

01179 260680

www.ssgreatbritain.org

Saltaire, West Yorkshire

*Nominated by John Styles, research professor in history,
University of Hertfordshire*

'Where you can see how Britain began to reach a
settlement after the Industrial Revolution'

There's something about Saltaire that makes it feel solid, amenable and welcoming. That could be because it is solid, amenable and welcoming, or it could be that's what you assume you'll find if you know a little about the history of the place. It's hard not to impose positive expectations if you've read the inscription ledger for Saltaire on the World Heritage List: 'Its textile mills, public buildings and workers' housing are built in a harmonious style of high architectural standards and the urban plan survives intact, giving a vivid impression of Victorian philanthropic paternalism.'

Just to the north of Bradford, Saltaire presents a clear counterpoint to its big industrial neighbour. It comes across as somewhat lost in time, with its uniform array of well-maintained terraced houses that appear to have been little altered since they were built some 150 years ago. This isn't a heritage theme park: people have continued to live here in the spacious, village-like environment ever since it was founded in the 1850s.

The paternal philanthropist behind Saltaire was Titus Salt, who gave not only his energy, vision and money, but also his surname to this community along the banks of the river Aire. Salt made a fortune out of the alpaca wool market, which he cornered in the 1840s. By 1850 he owned five mills in Bradford, but in that year he decided to transfer his business away from the city to a new mill and to build a model village along with it. Thus was born Saltaire.

According to John Styles, 'Aside from the fact that it's the best-known model industrial community in Britain and in many ways also the most architecturally uniform, integrated and strikingly beautiful, Saltaire matters because it sums up one of the key responses to the economic and social effects of the Industrial Revolution.'

By the time of Titus Salt, the Industrial Revolution had been in full swing for some time, with the northern English mills and factories producing cloth using powered machinery. In the rush to industrialise, social, cultural and political considerations had been broadly overlooked, which had led to a rash of new towns, quickly and badly built, offering poor living and working conditions for the flood of émigrés from the countryside. This provided the backdrop for early 19th-century radical politics, with activists, such as the Chartists, agitating for political and social reform. Bradford, Titus Salt's original business base, was noted as a centre for both squalor and radicalism.

Saltaire, in the view of Styles, represents one very important response to all that. 'Salt was one of a number of industrialists who felt a moral responsibility to their workers, and it's their response to the problems facing them that set the tone for the late Victorian settlement and stabilisation of the conditions that grew up in the Industrial Revolution. We think of Peterloo and Chartism and wonder why it all settled down. Well, I think one of the reasons is that these mill owners saw there was a problem and started to create a set of communities around their mills. As industrial culture in the cities began to stabilise, the pace of technological transformation slowed down, and you began to get more settled communities – the late 19th- and early 20th-century mill towns with the factory and community living round it. It was no socialist utopia, but it was a much more stable world.'

Saltaire is a particularly well-executed and sophisticated example of that kind of factory paternalism. It's a community created entirely by one self-made father figure. In fact, you can see just how much of a father figure Titus Salt was by the names of his numerous children that survive on the street signs today (his wife Caroline bore him 11 offspring). Walk along Amelia Street and Fanny Street and you get a little insight into the man. Stop in front of the solid Victoria Hall, with its proud lions on plinths in front, and you get another: this was the site of Saltaire's 1869 Institute, designed in compensation for the lack of public houses in the village, to educate and entertain Salt's workers. It had a library, reading rooms and a lecture theatre, plus dance hall, billiards room and gymnasium. Now, oddly, it houses a Reed Organ and Harmonium Museum.

Opposite, with its own pair of lions staring back across the road, is the old school, and around the corner is the site of the former public washhouse, which in 1863 came complete with a Turkish bath. At the top of the village there were almshouses and a hospital, but if you head down over the railway, towards the Leeds and Liverpool Canal and the river beyond, you get to the economic centre of the village, where the money came from to pay for the altruistic endeavours just described. On one side of the road you have the old allotments, where Salt's workers could grow their food; the company dining room, where they could take it to be cooked; and the Congregational church, where they could receive their spiritual sustenance.

On the other side of the road is the huge mill building, where they worked. This is Titus Salt's integrated factory, built in 1853. It was, when it opened, the largest mill of its kind in the world, and designed to combine in one place all the various manufacturing operations required to turn alpaca wool into cloth. At its zenith, it housed 1200 looms powered by four beam engines, with heat and light supplied by the neighbouring gasworks. It's still a fine, large and imposing building on the outside, but its factory days are far behind it. A small historical exhibition on the second floor gives you a taste of what went on inside before it was converted into the café and artistic hub that it's now become, happily open and free to all-comers to enjoy. It was given its new incarnation by a visionary called Jonathan Silver, who bought it and redeveloped it in the 1980s. Within this contemporary, airy, artistic space, it's hard to get much sense of Victorian factory life, though that is no criticism of this excellent rejuvenation of an historic building, enlivened as it is by an archaic lift system and the gallery devoted to works by local-born artist David Hockney.

It seems a reasonable legacy for Titus Salt, who gave his workers what they asked for. 'It's what the Chartists said the capitalists could never give them, but he did,' concludes Styles. 'Good housing, settled community, continuity of work and a sense that he owed responsibility to them.'

Saltaire thus represents a well-built and lasting memorial to the way that Britain began to reach an accommodation after the immense changes wrought by the Industrial Revolution.

Saltaire

Near Shipley, Bradford, West Yorkshire BD18 3LA

01274 531163

www.saltairevillage.info

HMS *Warrior*, Portsmouth
Nominated by Andrew Lambert, professor of history, King's College London
'Where you can experience 19th-century Britain's overwhelming naval strength'

When you're thinking about British history, it's as well to remember the impact that geography has on the national story. Andrew Lambert phrases it nicely: 'Britain is a maritime rather than a continental state, and therefore its icons of power are not fortresses or borders but warships and the dockyards that go with them.'

There's one dockyard in Britain that holds three such icons of power. Now a major heritage attraction, it goes under the umbrella title of Portsmouth Historic Dockyard. It famously holds Henry VIII's *Mary Rose* and Nelson's *Victory*, but the third member of the triumvirate, HMS *Warrior*, goes somewhat overlooked, even though she's hard to miss, sitting as she does just inside the entrance to the dockyard.

'*Victory* tells us how Britain got to be the masters of the ocean,' says Lambert. '*Warrior* shows us how, in the middle of the 19th century, the rising power of industrial technology was harnessed to maintain that status without the need to engage in conflict. Queen Victoria's little wars were fought, therefore, against the backdrop of Britain being at peace with the great powers between 1856 and 1914. The reason for that was overwhelming naval power, and the most potent emblem of that is this transformational ship, the first iron-hulled, armour-clad ship armed with breech-loading rifle artillery.'

Warrior – long, fast and powered by sail or by its 26-tonne propeller (which took 400 men to raise out of the water) – was launched in 1860. Steam power had been introduced to Royal Navy ships in 1821, and over the next couple of decades, by using paddle-wheel and then propeller, it had become an important propulsion technology, to the ire of some of the more traditional proponents of the sailing ship. With new technology came a brief arms race, with Britain and France tussling to fill their fleets with as many wooden-hulled, steam-powered battleships as they could manage. By the late 1850s, Britain had gained the upper hand, but the French then changed the rules by building a wooden-hulled, steam-powered, armour-plated battleship called *La Gloire*, which launched in 1859. The arms race was concluded when Britain quickly trumped this with the iron-hulled *Warrior*, which was, as Lambert notes, '...a massive technological solution to the problem of arms racing. The French simply gave up. It killed the competition stone dead. The British built half a dozen more like *Warrior*, and the French could do nothing about it.'

Interestingly, *Warrior* never actually saw much action. If it had been involved in battle, the navy would have hoped that its central armoured box design would have kept out the enemy's attacks, while its own fearsome range of cannon would have penetrated its opponent's defences. As it was, the most dangerous thing she ever did was to run into another Royal Navy battleship. Her great achievement was demonstrate Britain's position of overwhelming naval strength and thereby keep the peace. 'There was nobody out there who'd have dreamt of taking on Britain after they started producing ships like *Warrior*.'

You can see why when you pay a visit. She's a big ship and it will take you a while to walk around her and to climb up and down through her decks. What you get immediately when you step off the gangplank is a sense that she sits between two times: your line of sight is confused by steamship funnels, which are surrounded by huge, rope-ridden masts for sails.

Go below deck and the sense of transition is even more apparent. The gun deck, with its low ceilings and styling, feels and looks like that on the earlier, much smaller HMS *Victory* (which, of course, is also worth a visit), yet it's home to a long line of much more modern-looking cannon. If you're not quite sure which period you're standing in, descend to the boiler- and engine-rooms and you'll be in no doubt, as you walk along the row of ten iron boilers and into the huge engine room, that this is a 19th-century ship.

Warrior's transitional nature is underlined by the fact that she became obsolete within a decade. In 1883 she was withdrawn from sea service. After a few more decades of various naval roles, she then had a long and somewhat undignified life as a floating oil jetty in Pembroke Docks. This did at least mean that she survived broadly intact, unlike every other ironclad of her time.

Although Portsmouth has a long history as a naval dockyard, *Warrior* wasn't actually built here, but rather at the Thames Ironworks in London.

Nevertheless, she does fit in well with the rest of the naval heritage attractions at the Historic Dockyard, which, along with the other historic ships, also has several museum displays. The *Mary Rose*, for all her venerable age and exciting rediscovery story, and the *Victory*, for her central role in one of Britain's greatest maritime triumphs, both demand attention when you're visiting of course. But what you don't want to do is head straight past *Warrior* without a second glance because her story is just as interesting and important.

HMS *Warrior*

Portsmouth Historic Dockyard, Victory Gate, HM Naval Base, Main Road,

Portsmouth, Hampshire PO1 3QX

023 9277 8604

www.hmswarrior.org

Verdant Works, Dundee

Nominated by Maxine Berg, professor of history,
University of Warwick
'Where you can see the global nature of Victorian
industry in one place'

If you're visiting somewhere called Verdant Works, you might expect to find a bit of greenery around the place. When a mill was built here, back in 1833, it was indeed surrounded by fields, with a watercourse – the Scouring Burn – burbling past it. Now that stream is nowhere to be seen, but it's still there, hidden beneath the stone and cobbles that now encase this part of Dundee. The works' surroundings are not so verdant any more either, but the area it sits in, Blackness, is now a conservation zone, its narrow streets and close-packed industrial architecture giving it a different charm that has only recently come to be appreciated.

Blackness was at the heart of the jute industry, which made Dundee an international name during the 19th century. By 1900, there were over 100 jute-processing mills across the city, and over 50,000 people employed in them. Little wonder that Dundee's nickname was Juteopolis. Verdant Works was just one of those mills, but it's the only one that's now open as a heritage attraction, so in that sense it speaks for the rest of the industry.

As Maxine Berg observes, 'This is an area of Dundee that was crowded with mills during its heyday. Among its narrow streets and old stone buildings there are still a number of the old mills left, and it doesn't take much to imagine the great noise and clatter of the machines. People went deaf working in these mills. In fact, the Dundee working-class accent is said to derive from trying to speak over the noise of them.'

How did Dundee come to be so defined by jute? In the 1830s the city had a thriving linen industry, with the raw material being flax imported from the Baltic and Russia. When that began to become uneconomical, people looked for alternatives, and jute, derived from plants native to Bengal, was the answer. Dundee was particularly well placed for the jute-processing business because whale oil was required to soften the threads of the plant, and Dundee already had a whaling fleet. Also, the city was a major ship-builder, and thus readily able to supply the fast craft needed to bring the jute bales from India to Scotland.

The Crimean War in the 1850s proved a huge stimulus for the industry because jute was an ideal material for making tents, sails, sacks, horse-bags, rope and other items needed by the British troops encamped near the Black Sea. For 50 years or so after that, Dundee was the master of the industry, but its dominance was challenged in the 20th century by competition from Calcutta, where labour was cheaper and the raw material closer to hand. The death of Dundee's jute industry was a slow one, and it took until 1999 for the last mill to close.

What's perhaps particularly interesting about Dundee's jute industry is its global nature. Berg explains: 'There is a fascinating story about the cultivation of jute in India, and the way it was transported to a place that was all about shipping, whaling and linen. This industry was created in Dundee not just because of the skills it had acquired from the linen industry, but because of the connections it had formed with outposts of the empire. Scotland played a key part in the industrial story of Britain: it was very important from the late 18th century onwards.'

Just as the production process was international, so was the market for Dundee's jute. Gold-rush Australia and America, for instance, needed jute canvas for prospectors' tents. If you want to understand the global flavour of the Victorian imperial economy and Scotland's important contribution to it, Dundee's jute industry encompasses both. Verdant Works is the best surviving monument to that industry, and there you can see the original mill buildings preserved within the context of their Victorian streetscape. The place is now a museum devoted to the jute story, so you can walk around the former machine-rooms and be much informed about the business of making and selling jute in the 19th century.

The rise and fall of Dundee's jute mills in some ways mirrors the broader British experience, of Victorian heyday followed by 20th-century decline. In one respect, however, the industry is atypical, as it was women, rather than men, who did most of the work. According to Berg, 'This particular industry relied primarily on the work of women and children, and the museum vividly depicts the "mill lasses" as very raucous and totally self-confident; they were noisy and overdressed. Although they were not well-paid, they went out and earned their living and also ran their families. Dundee was very much a women's town.'

It was a female-led industry for the simple fact that women's labour was cheaper than men's. This led to an unusual dynamic within Dundee, where the husbands stayed at home to look after the children while the women assumed traditionally masculine roles and behaviour. In the museum buildings at Verdant Works, several original pieces of jute-processing machinery are preserved, along with photographs of the mill lasses operating them and their own oral testimonies about life in the factories and outside them. It's fascinating, but what's lacking, according to Berg, is one other audio element to the story. 'The noise is missing. It would be great if you could walk into one of these rooms and experience the din of the machinery.'

Modern health and safety regulations render that a rather unlikely scenario, so you'll have to imagine the cacophony. That aside, Verdant Works offers a first-rate insight to the Scottish contribution to Britain's imperial project, the global business of Victorian industry and enterprise, and the particular impact it had on individual people – three good reasons to pay a visit to Dundee.

Verdant Works

West Henderson's Wynd, Dundee, Angus DD1 5BT

01382 225282

www.rrsdiscovery.com

Porthcurno Telegraph Station, Cornwall

Nominated by Richard Noakes, lecturer in history, University of Exeter

'Where the cables came ashore to keep Britain in touch with its empire'

Porthcurno has a great little beach. Its gently sloping sand funnels out from a luxuriantly green Cornish valley without the sharp incline from cliff to sea that is a feature of much of the coastline around this far west tip of the country. It is only a short distance from Land's End, so it's always been a bit out of the way.

These are the factors that entice holidaymakers today, but they're also the elements that attracted the attention of the Scottish cotton magnate John Pender in the 1860s. He had seen the potential of the new technology of telegraphy, which, simply put, used electricity to send words over wires. Since 1839, telegraph lines had been strung alongside railway tracks, allowing for radically improved communication over land. And in the 1850s, after several attempts, engineers worked out a reliable way of laying these wires under the sea by insulating them with a rubbery substance called gutta-percha and wrapping them with armoured wire. In the mid 1860s such cabling had been laid across the Atlantic by Brunel's massive metal ship the SS *Great Eastern*, thereby linking Britain with the USA. The undersea opportunities were what piqued Pender's interest, particularly in terms of the communication needs of the widely dispersed British Empire. He had a plan to link Britain to India by telegraph, and he needed a suitable location for the landfall of his underwater cable. Richard Noakes explains why he plumped for Porthcurno.

'The cables needed to start as far west as possible in England, then to go around France, into the Mediterranean and on to India. The cable station was originally going to be at Falmouth because it had the infra-structure – a railway line with inland cables already strung along it. But in the 1860s Falmouth was still a busy port, and there was a risk that boats would catch the undersea cable with their anchors, so Pender picked the quiet and desolate cove at Porthcurno, where there was nothing more than a few farmyards.'

The cable was laid in 1870. It worked, and became the start of big things for Porthcurno. From a place with frankly very little going on at all, it became a vital cog in the 'Victorian Internet', the largest cable station in the world. It was operated under the auspices of the Eastern Telegraph Company for half a century, and a further dozen or so cables were trained into the little valley from all around the globe. The cable station survives today as the centre of the Porthcurno Telegraph Museum, and its substan-tial flat, white presence dominates the rest of the little settlement.

According to Noakes, 'This building symbolises Britain's dominance of the submarine telegraph network. There was a very complicated rela-tionship between imperialism and technology from the 1850s onwards, and you see that in Porthcurno. The British need to keep its empire together created a demand for long-distance submarine cables, but the cables created new political and economic possibilities for imperial expansionism. They changed politics because they made it easier for communication, but that connection was driven by the need of British governments to talk to foreign businesses and governments.'

So Porthcurno was a key site in the running of Britain's empire, which is quite a claim for such an isolated hamlet. Stroll down to the beach from the cable station (it's not far) and not only can you enjoy the very pleasant sandy bay, but you can dwell on the fact that under the sand ran the cables that enabled Britain's army of imperial administrators to communicate with one another. The small cable hut at the head of the beach, into which the cables were all fed, brings home the global significance rather nicely.

From the early years of the 20th century, cable telegraphy was threatened by a new technology, wireless telegraphy, whose most famous proponent was Guglielmo Marconi. He carried out some of his early experiments in wireless transmission at nearby Poldhu on the Lizard Peninsula, and by the 1920s he had developed a thriving radio communications network. This was such a threat to cable telegraphy that the Eastern Telegraph Company was merged with Marconi's business, becoming Cable & Wireless in 1934.

Despite the success of wireless technology, cables were far from redundant in the 1930s and 1940s, a fact not lost on the Germans during the Second World War, says Noakes: 'Porthcurno became a major target for the Luftwaffe because it was still a major cable station, so Cable & Wireless decided to shift the operations underground.'

The company built two tunnels into the valley wall behind the cable station, and this secret wartime facility is now the major attraction at the museum. Once you're through the thick metal doors, you're into a world of strange and archaic electrical apparatus, with all manner of curious telegraphic devices on display. The great thing is that quite a few of them still work, as demonstrated in a splendid and very informative short talk that's held in the tunnels a few times every day. If you don't understand how telegraphy works when you go in, you will when you come out.

There's also a good bit of social history on display here. Aside from Porthcurno being a working telegraph station (until 1970), it was also a training school for telegraph engineers (until 1993), which turned out thousands of young men to operate the global telegraph empire. Here they were removed from worldly distractions and could focus on learning their trade. The effect of dropping these young men into an isolated Cornish community is also explored in the museum.

The place is not quite so isolated now. The large car park for the museum and beach is testament to that, but it's still a lovely place to explore. If you take a walk around, you'll find the remains of the antenna that was set up in 1902 to spy on Marconi's trials at Poldhu, the white stone pyramid that marks the point where the cable from Brest in France was brought ashore in 1880, and the pillboxes on the beach to keep the enemy at bay in the Second World War. And, on a different tack entirely, just around the corner is the open-air Minack Theatre, with its dramatic ocean backdrop – as good a place as any to contemplate the power of communication.

Porthcurno Telegraph Station
Porthcurno Telegraph Museum, Eastern House, Porthcurno, Penzance,
Cornwall TR19 6JX
01736 810966
www.porthcurno.org.uk

People's Palace, Glasgow

Nominated by Jacqueline Jenkinson, lecturer in history,
University of Stirling
'Where you can see a city celebrating its role in
Britain's global prominence'

If you're going to be the only building in the middle of a great big open space, you'll need to exude a certain confidence. Glasgow's People's Palace, plumb in the middle of Glasgow Green, does indeed have a certain swagger to it. Its red sandstone façade makes for a very imposing sight, particularly as it's offset by the equally impressive terracotta marvel that is the Doulton Fountain outside the front door.

Around the back of the People's Palace is a huge glass conservatory housing the Winter Gardens, and inside the main building today is a museum dedicated to the social history of Glasgow from 1750 onwards. That's a very appropriate use for the palace because its original purpose, when it was opened at the end of the 19th century, was to be a place where people could go for recreation and self-improvement.

It doesn't take more than a quick glance to get the message that the People's Palace was built at a time when Glasgow had a lot to celebrate and be proud of. In the 1890s, it could make a claim with some justification to be the 'Second City of Empire', with a thriving range of heavy industries, and particular dominance in the shipbuilding business. Glasgow was replete with parks and gardens, and boasted other civic modernities, such as a telephone network and gas and electricity supplies. At a time when Britain's empire was at its height, Glasgow was one of its key cities.

Jacqueline Jenkinson explains: 'The period of Glaswegian power was from the 1860s to 1914, when Britain was exporting its industrial, technical and financial products. Glasgow was very prosperous then, and the People's Palace sits squarely in the middle of it. The city was making money from shipbuilding, iron and steel, and coal mining.'

To look at the grand façade of the People's Palace is to get an idea of the importance of Glasgow – and Scotland – to the British imperial project. This city was at the heart of the extraordinary period of global dominance that ran roughly in tandem with the long reign of Queen Victoria, and the architecture of the place sums up the confidence that stemmed from that. It's appropriate, then, that atop the Doulton Fountain just outside it is a statue of Queen Victoria herself, with something of a regal glare on her face. On the tiers below her are sculptures representing imperial achievements around the world; Australia, Canada, India and South Africa are all depicted. It's a paean to imperial greatness.

There is a bit of historical licence in play here, though, as the fountain has not always neighboured the People's Palace. Originally it stood in Kelvingrove Park, another of Glasgow's green spaces. It was unveiled at the Empire Exhibition held there in 1888. That exhibition was so successful that the city ran a second one, in 1901. The People's Palace was opened in 1898, between these two major festivals of empire, so again it's bang in the middle of Glasgow's imperial power play, when the city was in celebratory mood.

Inside the building, on the second floor of the museum, is an artefact revealing an earlier period in Glasgow's history, when the city began to become a really serious global operator. It's a portrait of the Glassford family, painted in the 1760s. The large canvas shows a very respectable

Georgian gentleman, with wig and suit as fashion dictated, surrounded by his doting family. What you wouldn't immediately spot is that at Mr Glassford's shoulder is a black slave. He's very faint, his identity is unknown, and his presence was only recognised at all after a recent conservation project on the picture. Glassford was one of Glasgow's tobacco lords, who in the 18th century had cornered the tobacco trade, importing from America and exporting to Europe, and making himself a millionaire in the process. When the American Revolution disrupted supply, he turned to Caribbean sugar. Both these lines of trade relied on African slave labour – hence the significance of that black figure in the Glassford portrait.

As with many aspects of Britain's history, the slave trade does linger in the background, and as Jenkinson points out, 'In the city centre there are a number of key streets that are named after the tobacco lords. For example, Glassford had a street named after him, and nearby are Virginia Street and Jamaica Street, which take their name from places that supplied the vital products.'

You can go further back into Glasgow's history by taking a stroll around the Green surrounding the People's Palace. It's long been a public space devoted to Glaswegian gatherings of various kinds. Animal grazing, clothes washing, sport playing, political meetings and public executions have all been carried out here down the centuries. The exhibitions inside the palace offer interesting commentary on much of the social history involved, and, indeed, tackle the tobacco lords and the broader Atlantic trade, plus the heyday of heavy industry and shipbuilding that followed.

One final building that you will struggle to miss if you visit the People's Palace is the rather exotic edifice that overlooks it from a distance at the edge of the park. It resembles, and was in fact designed to mimic, the Doge's Palace in Venice. With its polychromatic bricks and ornate Mediterranean windows, it's something of a surprise to find such a thing on the edge of a park in Glasgow, and perhaps more surprising still to note that it was originally built as a carpet factory. It was constructed by one of Glasgow's Victorian grandees, James Templeton, towards the end of the 19th century, and the carpets produced here were another of the city's global exports. It apparently owes its unusual appearance to the fact that Templeton was having trouble getting plans for a more conventional factory past the city's planning authorities. As a dark footnote however, the partially built factory collapsed in 1889, killing 29 women and girls. Glasgow's, and indeed Britain's, drive to global imperial dominance was not without its casualties.

People's Palace
Glasgow Green, Glasgow G40 1AT
0141 276 0788
www.glasgowlife.org.uk/museums

Pankhurst Centre, Manchester
Nominated by June Purvis, professor of women's and gender history, University of Portsmouth
'Where the suffragette movement was born'

Aside from the television in the corner, the parlour in the Pankhurst house feels like a room from the 1900s. That's very much the idea because, as June Purvis notes, 'It was here, in the parlour, that the most important women's group campaigning for the parliamentary vote in Britain was founded. On 10 October 1903 Mrs Emmeline Pankhurst and some local socialist women, such as Mrs Scott, Mrs Harper and Mrs Hall, founded the Women's Social and Political Union (WSPU). It was the beginning of the suffragette movement.' (Incidentally, the television in the room is not an oversight; it's there to show an archive film of the suffragettes in action.)

The house at 62 Nelson Street was where Emmeline Pankhurst lived with her children in the early years of the 20th century. There's a plaque by the front door that records this fact because the Pankhurst name has since become synonymous with the cause of women's suffrage. The property was saved from the threat of demolition in the 1980s to become, with its neighbour, number 60, the Pankhurst Centre. The pair of Georgian brick houses now stand somewhat isolated among the modern buildings of the Manchester Royal Infirmary. Part of the downstairs has been set up as a museum, with the parlour as the star attraction, while the rest of it is now a women's centre.

When the Pankhursts lived here, Britain was a divided society, particularly with regard to the right to vote. Traditionally, the franchise had been the preserve of the landed, propertied elite, but during the 19th century, campaigners challenged the status quo and gradually brought about a more equal voting system through a series of Reform Acts in 1832, 1867 and 1884. However, nearly 40 per cent of men were still disenfranchised because of property qualifications in the 1884 Act, and all women were excluded from voting as the 20th century dawned.

Inequitable voting rights were a subject that exercised the minds of middle-class reformers such as Mrs Pankhurst and her husband Richard, a radical Manchester lawyer. The couple married in 1879 and lived in

Buckingham Crescent. As prominent socialist activists, they quickly became fully engaged in the politics of reform. When her husband died unexpectedly in 1898, Mrs Pankhurst was left with financial difficulties, so moved with her family to a smaller house in Nelson Street. Obliged to take a job, she became a registrar of births and deaths, and through this occupation came into contact with the hard lives of the working-class women of Manchester. This cemented her opinion that women were unfairly treated, but it was an incident relating to her husband's memorial that pushed her into taking a stand.

'Mrs Pankhurst had been active in campaigning for women's suffrage for a number of years,' says Purvis. 'She and her husband had been soul-mates, involved politically as well as emotionally. Both were active in the Independent Labour Party (ILP), and after Richard's death, an ILP hall was named in his memory. When she later heard that women were not allowed to become members of that particular branch of the ILP, she was so enraged that she said, "Women, we must do the work ourselves. We must have an independent women's movement. Come to my house tomorrow and we will arrange it."'

The WSPU was not the first organisation dedicated to the cause of women's suffrage. There had been campaigns for better rights since the 1860s, and in 1897 the National Union of Women's Suffrage Societies (NUWSS) brought together various local suffragist groups under one banner. The NUWSS worked through conventional political channels and convinced most MPs of the principle of women's suffrage, but failed to achieve any actual change in the law. Seeing that the talking was going nowhere, Mrs Pankhurst's WSPU took as their motto 'Deeds, not Words', but it was to be a couple of years before the actions of WSPU campaigners attracted much attention. It was, in fact, Mrs Pankhurst's daughter Christabel and the mill worker Annie Kenney who sparked things off.

'It wasn't until 1905, when Christabel Pankhurst and Annie Kenney protested in favour of votes for women at a Liberal Party meeting in the Manchester Free Trade Hall, that the movement took off,' says Purvis. 'They planned to create a disturbance whereby they would be arrested, but they were merely roughly ejected. Outside, Christabel spat at a policeman, technically an offence, so the two women were sent to prison – Christabel for seven days and Annie for five. Their actions hit the newspaper headlines, and from that moment on, more and more women began to join the WSPU.'

You can see a plaque commemorating this event inside the lobby of the hotel that now stands on the site of the Free Trade Hall (page 284). Following their media coup, the suffragettes adopted the militant approach for which they became famous. From heckling politicians, WSPU activists moved on to a campaign of window smashing, arson and violence that shocked and enraged sensibilities in Edwardian Britain, and certainly garnered the cause considerable publicity. As militancy increased, WSPU supporters took on the term 'suffragette' to distinguish themselves from the more moderate 'suffragists', some of whom disapproved of direct action.

The pressure on government to respond to their demands was increased in 1909 when imprisoned suffragettes started going on hunger strike, and culminated in 1913 when Emily Wilding Davison ran in front of the king's horse at the Epsom Derby, suffering mortal injuries and dying a few days later.

With the advent of the First World War in 1914, the suffragettes called a halt to their campaign. At the end of the conflict, in 1918, limited female suffrage was granted by parliament. Ten years later, the vote was extended to all women over the age of 21. The significant and valuable contribution of Britain's women to the war effort has been seen as one reason for the eventual success of the suffrage campaign, but undoubtedly the suffragettes did much to make it an issue of national interest in the run-up to the war. As Purvis reminds us, 'It all started in the house on Nelson Street – an important symbol of how, from very humble beginnings in a parlour, a major movement was founded that mobilised thousands of women to campaign for their democratic rights.'

Pankhurst Centre

60–62 Nelson Street, Chorlton on Medlock, Manchester M13 9WP

0161 273 5673

www.thepankhurstcentre.org.uk

Titanic's Dock and Pump-house, Queen's Island, Belfast

Nominated by Cormac Ó Gráda, professor of economic history, University College Dublin

'Where you can see the footprint of *Titanic*, and Belfast's shipbuilding heritage'

A very big hole in the ground might not seem that much of a draw, but it becomes more enticing when you know what once sat in it. The Thompson Graving Dock on Queen's Island in Belfast is where one of the most famous ships in history, the *Titanic*, was fitted out.

When the *Titanic* was built, from 1909 to 1912, Belfast led the world in shipbuilding. A staggering 176 ships were launched from here in the first decade of the 20th century. Through the preceding century, the city had been developing at a rapid pace, with shipbuilding emerging as the leading industry. A considerable amount of money was invested to overcome some natural obstacles to ship construction, most notably the straightening of the river Lagan in the 1840s. Dargan's Island (named after Irish-born engineer William Dargan, who oversaw its creation) was formed from the mud dredged up in this straightening operation. It was renamed Queen's Island in 1849, and a few years later it became the base of the newly formed Harland & Wolff business. Along with the rival firm of Workman Clark, it came to dominate the Belfast shipbuilding scene in the second half of the 19th century.

'The interesting thing about the site is that it was an unpromising place to begin with, and Belfast was an unlikely location for a world-beating shipbuilding industry,' notes Cormac Ó Gráda. 'The place is a testament to the forward-looking policies of the powers-that-were in mid 19th-century Belfast. They had two companies operating there for about half a century, and both of them would have been among the top ten shipbuilders in the world. Harland & Wolff was very near the top.'

It was no surprise, then, that when the head of the White Star Line, Bruce Ismay, decided he wanted new craft to compete with the *Mauretania* and the *Lusitania*, steamships recently launched by his rival Cunard to ply the North Atlantic route between Britain and America, he turned to Belfast and Harland & Wolff. The ships he asked to have built were to be the largest ever to grace the oceans.

By 1909, work had begun on two of the three ships, the *Olympic* and the *Titanic* (the *Britannic* came later), but considerable upgrades to the facilities on Queen's Island were required to accommodate the construction of these enormous new vessels. Three existing slipways were merged into two, and a huge steel gantry erected over them so that the ships could be built side by side. Nearby were the barrel-ceilinged drawing offices of the Harland & Wolff headquarters where the construction plans were drawn up. The building process involved putting the hull frames together on the slipway, then steel-plating them, still on dry land. When the superstructure was completed, the ships were launched into the river and towed to the deep-water fitting-out wharf, then returned to dry dock for final work before sea trials.

That's where the big hole in the ground comes in. The Thompson Graving Dock was built in 1904, a little downstream of the drawing office and slipways, to accommodate the huge new ships. It's a very big space – 259 metres (415 feet) long, 13 metres (21 feet) deep and 29 metres (46 feet) wide. Today it's within the confines of the Northern Ireland Science Park. You can walk around it, look down into its great, brick-lined stepped maw, and consider that when the *Titanic* had been towed in, the gates at the end shut, and the water pumped out, the ship would still have been towering way above your head. You can see the great keel blocks that the ship would have rested on, the capstan that wound in the cable to bring it to dock, and the grilles way down at the base through which the water would drain as it was pumped away. Astonishingly, the dock could be pumped dry of its 26 million gallons of water in just an hour and a half – a rate of two swimming pools per minute.

The machinery that facilitated such a powerful operation is to be found in the pump-house alongside the dock. This building is a fine example of late Victorian architecture: red bricks with a cream façade, great arched windows and a handsome clock tower. Part of the pump-house today is a café, with some display material about the history of the dock, and part of it retains the pumping machinery. An organised tour will take you into the machinery room, a worthwhile experience. The blue engines sit at the bottom of another deep hole, this time lined with white tiles that, appropriately enough given the speed of pumping, make it look like a glorified old swimming pool.

The dry dock here has been branded as the 'physical footprint of the *Titanic*', which is a reasonable enough bit of marketing. It was on those keel blocks that the ship last rested on dry ground before she embarked on her fateful maiden voyage in April 1912. As is well known, she did not reach her destination of New York; instead, she struck an iceberg and sank, resulting in the loss of over 1500 lives.

The sinking of the *Titanic* is a story of enduring fascination and one that attracts a considerable number of visitors to this part of Belfast. The area suffered with the decline in shipbuilding from the 1970s onwards, and Belfast's last ship, a roll-on roll-off merchantman, convertible to naval use in time of need, was launched in 2003. But work is under way to re-develop the area as the Titanic Quarter, and the Titanic Signature Building is being built at the head of the *Titanic/Olympic* slipways, near the Harland & Wolff HQ. The plan is to have a *Titanic* museum on site by 2012, the centenary of the sinking. Currently, you can visit the drawing offices and slipways as part of an organised tour, construction on the new buildings permitting.

Of course, Belfast's shipbuilding heritage is not about just one ship, even though the *Titanic* does tend to overshadow everything else. Not far from the Thompson Dock and pump-house you can still see the great yellow Harland & Wolff cranes called Goliath and Samson standing tall above Queen's Island. They were erected in 1969 and 1974 respectively, when the shipbuilding industry was still strong here. Since then, the industry has suffered a serious decline in Belfast, but the cranes are a reminder of the time when tens of thousands of people were working here building ships that crossed the world.

As Cormac Ó Gráda concludes, 'The location has a double resonance. It is inseparable from Belfast's brilliant past as a leading city of the British Industrial Revolution, and the central role of shipbuilding in that past. But it also recalls the tragic story of the *Titanic*, sometimes retold as a parable for thwarted ambition, sometimes as a metaphor for Ulster's troubled history.'

Titanic's Dock and Pump-house
Queens Road, Belfast BT3 9DT
02890 737813
www.titanicsdock.com

The Cenotaph, London
Nominated by Mark Connelly, professor of modern British military history, University of Kent
'Where you are transported back to a weary Britain after the First World War'

The obvious thing to do at the Cenotaph is to stand and think about the war dead that it commemorates, though admittedly, on a normal London day, the traffic rushing past on either side of the monument doesn't really make for a reflective environment. Perhaps it would be worth trying to make your visit outside the busiest working times because, for Mark Connelly, reflection is required. 'Warfare has been the crucial defining element for Britain and its empire in the 20th century. There have been only two years since 1945 that a serving member of the armed forces has not been killed.

'The Cenotaph is a key anchoring point of everything that the British people have stood for in the 20th century. While it was originally designed to be a temporary structure in wood and plaster for the 1919 peace cele-bration, there was such a sense of the need for something to grieve around after the bloodletting of the First World War that the monument was made permanent. It was unveiled in 1920 after massive public demand.'

To look at the Cenotaph, then, is to be taken back to the years imme-diately after the First World War, and a time when the nation was still reeling from the huge loss of life and the sight of scarred soldiers, lacking limbs or with disfigured faces, on the streets of London and throughout Britain. The reality of war would have been a first-hand experience for those who saw the Cenotaph being constructed, and many among them would have found their faith in state and religion sorely shaken by combat on the battlefield. The Cenotaph designer, Edward Lutyens, appears to have taken that into consideration. 'Lutyens made something so simple so that it means anyone can project their own ideas and feelings on to it. Deliberately, it has no overt religious symbolism. It just has the words 'The Glorious Dead' on it, and merely hints at a concept of eternal life. However, to make sure no offence was committed, the inscription on the tomb was checked with religious leaders throughout Britain's empire.

The Cenotaph: a memorial that put remembrance at the heart of governance

'The word "cenotaph" comes from the Greek for "empty tomb", and that's what it is – there's no one buried under it. The comforting idea for the people of the 1920s and 1930s was that the dead had already risen and gone on to somewhere better.'

The lack of religious overtones, though perhaps in tune with the attitudes of many veterans, was controversial at the time. The Church response was to provide a Tomb of the Unknown Warrior in Westminster Abbey, just a short walk away from the Cenotaph. You can go and look at that tomb in the nave of the abbey, and as you walk from one monument to the other, it's hard to miss the fact that you are in Westminster, the heartland of government; the Houses of Parliament are opposite the abbey, while the road on which the Cenotaph stands has various Cabinet offices along its length. This was deliberate, says Connelly: 'What these two monuments do is basically turn the key legislative part of the empire into one massive war memorial. On the unveiling day in November 1920, King George V pulled the cord on the Union Jack that shrouded the Cenotaph, then fell into line as chief mourner behind the gun carriage that was taking the unknown warrior to the tomb in Westminster Abbey.'

Well over a million people filed past the Cenotaph in the week following its unveiling, continuing into the abbey to pause at the Tomb of the Unknown Warrior. The Cenotaph has remained a focus for national remembrance of military sacrifice, and every successive conflict has added its own patina to the national day of remembrance that is now firmly set on the anniversary of the First World War's Armistice. Clearly, the Second World War gave a new generation further cause for remembrance on 11 November. Even though there are no more survivors from the First World War to file past the Cenotaph now, the place continues to resonate as somewhere that, says Connelly, 'forces us to think about what we're doing now as a nation, and the kind of values we're projecting through our armed forces'.

While you're reflecting on that, and perhaps letting your mind wander back to the end of the First World War, perhaps think too about Connelly's final observation: 'The Cenotaph allows people to play a complex architectural game with themselves because although it looks like a standard ascending oblong that's tapering, none of the points on it are perfectly straight – they are all parts of radials. Lutyens was a theosophist [one who professes knowledge of God by inspiration] and one of his big concepts was that things should be part of a circle representing the eternal cycle of birth, death and regeneration.' Frankly, it's pretty hard to see the circular trickery on the Cenotaph because the curvature was very slight to begin with and the edges of the monument have become worn over time, but if you can see spherical stirrings, then you've got Lutyens' message, which is that the Cenotaph is 'meant to be part of a circle that embraces us all'.

The Cenotaph
Whitehall, London SW1

Dover War Tunnels, Kent
Nominated by James Holland, writer and historian
'Where Britain's Second World War army was saved to fight another day'

You can't beat a good tunnel for historic atmosphere, and Dover boasts a lot of them. This isn't surprising. Its cliffs are famously white because they are composed of chalk, which is a nice soft medium in which to plunge one's pickaxe. That's part of the reason why, beneath the great medieval shell of Dover Castle, there is a multi-level tunnel network. The other reason is that this cliff looks out on the Straits of Dover, the shortest stretch of Channel separating Britain from the Continent, and was therefore of immense strategic value down the centuries.

When Napoleon loomed large across Europe (and, indeed, he looked out from Boulogne in 1805 with his Grande Armée massed to attack, but in the end he turned away), Britain needed men ready to repulse him. Dover was thought a likely target, so the medieval castle defences were remodelled and brought into the artillery age. But there wasn't space to house the men to man the guns. The solution was to go underground. Tunnels were dug into the cliffs, seven in all, parallel to one other below the cliff-top. By 1803 this ingenious underground barracks was opened, housing at its peak some 2000 officers and soldiers.

Ultimately, Napoleon never invaded, so that might have been an end for the tunnels. However, in 1938, when the threat of war with Nazi Germany hung heavy in the air, the tunnels were brought back into action as the headquarters for the newly constituted Dover Naval Command, charged with protecting the Channel from enemy action. It became a rather more important place much sooner than the British military top brass would have hoped, after Germany's lightning-quick advance in the Battle of France in May 1940 left the entire British Expeditionary Force surrounded and in imminent danger of annihilation, backed up against the wrong side of the Channel at Dunkirk.

Responsibility for getting the stranded army home was dropped on the shoulders of Vice Admiral Bertram Ramsay, head of Dover Naval Command, from his base within those old tunnels. As James Holland says, 'In 1940 it was a key place because it was where the Dunkirk evacuation – code-named Operation Dynamo – was organised.'

The speed of Hitler's success meant that Ramsay had precious little time to come up with answers to the terrifying logistical exercise that faced him. Yet over the course of just nine days, starting on 26 May 1940, he and his tunnel-based team orchestrated the evacuation of some 338,000 soldiers in as many Royal Navy vessels as he could muster, along with the now-famous flotilla of civilian 'little ships'. Churchill called it a 'miracle of deliverance', and given that initial estimates

Operations were planned in the safety of Dover's war tunnels

suggested that only 45,000 men were likely to be rescued, a miracle it must have seemed.

Before you take the tunnel tour, you'd find it instructive to poke your nose inside the Admiralty lookout buildings on the cliff-top and take in the view of the great harbour below. This is where Ramsay's lookouts had to monitor the tremendous volume of seaborne traffic during the evacuations. There were so many ships that they had to abandon the naval niceties of harbour management and just let the vessels enter as best they could.

Once you've looked out to sea, head down to the tunnels. You're obliged to take a guided tour for fear of taking a wrong turn (apparently there are, even now, tunnels that have not been fully explored by English Heritage). On your tour, you'll be taken into areas that have mocked-up re-creations (based on contemporary photographs) of the tunnels' various wartime uses – from hospital bays and catering corridors to communications nerve centres.

Slightly confusingly, there are more tunnels on show to present-day visitors than existed in the days of Dunkirk. As the Second World War progressed, two further levels of tunnels were added into the network, above and below those created in Napoleon's time. That original early level, known as Casemate, housed Admiral Ramsay's control staff in May 1940. A further level above, Annexe, was dug in 1941 to house hospital facilities; and in 1943 a basement level, codenamed Dumpy, was excavated. On your tour you'll walk through part of Annexe, then down into Casemate, but Dumpy is off-limits. (There is an instructive film and several good plans of the site to help you get your bearings.)

The tunnels are fascinating places to visit, particularly when you think of how pivotal a role they played in the army rescue from Dunkirk. It's worth mulling on the fact that in those hectic evacuation days, Ramsay's staff pulled 24- or 36-hour shifts, working in rather dim light under what must have been pressure of an intensity that's hard to imagine today. Had they not been able to sort out the logistics of Operation Dynamo so quickly and effectively (and had the German forces moved in for the kill with more rapidity when they had the British cornered), the outcome of the entire war might have been rather different.

If you're not pining for natural light after the tour, go and take a look at the medieval tunnels on the landward side of Dover Castle, dug in the aftermath of another foreign invasion, when Prince Louis of France besieged the castle in 1216. Admittedly, that foreigner was invited in by the rebellious barons in their battle with King John, so comparisons with Napoleon and Hitler are not strictly accurate, but it does drive home the fact that Dover was, throughout its military history, very much a frontier fortress. In 1940 that frontier must have felt very close to home indeed. Although the success of Operation Dynamo had at least rescued the bulk of British troops, it was far from clear if that was going to be enough to dissuade Hitler from carrying out his plans to invade.

Dover War Tunnels

Dover Castle, Harold's Road, Dover, Kent CT16 1HU

01304 211067

www.english-heritage.org.uk/daysout

Battle of Britain Memorial, Capel-le-Ferne, Kent

Nominated by Jeremy Crang, senior lecturer in history, University of Edinburgh

'Where you can consider the battle that boosted morale throughout Britain during World War II'

Ask a historian when the last pitched battle was contested on British soil and you'll tend to get the answer, 'Culloden in 1746'. That may be strictly accurate, but it was of course before the days of air power. During the Second World War, one battle was carried out, if not actually on British soil, then not too far above it.

As Jeremy Crang explains, 'The Battle of Britain was an air battle fought in the skies over the Channel and southern England between July and October 1940. The Germans needed to obtain air supremacy as a prerequisite for an invasion, and the gallant deeds of the RAF fighter crews in defeating the Luftwaffe during that epic summer played a vital role in deterring Hitler from invading Britain and keeping alive an armed anti-Axis presence in Europe.'

The memorial to those who served in the skies to protect Britain is very well located at Capel-le-Ferne, between Dover and Folkestone on a cliff overlooking the Channel. This was Hellfire Corner in 1940, scene of some of the fiercest fighting of that summer. It's interesting to dwell on the fact that the British public, particularly in this part of Kent, would have seen the battle played out above their own homes. Archive BBC news footage survives of a reporter commentating on a dogfight above Dover, while in the background, spectators oohed and aahed as if they were at a fireworks display. Of course, they would also have seen the casualties that came down on home soil.

The memorial at Capel-le-Ferne was the brainchild of one such casualty, Wing Commander Geoffrey Page, who had fought in the battle and been badly burnt. Inaugurated in 1993, it features a sculpture of a solitary pilot looking out to sea within an amphitheatre of raised earthen banks. When viewed from the air, the three paths that radiate from the central sculpture resemble a propeller. In 2005, the curving memorial wall, with the names of those who fought in the battle, was completed thanks to a generous donation from Air Chief Marshal Sir Christopher Foxley-Norris, chairman of the Battle of Britain Fighter Association. The wall features the names of nearly 3000 aircrew who flew at least one operational sortie between 10 July and 31 October 1940 with one of the 71 RAF fighter squadrons, units and flights that participated in the battle.

Crang once visited the memorial and reviewed the names on that wall in the company of a veteran of the battle, Wallace Cunningham, who flew a Spitfire with 19 Squadron and was awarded the Distinguished Flying Cross for 'great personal gallantry and splendid skill in action'. As Crang recalls: 'The list includes not only the pilots who hailed from the United Kingdom, but also those from Canada, New Zealand, Australia, South Africa, Poland, Czechoslovakia and elsewhere who fought with the RAF that summer. Casting one's eyes down the roll-call, one cannot help but wonder about the personal histories of these young flyers. But to visit Capel-le-Ferne *with* one of those so honoured, to see him gaze up at his name on the wall and to hear him recount anecdotes of some of his 19 squadron comrades listed alongside him – "Grumpy" Unwin, "Farmer" Lawson and "Admiral" Blake – was a very special experience.' As for 'Jock' Cunningham himself, he was shot down in August 1941 while escorting bombers across the Channel and crash-landed his Spitfire on Rotterdam beach. He spent the rest of the war in German POW camps, and while in Stalag Luft III, he jumped for many hours over a vaulting horse in order to assist in the renowned 'wooden horse escape' (the horse was cover for a tunnel that was being dug beneath it).

We can't all experience the memorial in such company, but it's a splendid site to sit in quiet contemplation of the contribution of the airmen to the survival of Britain. Winston Churchill, of course, paid his famous tribute to them while the battle was still raging, declaring in the House of Commons on 20 August that 'Never in the field of human conflict was so much owed by so many to so few'. 'Although the "few", with their typically laconic sense of humour,' notes Crang, 'were said to have interpreted this accolade as a reference to the size of their unpaid drinks bills in the mess, they have come to play a central role in the story of Britain's "finest hour".'

There are replicas of the two planes most closely associated with the battle, a Hurricane and a Spitfire, next to the little visitor centre by the memorial. All of this stands on the site of a Second World War gun battery, and there is still a network of tunnels nearby that was used as a hospital and lookout point (though these are in private hands). The Battle of Britain, of course, followed hard on the heels of the evacuation from Dunkirk, so while you're in the area to see the memorial, you should take the opportunity to visit the wartime tunnels under Dover Castle, from which the evacuation was orchestrated.

Battle of Britain Memorial
New Dover Road, Capel-le-Ferne, Folkstone, Kent CT18 7JJ
01303 249292 or 01732 870809
www.battleofbritainmemorial.org

Spean Bridge Commando Memorial, Highland

Nominated by Ewen Cameron, reader in history, University of Edinburgh
'Where you can see how the British state incorporated the rebellious Scottish Highlands'

There are not many war memorials that attract visitors by the coachload. Spean Bridge Commando Memorial does. But then it is in a beautiful part of the country and firmly on the tourist route through the Scottish Highlands, on the main road that ploughs up from Fort William to Loch Ness.

The memorial stands at the crest of a hill beside the road winding up from Spean Bridge in the valley below. It commemorates the Commandos of the Second World War with a large and imposing statue of three of their number in battledress looking out across the mountains.

In 1940 Winston Churchill ordered the creation of an elite body of British army troops to add some steel to what appeared to be shaping up to be a desperate fight for survival against Hitler's Germany. The Commandos were the result, volunteers taken from every part of the British army. Subsequently, Royal Navy and Air Force troops were also brought in, under leadership from the Combined Operations Headquarters. The Commandos performed with considerable distinction during the war, particularly in the Normandy landings of 1944 that led to the liberation of Europe. A few years after the end of the conflict, a competition was held for a suitable monument to their endeavours. The Scottish sculptor Scott Sutherland won the commission, and his statue, 5 metres (17 feet) high, was unveiled in 1952 by the Queen Mother.

The location of the memorial is significant. A few miles down the road is Achnacarry Castle, ancestral home of the chiefs of Clan Cameron and, from 1942, training centre for the Commandos. Prospective recruits would arrive by train at Spean Bridge, then march to Achnacarry to commence their training. The castle is not open to the public, though there is a Clan Cameron Museum in its grounds, while at Spean Bridge there are coffee and souvenir shops, and an exhibition of Commando memorabilia.

The monument itself is the big draw, though, surrounded as it is by magnificent views. Indeed, there is a panoramic table beside the statue that will help you identify which of the mountains in front of you is Ben Nevis. The monument is right in the heart of the Highlands, as Ewen

Cameron explains: 'It's placed on a very interesting point in the landscape – at the junction of the Great Glen, Glen Spean and Glen Roy. You have views to the west, south and east, so you get a wonderful panorama.'

It's clearly tough terrain, and a testing landscape in which to train as a soldier. That was, of course, the idea: a demanding location was needed in which to hone the skills of the elite force. But the Commandos were not the first soldiers to operate in the region. 'This is a landscape that has quite a deep military history,' notes Cameron, 'but if you go back to the 17th and 18th centuries, it's also a place of civil war. The area had a strong Jacobite link – Cameron of Lochiel, whose home was Achnacarry Castle, was on the Jacobite side in the 1745–6 rebellion – so it's ironic that an area with that rich anti-British, anti-state history was used in the Second World War for the defence of the state.'

At the end of the road through the Great Glen, you get to Inverness, Culloden and Fort George (page 236), where the Jacobite threat was extinguished in 1746. Interestingly, the first shots in that rebellion were fired in the vicinity of Spean Bridge. A footpath will take you from the Commando Memorial along a 3-km (2-mile) route to the High Bridge on the Spean, where the Highbridge Skirmish of 1745 opened hostilities in the Jacobite Rising (there's a signboard just below the car park that points the way).

'United we conquer' reads the inscription around the top of the plinth of the Commando Monument. This was the motto of Combined Operations during the Second World War. However, you could read that statement as a reference to the longer history of the United Kingdom because in Cameron's view, 'The memorial reflects the way in which the British state has effectively incorporated the Scottish Highlands since

1745. During the 18th century the landscape was seen as threatening, as the source of support for opposition to the state, but by the 1940s, not only had the people and the region been incorporated into the state, but the landscape was seen as something that could be turned to good use, for training special forces, for warfare.'

The inscription on the plinth below the statue relates the Commando story of the Second World War, while the recently opened memorial garden that's adjacent to it brings things up to the present day. Most of the regiments were disbanded after the war, but Commandos have served in British military operations throughout the 20th and 21st centuries. Plaques in the memorial garden to soldiers killed in more recent conflicts highlight that sad fact.

Spean Bridge Commando Memorial

Beside the A82, 3 km (2 miles) north of Spean Bridge, Kilmonivaig, Highland PH34

Grid reference: NN 224818

www.undiscoveredscotland.co.uk/speanbridge

Bletchley Park, Buckinghamshire

Nominated by Patricia Fara, senior tutor,
Clare College, University of Cambridge
'Where code-breaking heroes shortened the
Second World War'

There are very few pre-fabricated huts in this book's selection of significant historic places. But the wooden buildings that were erected in 1939 on the lawn of the mansion of Bletchley Park, now on the outskirts of Milton Keynes, deserve their place. They were at the heart of the operation to break the codes of the German and Japanese forces during the Second World War.

What happened at Bletchley was kept secret for decades after the war, and it wasn't until the 1970s that information began to come out. The 1991 film *Enigma* brought the story to wider attention, but it's only in the last few years that the place has opened as a heritage attraction and museum. What visitors see now is the curious 19th-century Gothic mansion surrounded by a mass of wooden huts and later brick extensions from the war years. If you want an authentic wartime experience, here is as good a place as any to come. It feels in parts as if the site were still stuck in the 1940s. As Patricia Fara observes: 'In most museums you see all the objects laid out in cases, often modern cases, so there's very little connection between what you see inside the case and the building itself. But when you go to Bletchley, the buildings themselves are part of the museum. You're wandering around these old huts exactly where everything was happening.'

So what *was* happening? Bletchley Park was taken over by the Government Code and Cypher School in 1938. Initially, the staff worked in the mansion and its adjoining buildings, but as the scale of the operation increased, the wooden huts and brick buildings were erected. Thousands of people were employed here by the end of the war, and they were engaged in the business of decoding, translating and analysing the correspondence of the German armed forces. The information they gathered was dispatched from here to intelligence officers in London.

The most famous person to have worked at Bletchley was Alan Turing, a key figure in the development of the modern computer. You can pop your head around the door of the office where he worked within one of the pre-fab huts. He devised a machine called a Bombe that was used to break the codes of the famous German Enigma encryption machine. The Bombe, a large and complicated-looking contraption of rotors, colour-coded drums and great snakes of wire, was developed from a device created by Polish code-breakers before the war (there is a memorial to the important Polish contribution in the stable yard at Bletchley). A rebuilt Turing Bombe is on display in the museum in Block B. To look at it is to be in awe not only of Turing's inventiveness, but also of the skill of the Wrens who had to operate these room-sized machines (there were some 200 or so in use during the war). It looks to have been a devilish job of rewiring and resetting every time a new batch of codes was to be worked on.

In the museum you can also see various Enigma machines (which look like typewriters with rotors) of the sort that the Bombe was designed to counter. One of these was famously stolen from the museum in 2000 and then bizarrely posted to the BBC journalist Jeremy Paxman. It is now displayed in what one presumes is a very strong glass case.

The intelligence provided by the Bletchley Park code-breakers is now recognised by historians as a vital contribution to the Allies' successful conclusion of the war. It has been suggested that the quality and quantity of information the code-breakers were able to pass on might have shortened the war by two years. According to Fara, 'Although a lot of it is still classified, there's more and more information coming out that shows we knew in advance what a lot of the German plans were, and so were able to take pre-emptive action. It's pretty clear that Bletchley did have a decisive role to play in the war.'

Having provided critical intelligence that, among other things, helped protect shipping in the Battle of the Atlantic in the early 1940s, the success of the code-breaking operation was challenged in 1942. The Germans brought in a new version of the Enigma machine, which Turing and others had to deal with through improvements to the Bombe, and meanwhile a different cipher (the Lorenz) was adopted for messages between Hitler and his high command. Another hero of Bletchley Park, Tommy Flowers, built Colossus, the first programmable electronic computer to counter Lorenz. This machine helped break the new German codes, and also paved the way for the computer revolution.

A Colossus machine has been rebuilt at Bletchley Park. Housed in one of the huts, like the Turing Bombe it takes up most of a room, and it's all valves, whirring tapes, switches and wires. If you're lucky, there will be one of the rebuild project volunteers there, delving into the innards of the device. Indeed, part of the atmosphere of the place today derives from the volunteers and enthusiasts who've been rebuilding the wartime machines. It's taken a lot of skilled work over many years from these people to recreate them. Their involvement gives Bletchley Park a friendly, low-key atmosphere that feels somehow particularly appropriate to the story; it lends it the sort of understated Britishness that one tends to associate with the war years. That sensation is accentuated by the bike sheds, some with archaic bicycles on racks, that proliferate around the site: the staff were not billeted at Bletchley Park, so these clandestine code-breakers were cycling in from their lodgings every day to get to work on their classified mission.

If it sounds more bike-clip and spectacles than cloak and dagger, the secrecy that nevertheless surrounded what went on here was jealously protected after the end of the Second World War. It was deemed crucial that the Soviet Union, Britain's one-time wartime ally but latterly Cold War adversary, did not learn the extent of the code-breaking work. As everything was kept hush-hush for decades, Bletchley perhaps still doesn't get quite the recognition it should for its place in the Second World War, and indeed in computing history. All the more reason to pay a visit now.

Bletchley Park

The Mansion, Bletchley Park, Milton Keynes, Buckinghamshire MK3 6EB

01908 640404

www.bletchleypark.org.uk

Royal Festival Hall, South Bank, London
Nominated by Paul Addison, honorary fellow, School of History, Classics and Archaeology, University of Edinburgh
'Where you can see how a more modern Britain began to emerge after the Second World War'

When it was built, the Royal Festival Hall was a Modernist shock in war-ravaged London. Today it doesn't seem quite so modern or shocking, but then we've had 60 years to get used to it, and the style of architecture it employed has spread across Britain. Its long and glassy river Thames frontage, combined with its straight and unadorned lines of Portland stone, does not feel especially unfamiliar.

The hall was built as part of the 1951 Festival of Britain, the 'tonic for the nation', that was designed to give the country a lift after the battering of the Second World War. That conflict had ended just six years earlier, and Britain, though on the side of the victors, was still very much in recovery. The nation's cities had been pounded by Luftwaffe bombs and were still building sites, while its finances were in such poor shape that austerity and rationing were the order of the day.

In May 1941 an incendiary bomb destroyed the Queen's Hall, a much-loved concert venue that had stood in Langham Place in central London. In 1943 the neglected South Bank of the Thames was proposed as a potential location for a new concert hall, and in 1948, when plans for the Festival of Britain were initiated by the Labour government, a new concert venue, the Festival Hall, was revealed as a key element of the main exhibition site between Waterloo Bridge and London County Hall.

The Festival of Britain was a nationwide gala, with events across the country, a touring show and even a festival ship stopping at ports. But the flagship event was on the South Bank, with colourful pavilions dedicated to different aspects of Britain's national character and achievements dotted around the site. A quarter of the population, some 8.5 million people, came through the turnstiles. With its bold use of colour and water features, Paul Addison feels it must have been akin to entering another world for Britons, whose everyday life was so drab and dilapidated. The highlight for many was the huge aluminium Dome of Discovery, within which the British contributions to discovery and exploration were displayed. The wondrously suspended metal rocket called the Skylon that stood outside the Dome was 90 metres (300 feet) high and perhaps the most eye-catching architectural feature, but the most enduring one was the Royal Festival Hall. It was the only element of the whole festival that

The Royal Festival Hall in 1951, with the Skylon far right

was destined to be permanent – everything else was temporary, designed to exist just for that summer of 1951.

The fate of the site was sealed when Labour lost the election in the autumn of 1951. Despite its reforming social programme, which included the foundation of the National Health Service, Clement Attlee's administration could not hang on to power, and the incoming Conservatives had no interest in prolonging the life of the festival site. The pavilions were swept away, leaving only the Royal Festival Hall. It still stands as a symbol of the post-war vision, a New Jerusalem built from the wreckage of battle.

'Of course, people today remember the welfare reforms,' says Addison, 'but the Royal Festival Hall represents a different aspect of the New Jerusalem – about planning, architecture and design, and modernity in all those things. It's a kind of cultural dimension of the welfare state. It's about a movement of people who were not necessarily socialists, but who believed that the best in arts and material culture should be made available to all.'

So the hall was, in 1951, a very exciting building. Now, however, it's rather understated in contrast to the concrete brutalism of the neighbouring Hayward Gallery and Queen Elizabeth Hall, built in the 1960s. The actual auditorium is in the heart of the building, and you'll be able to get in there only if you're attending a concert. During renovations in 2005–7, it was taken apart so that the acoustics could be improved, but the original materials were conserved and replaced, so it is not that different from its earlier design. The foyers that surround the auditorium are open and free to the public every day. They give a feel for what the designers were hoping to achieve – a democratic space, in keeping with the new order of post-war Britain, where everyone could enjoy the arts. In practice, during the first decades of its existence, it was only really open to those paying to attend the evening concerts, but since 1983 and the introduction of the Open Foyer programme, it has come closer to those original aspirations. With its cafés and restaurants, it has a welcoming feel, certainly for the army of coffee-drinking laptop lunchers scattered about the place, and there's every chance you'll come across a performance of some sort as you walk around.

There are several floors to explore, and the predominance of polished wood throughout the interior does lend it a 1950s' air. Don't forget to look down at the carpet: the net and ball design is an exact replica of the original pattern by the architect Peter Moro. As Addison notes, design innovation was one of the legacies of the Festival of Britain. 'It's important in terms of consumerism. It popularised new styles of furniture, for example. The famous design couple Robin and Lucienne Day were part of this: he did the chairs, his spindly Scandinavian design becoming something of a standard look, while she produced abstract curtains to go with them. These were things that would have been introduced to any modern home in the 1950s and 1960s. In terms of design, it's a straight line from the Festival of Britain to Habitat – one definitely informed the other. The festival was an attempt to show people that beyond austerity lay a much more enjoyable future, with more prosperity and many more consumer goods, but it didn't cheer people enough to ensure a Labour victory at the next election. It was the Tories, therefore, who inherited the "Never had it so good" moment.'

So if you want to see how Britain emerged from the Second World War and began to build itself anew, the Royal Festival Hall, the sole reminder of the Festival of Britain, is the place to go. It's a shame that there is so little left of the rest of the festival site, though if you take a stroll around the area, you will find the place on which the Dome of Discovery once stood in Jubilee Gardens, now overshadowed by the London Eye above it. Nearby, a Canadian flagpole that graced the original festival has been re-erected, but it doesn't provide the vertical visual impact that the long-lost Skylon would have had back in 1951.

Royal Festival Hall

Southbank Centre, Belvedere Road, London SE1 8XX

020 7960 4200

www.southbankcentre.co.uk

Free Derry Corner, Derry/Londonderry

Nominated by Claire Fitzpatrick, lecturer in history, University of Plymouth

'Where you can stand witness to Northern Ireland's Troubles'

There are very few places in Britain where the past is quite so close to the surface as Derry/Londonderry. The walls that ring the old town date back to the 17th century (see Derry City Walls, page 183) but it's for more recent historical events, specifically its role in the Troubles of the 20th century, that the place is widely known.

When those now venerable walls were still young in 1689, the city was besieged by a Catholic army, supporters of King James VII and II, who had recently fled his throne following the invasion on England's south coast by William and Mary. The Protestant defenders inside held out for over 100 days, and 'No surrender' became their motto. From those same city walls today, you can still see that slogan; the events of 1689 have had a long resonance for Protestants in Northern Ireland. Painted on the gable end of a house in the Protestant Fountain area of the city, outside the walls, but clearly visible from them, there is the statement: 'Londonderry West Bank Loyalists still under siege. No Surrender.' The kerbstones are painted red, white and blue, and Union flags are dotted around.

Further around the wall, you look out over Bogside, another housing estate outside the walled city, but this time with a Catholic majority, where the flags of the Irish Republic fly, and the gable ends of houses are painted with murals depicting events from the Troubles. That word, of course, is the rather muted label given to the 30 years of conflict from the late 1960s to the late 1990s, between loyalists who wanted to remain part of the United Kingdom and nationalists pressing for a united Ireland, which resulted in thousands of deaths.

Just by walking the city walls here, it's quite apparent that Northern Ireland is still coming to terms with deep divisions. Following the failure of James VII and II to regain his crown, penal laws were passed in Britain that limited the rights of Catholics. Ireland and Britain were joined in union in 1801, and Ireland's Catholics finally granted emancipation in 1829. Then the debate moved to the question of whether Ireland should rule itself. That continued for another century, until Ireland was partitioned between north and south in 1921, with the south achieving full independence in 1949 as the Republic of Ireland, while the north remained part of the United Kingdom. Twenty years of relative calm passed before the Troubles flared up in the 1960s.

While it's hoped that the peace process, ongoing since 1998, means that those darkest days are history, the past here is still very raw. That's not surprising, as probably the most infamous event of that period took place in Bogside on 30 January 1972: Bloody Sunday. This was when, in the streets you can see below the walls, 13 demonstrators were shot dead by the British army, with a further casualty dying later from his wounds.

The backdrop to this event can be seen from the Double Bastion on the city walls. From there you can look down on a mural that says 'You are now entering Free Derry'. This is what's known as Free Derry Corner, and in 1969 it was the scene of riots as nationalists protested for civil rights, eventually barricading the area and refusing access to the authorities. The Free Derry slogan was painted on a wall at that time, and the message stuck. What followed in August 1969 became known as the Battle of the Bogside, when police entered the area with armoured vehicles and water cannons to disperse the protestors. Soon afterwards the British army was called in to Northern Ireland, but violence escalated, particularly in the aftermath of Bloody Sunday. Although the first sectarian murders of the Troubles happened in 1966, it was from 1969 onwards that the situation really degenerated, and Derry/Londonderry was central to the story.

'In a place like Northern Ireland, which is big on commemoration, it was symbolic to write on that Free Derry wall,' says Claire Fitzpatrick. 'This is a nationalist area and they felt locked out of the city, so Free Derry Corner is the ironic response to the city walls. It's an important part of British history, within the context of British identity. This small enclave was setting itself apart from the UK, and quite defiantly so. In terms of the country, it's a symbolic place. I would definitely recommend people go there and look at it. It became an important part of Republican publicity and mythology.'

Today, as the army has left and the checkpoints and barricades are gone, Bogside has become something of a tourist attraction. If you linger too long over the various memorials in the area, or the sequence of gable-end murals depicting various events in the story of the Troubles, you'll likely find yourself surrounded by an incoming coach party. You shouldn't miss the powerful Free Derry Museum, which tells the story of the Troubles here. An audio recording made as Bloody Sunday unfolded plays as the soundtrack to the museum, which helps to make it a singularly affecting place.

The legacy of Bloody Sunday was for years an open sore in Northern Ireland: the initial investigation in 1972 into the events of the day, which

Free Derry Corner: a significant site in Northern Ireland's Troubles

concluded that the soldiers were fired on first and that the victims had been handling weapons, was regarded as a whitewash by nationalists. The Saville enquiry, which took another look into what happened, and reported in 2010, stated that the victims were not posing a threat of causing death or serious injury. This verdict has gone some way to bringing the story to a close, and the city is moving on (for example as the 2013 UK City of Culture) but nevertheless, you'll still be in no doubt that you're not far removed from a very troubled past if you visit Free Derry Corner today.

Museum of Free Derry

Bloody Sunday Centre, 55 Glenfada Park, Derry BT48 9DR

028 7136 0880

www.museumoffreederry.org

Cavern Club, Liverpool

Nominated by Peter Catterall, lecturer in history,
Queen Mary University of London
'Where you can get a sense of how the Swinging
Sixties took off'

The Cavern Club must be one of the most famous music venues in the world. It was the place that launched the Beatles from Liverpool on to the world, and today it helps bring the world to Liverpool, as a place of pilgrimage for fans of the Fab Four. But the original Cavern Club was actually demolished in 1973, 12 years after the Beatles first played there in 1961.

The club was originally in the cellar of one of the many warehouses that lined the then fairly innocuous Mathew Street in the centre of the city. Before it opened as the Cavern in 1957, the building had been variously a fruit warehouse, a Second World War air-raid shelter, and an egg-packing facility. The club closed in 1973, a curiously short-sighted move, when a compulsory purchase order was served on the place so that it could make way for a ventilation shaft for an underground railway. Even more curiously, the ventilation shaft was never built, but the warehouse was knocked down and the Cavern left full of rubble. It wasn't until the early 1980s that the area was redeveloped, but the club could not be reopened as it was unable to bear the weight of the building planned to stand above it. Enterprisingly, a new Cavern was opened a few metres away from the original, using many of the same bricks, and to the same design. On Mathew Street today you can therefore see a Cavern Club reconstruction very similar to the venue that the Beatles played in, and a few doors down you can see the doorway to the original site, now marked with an information board and photo montage of how it was in the 1960s.

The rest of the area, rebranded as the Cavern Quarter, has received quite a makeover and virtually everything in it is a homage to the band. Pedestrianised and modernised, it has shops, pubs, statues, memorials, even a themed hotel – in short, enough to keep devoted fans distracted for a few hours at least. Clearly, this is an obvious destination for admirers of the Beatles, but what's the broader historical significance?

Peter Catterall says: 'What you've got with the Cavern Club is a way of trying to convey in bricks and mortar a particular aspect of post-war Britain that might otherwise get overlooked – namely, the role of popular culture. In this case, it's obviously the Beatles, who are in many ways Britain's most successful cultural export of the post-war years.'

The Beatles formed in 1960 and played 292 gigs at the Cavern, but they came to serious prominence three years later, when "Please Please Me" became a number one hit. Beatlemania struck Britain hard, and the band went on to achieve global fame the following year, when they made it big in the USA. The 1960s were the decade when conventional attitudes to music, sex, fashion, class and much else were challenged as a new youth culture came to prominence. Music, believes Catterall, was in the vanguard of all this: 'I don't think music was the only element of the 1960s, but it came to be emblematic of it. You can't imagine Swinging London without the music. In a sense the band that made everything possible was the Beatles – it was they who paved the way for the idea that the British were good at music.'

Many bands followed in the wake of the Beatles, with Liverpool being a centre of creativity for the Merseybeat sound. Meanwhile, London grabbed its 'Swinging' tag because of the flourishing music and fashion scene there. If you take the view that music was a spark to the wider cultural and social changes of the 1960s, the Cavern Club is the place to go to see where it all began. After all, this was where, in 1961, the man who was to become the Beatles' visionary manager, Brian Epstein, first saw them play, and it was where they built up their fan base and honed their skills (though their time in Hamburg at the start of their career was also pivotal in the latter respect).

Visit the new Cavern Club today and you can get a decent sense of what an early Beatles gig must have been like (particularly if you go when live music is being played, as it regularly is). Standing in the low, arched brick cellar facing the cramped stage, you can readily imagine the place packed and sweaty, with dancing in the aisles on either side of the main vault, and condensation dripping off the walls.

If that isn't enough of a Beatles immersion experience for you, Liverpool does not want for other tourist attractions on this theme. There are numerous taxi and bus tour options available, which will take you past the various places associated with the Beatles' childhoods and their musical links with the city. The National Trust now owns both John Lennon's and Paul McCartney's former homes, so you can visit them if you wish (though you'll need to book in advance). Alternatively, a ten-minute walk away from the Cavern Quarter you'll find the Beatles Story Experience on Albert Dock, where you can review the full history and visit another replica of the Cavern Club.

While the city retains many memories of the Beatles, their influence goes far beyond Liverpool. The band continued to be, arguably, the defining musical presence of the 1960s, until their break-up at the end of the

McCartney and Lennon photographed at the Cavern Club

decade. Their sway spread from music into fashion and even politics (John protested against British support for the Vietnam war by returning the MBE he'd been given in 1965). As Catterall notes, 'The Beatles did go on to become the full cultural package, so they had a deep cultural resonance in the UK and elsewhere.'

The 1960s have become a much-mythologised time. In fact the social changes that were wrought across Britain, which have come to be tied to the 1960s, started before the decade began and continued after it. Certainly, though, it was a period when established and traditionally cherished ideas were challenged and new mores created, and many of the values that came out of that process remain with us today. Music was a big part of this movement, and the Beatles were a very big part of the music. So although there are many significant moments on the road to the creation of 21st-century Britain, the venue where the Beatles made their name, the sweaty brick-lined cellar that was the Cavern Club, is as good a place as any to dwell on how much the country has changed since the middle years of the last century, and, indeed, on what it might become in the years ahead.

Cavern Club
10 Mathew Street, Liverpool L2 6RE
0151 236 1965
www.cavernclub.org

NOMINATING HISTORIANS

Andrew Abram is a lecturer in medieval history at the University of Wales Trinity Saint David.

John Adamson is a fellow in history at Peterhouse, University of Cambridge. His books include *The Noble Revolt: The Overthrow of Charles I* (Phoenix, 2009) and the edited collections: *The Princely Courts of Europe 1500–1750* (Sterling, 1999) and *The English Civil War: Conflict and Contexts* (Palgrave Macmillan, 2009).

Paul Addison is honorary fellow in the School of History, Classics and Archaeology at the University of Edinburgh. His books include (co-edited with Harriet Jones) *A Companion to Contemporary Britain, 1939–2000* (Blackwell, 2005).

David Allan is reader in history at the University of St Andrews. His books include *Commonplace Books and Reading in Georgian England* (Cambridge University Press, 2010)

Thomas Asbridge is reader in medieval history at Queen Mary, University of London. His books include *The Crusades: The War for the Holy Land* (Simon & Schuster, 2010) and *The First Crusade: A New History* (Simon & Schuster, 2004).

John Belchem is professor of history at the University of Liverpool. His books include *Merseypride: Essays in Liverpool Exceptionalism* (Liverpool

University Press, 2006) and *Liverpool 800: Culture, Character and History* (Liverpool University Press, 2007).

Harry Bennett is reader in history at the University of Plymouth. His books include *Survivors: British Merchant Seamen in the Second World War* (Continuum, 2007).

Maxine Berg is professor of history at the University of Warwick. Her books include *The Age of Manufacturers 1700–1820: Industry, Innovation and Work* (Routledge, 1994) and *Luxury and Pleasure in Eighteenth-Century Britain* (Oxford University Press, 2005).

Tracy Borman is chief executive of the Heritage Education Trust. Her books include *Elizabeth's Women: The Hidden Story of the Virgin Queen* (Jonathan Cape, 2009) and *Henrietta Howard: King's Mistress, Queen's Servant* (Jonathan Cape, 2007).

Peter Borsay is professor of history at Aberystwyth University. His books include *A History of Leisure: The British Experience Since 1500* (Palgrave Macmillan, 2006).

Joanna Bourke is professor of history at Birkbeck College, University of London. Her books include *Rape: A Cultural History* (Virago, 2008) and *Are Women Animals? Historical Reflections on What It Means to Be Human, 1791 to the Present* (Virago, 2011).

Alixe Bovey is a lecturer in medieval history at the University of Kent. Her books include *Monsters and Grotesques in Medieval Manuscripts* (British Library, 2002).

Lloyd Bowen is senior lecturer in early modern and Welsh history at Cardiff University. He is the author of *The Politics of the Principality: Wales, c.1603–1642* (University of Wales Press, 2007).

Mike Braddick is professor of history at University of Sheffield. His books include *God's Fury, England's Fire: A New History of the English Civil Wars* (Penguin, 2008).

Jerry Brotton is professor of Renaissance studies at Queen Mary, University of London. His books include *The Sale of the Late King's Goods: Charles I and His Art Collection* (Macmillan, 2006).

Alyson Brown is reader in history at Edge Hill University. She is the author of *English Society and the Prison* (Boydell, 2003).

Michael Brown is a lecturer in history at the University of St Andrews. His books include *Bannockburn: The Scottish War and the British Isles, 1307–1323* (Edinburgh University Press, 2008).

Barry Burnham is professor of archaeology at the University of Wales Trinity Saint David.

Chris Callow is a lecturer in early medieval history at the University of Birmingham.

Ewen Cameron is reader in history at the University of Edinburgh. His books include *Impaled Upon the Thistle: Scotland Since 1880* (Edinburgh University Press, 2007).

David Carpenter is professor of medieval history at King's College London. His books include *The Struggle for Mastery: Britain 1066–1284* (Penguin, 2004).

Helen Castor is a fellow in medieval history at Sidney Sussex College, University of Cambridge. Her books include *She Wolves: The Women Who Ruled England before Elizabeth* (Faber, 2010).

Peter Catterall is a lecturer in history at Queen Mary, University of London. His books include (co-edited with James Obelkevich) *Understanding Post-war British Society* (Routledge, 1994).

Malcolm Chase is professor of social history at the University of Leeds. His books include *Chartism: A New History* (Manchester University Press, 2007).

Mark Connelly is professor of modern British military history at the University of Kent. His books include *The Great War: Memory and Ritual: Commemoration in the City and East London 1916–1939* (Boydell & Brewer, 2002).

Ted Cowan is emeritus professor of Scottish history at the University of Glasgow. His books include *For Freedom Alone: The Declaration of Arbroath 1320* (Tuckwell Press, 2003).

Jeremy Crang is senior lecturer in history at the University of Edinburgh. His books include *The British Army and the People's War, 1939–1945* (Manchester University Press, 2000).

Pauline Croft is professor of early modern history at Royal Holloway, University of London. Her books include *Patronage, Culture and Power: The Early Cecils* (Yale University Press, 2002).

David Dabydeen is professor in the Centre for Translation and Comparative Cultural Studies at the University of Warwick. He is co-editor (with John Gilmore and Cecily Jones) of *The Oxford Companion to Black British History* (Oxford University Press, 2010).

Saul David is professor of war studies at the University of Buckingham. His books include *The Indian Mutiny* (Penguin, 2003) and *Victoria's Wars* (Penguin, 2007).

Gerard De Groot is professor of history at the University of St Andrews. His books include *The Sixties Unplugged: A Kaleidoscopic History of a Disorderly Decade* (Macmillan, 2008) and *The Seventies Unplugged: A Kaleidoscopic Look at a Violent Decade* (Macmillan, 2010).

Malcolm Dick is director of the Centre for West Midlands History at the University of Birmingham. His books include *Birmingham: A History of the City and Its People* (Birmingham City Council, 1995), *Joseph Priestley and Birmingham* (Brewin Books, 1995) and *Matthew Boulton: A Revolutionary Player* (Brewin Books, 2009).

Clare Downham is a lecturer at the Institute of Irish Studies, University of Liverpool. Her books include *Viking Kings of Britain and Ireland: The Dynasty of Ívarr to AD 1014* (Dunedin Academic Press, 2007).

Madge Dresser is reader in history at the University of the West of England. Her books include *Slavery Obscured: The Social History of the Slave Trade in an English Provincial Port c.1698–c.1833* (Redcliffe Press, 2001, reprinted 2007).

Christopher Dyer is professor of regional and local history at the University of Leicester. His books include (co-edited with Dr Richard Jones) *Deserted Villages Revisited* (University of Hertfordshire Press, 2010).

Paul Elliott is a lecturer in modern history at the University of Derby. His books include *The Derby Philosophers: Science and Urban Culture in Britain c.1700–1850* (Manchester University Press, 2009); *Enlightenment, Science and Modernity: Geographies of Scientific Culture and Improvement in Georgian England* (I.B. Tauris, 2010); and (with Charles Watkins and Stephen Daniels) *The British Arboretum: Trees, Science and Culture in the Nineteenth Century* (Pickering & Chatto, 2011).

Chris Evans is professor of history at the University of Glamorgan. His books include *Slave Wales: The Welsh and Atlantic Slavery, 1660–1850* (University of Wales Press, 2010).

Patricia Fara is senior tutor of Clare College, University of Cambridge. Her books include *Science: A Four Thousand Year History* (Oxford University Press, 2009).

Claire Fitzpatrick is a lecturer in history at the University of Plymouth.

Sarah Foot is Regius Professor of Ecclesiastical History at Christ Church, University of Oxford. Her books include *Monastic Life in Anglo-Saxon England* c.600–900 (Cambridge University Press, 2006).

Vic Gatrell is a former professor of history at the University of Essex, and is now a life fellow at Gonville and Caius College, University of Oxford. His books include *City of Laughter: Sex and Satire in Eighteenth-century London* (Atlantic Books, 2006).

James Gregory is a lecturer in modern British history at the University of Bradford. His books include *Of Victorians and Vegetarians: The Vegetarian Movement in Nineteenth-century Britain* (IB Taurus, 2007) and *Reformers, Patrons and Philanthropists: The Cowper-Temples and High Politics in Victorian England* (IB Taurus, 2009).

Hannah Greig is a lecturer in history at the University of York, and a historical adviser to film and television productions.

Emma Griffin is senior lecturer in history at the University of East Anglia. Her books include *A Short History of the British Industrial Revolution* (Palgrave Macmillan, 2010).

Ralph Griffiths is professor emeritus of history at Swansea University. His books include *The Reign of King Henry VI* (History Press, 2004); *The Oxford Illustrated History of the British Monarch,* co-authored with J. Cannon (History Press, 2004); *The Making of the Tudor Dynasty,* co-authored with Roger Thomas (History Press, 2005); *King and Country: England and Wales in the Fifteenth Century* (Hambledon Continuum, 1991).

Stephen Halliday is a lecturer in history for the Institute of Continuing Education at the University of Cambridge. His books include *The Great Stink of London: Sir Joseph Bazalgette and the Cleansing of the Victorian Metropolis* (History Press, 1999) and *Amazing and Extraordinary London Underground Facts* (David & Charles, 2009).

James Holland is a writer and historian whose books include *The Battle of Britain* (Bantam, 2010).

Mark Horton is reader in archaeology at the University of Bristol, and a regular expert presenter on television and radio.

John Hudson is professor of legal history at the University of St Andrews. His books include *The Formation of English Common Law* (Pearson, 1996).

Pat Hudson is professor emeritus of history at Cardiff University. Her books include *The Genesis of Industrial Capital: A Study of the West Riding Wool Textile Industry c.1750–1850* (Cambridge University Press, 1986), *Regions and Industries: A Perspective on the Industrial Revolution in Britain* (Cambridge University Press, 1989) and *The Industrial Revolution* (Hodder Education, 1992).

Ronald Hutton is professor of history at Bristol University. His books include *Blood and Mistletoe: The History of the Druids in Britain* (Yale University Press, 2009) and *Debates in Stuart History* (Macmillan, 2004).

Eric Ives is emeritus professor of English history at the University of Birmingham. His books include *Henry VIII* (Wiley-Blackwell, 2010).

Jacqueline Jenkinson is a lecturer in history at the University of Stirling.

Bill Jones is reader in Welsh history at the School of History, Archaeology and Religion, Cardiff University, and co-director of the Cardiff Centre for Welsh-American Studies. His books include *Wales in America: Scranton and the Welsh, 1860–1920* (University of Wales Press, 1993) and *Welsh Reflections:*

Y Drych and America, 1851–2001, co-authored with Aled Jones (Gomer Press, 2001).

Richard Jones is a lecturer in landscape history at the University of Leicester. His books include *Medieval Villages in an English Landscape* (Windgather Press, 2006) and (with Christopher Dyer) *Deserted Villages Revisited* (Hertfordshire University Press, 2010).

William Kelly is a lecturer in early modern Irish and British history at the University of Ulster. His books include *Atlantic Gateway: The Port and City of Londonderry Since 1700*, co-authored with Robert Gavin and Dolores O'Reilly (Four Courts Press, 2009).

Andrew Lambert is professor of history at King's College London. His books include *Admirals: The Men Who Made Britain Great* (Faber, 2008).

Tony Lane is emeritus professor of social science and former director of the Seafarers International Research Centre at Cardiff University. His books include *Liverpool: City of the Sea* (Liverpool University Press, 1997).

Seán Lang is senior lecturer in history at Anglia Ruskin University. His books include *Parliamentary Reform, 1785–1928* (Routledge, 1999), *Nazi Foreign Policy 1933–1939* (Hodder, 2009), and *British History for Dummies* (John Wiley, 2006).

Ryan Lavelle is a lecturer in history at the University of Winchester. His books include *Alfred's Wars: Sources and Interpretations of Anglo-Saxon Warfare in the Viking Age* (Boydell Press, 2010).

Brian Lavery is a curator emeritus at the National Maritime Museum, Greenwich. His books include *Empire of the Seas* (Conway, 2009).

Stuart Laycock is a classicist and writer. He is the author of *Britannia: The Failed State* (History Press, 2008), and co-author with Miles Russell of *UnRoman Britain* (History Press, 2010).

Diarmaid MacCulloch is professor of the history of the Church at St Cross College, University of Oxford. His books include *Thomas Cranmer: A Life* (Yale University Press, 1997), *Reformation: Europe's House Divided 1490–1700* (Penguin, 2004) and *A History of Christianity: The First Three Thousand Years* (Penguin, 2009).

Gillian MacIntosh is a research fellow at the University of St Andrews. She is project manager of the online resource *Records of the Parliaments of Scotland to 1707* (www.rps.ac.uk) and author of *The Scottish Parliament under Charles II, 1660–1685* (Edinburgh University Press, 2007).

Stephen Marritt is a lecturer in history at the University of Glasgow, specialising in 11th- and 12th-century political and ecclesiastical history in Britain and northern Europe.

David Mattingly is professor of Roman archaeology at the University of Leicester. His books include *An Atlas of Roman Britain*, co-authored with Barri Jones (Oxbow, 2002), and *An Imperial Possession: Britain in the Roman Empire* (Penguin, 2007).

K.A.J. McLay is head of history and archaeology at the University of Chester, where he teaches early modern British and European history. He has previously published articles on the early modern military and warfare in *Historical Research, Journal of Imperial and Commonwealth History, Journal of Mediterranean Studies* and *War in History*.

John Morrill is professor of British and Irish history at Selwyn College, University of Cambridge. His books include *Uneasy Lies the Head That Wears a Crown: Dynastic Crises in Tudor and Stuart Britain 1504–1746* (University of Reading Press, 2005) and *Oliver Cromwell* (Oxford University Press, 2007).

Anne Murphy is a lecturer in history at the University of Hertfordshire. She is the author of *The Origins of English Financial Markets* (Cambridge University Press, 2009).

Helen Nicholson is reader in history at Cardiff University. Her books include *A Brief History of the Knights Templar* (Constable & Robinson, 2010).

Richard Noakes is a lecturer in history at the University of Exeter. He is co-author with Geoffrey Cantor, Gowan Dawson and Graeme Gooday of *Science in the Nineteenth-Century Periodical* (Cambridge University Press, 2004) and the co-editor with Stephen W. Hawking and Kevin C. Knox of *From Newton to Hawking* (Cambridge University Press, 2003).

Cormac Ó Gráda is professor of economic history at University College Dublin. His books include *Famine: A Short History* (Princeton University Press, 2009).

Nicholas Orme is emeritus professor of history at the University of Exeter and his books include *Medieval Children (Yale University Press, 2001),*

Medieval Schools (Yale University Press, 2006) and *The Saints of Cornwall (Oxford University Press, 2000).*

Mark Ormrod is professor of history at the University of York. He is co-editor with Gwilym Dodd and Antony Musson of *Medieval Petitions: Grace and Grievance* (York Medieval Press/Boydell & Brewer, 2009) and co-editor with Rosemary Horrox of *A Social History of England, 1200–1500* (Cambridge University Press, 2006).

Micheál Ó Siochrú is a lecturer in early modern Irish and British history at Trinity College Dublin. His books include *God's Executioner: Oliver Cromwell and the Conquest of Ireland* (Faber & Faber, 2008).

Derek Patrick is a lecturer in history at the University of Dundee. His books include *History of the Scottish Parliament, Vol. III: Parliament and Politics in Scotland, 1567–1707* (Edinburgh University Press, 2004).

Michael Penman is senior lecturer in history at the University of Stirling. His books include *David II, 1329–71: The Bruce Dynasty in Scotland* (Birlinn, 2004).

Huw Pryce is professor of Welsh history at Bangor University. His books include *Native Law and the Church in Medieval Wales* (Clarendon Press, 1993), *The Acts of Welsh Rulers 1120–1283* (University of Wales Press, 2005), and *J.E. Lloyd and the Creation of Welsh History* (University of Wales Press, 2011).

June Purvis is professor of women's and gender history at the University of Portsmouth. Her books include *Emmeline Pankhurst: A Biography* (Routledge,

2002), and she is co-editor with S.S. Holton of *Votes for Women* (Routledge, 2000).

Carole Rawcliffe is professor of medieval history at the University of East Anglia. Her books include *Medicine for the Soul: The Life, Death and Resurrection of a Medieval English Hospital* (Sutton, 1999) and *Leprosy in Medieval England* (Boydell, 2006). She is also co-editor with Richard Wilson of *Medieval Norwich* and *Norwich Since 1550* (Hambledon Continuum, 2004).

Julian D. Richards is professor of archaeology at the University of York. His books include *Viking Age England* (NPI Media, 2004) and *The Vikings: A Very Short Introduction* (Oxford University Press, 2005).

Dominic Sandbrook is a historian whose books include *Never Had It So Good: A History of Britain from Suez to the Beatles* (Allen Lane, 2006), *White Heat: 1964–1970, Vol. 2: A History of Britain in the Swinging Sixties* (Allen Lane, 2007), and *State of Emergency: The Way We Were: Britain, 1970–1974* (Allen Lane, 2010).

Gary Sheffield is professor of history at the University of Birmingham. His books include *Forgotten Victory: The First World War – Myths and Realities* (Headline, 2001).

Keith Snell is professor of rural and cultural history at the Centre for English Local History, University of Leicester. His books include *Rival Jerusalems: The Geography of Victorian Religion* (Cambridge University Press, 2000), and *Parish and Belonging* (Cambridge University Press, 2006).

David J. Starkey is director of the Maritime Historical Studies Centre at the University of Hull. His books include *British Privateering Enterprise in the 18th Century* (University of Exeter Press, 1990) and *Oceans Past: An Environmental History of World Fisheries*, with Poul Holm (Palgrave Macmillan, 2011).

Mark Stoyle is professor of history at the University of Southampton. His books include *Soldiers and Strangers: An Ethnic History of the English Civil War* (Yale University Press, 2005) and *The Black Legend of Prince Rupert's Dog: Witchcraft and Propaganda During the English Civil War* (University of Exeter Press, 2011).

John Styles is research professor in history at the University of Hertfordshire. His books include *Design and the Decorative Arts: Britain 1500–1900*, co-authored with Michael Snodin (V&A Publications, 2001), *The Dress of the People: Everyday Fashion in Eighteenth-Century England* (Yale University Press, 2008), and *Threads of Feeling: The London Foundling Hospital's Textile Tokens, 1740–1770* (Foundling Museum, 2010).

Pat Thane is emeritus professor in the Centre for Contemporary British History at King's College London. Her books include: *Foundations of the Welfare State* (Longman, 1996), *Old Age in English History* (Oxford University Press, 2001), and *Unequal Britain: Equalities in Britain since 1945* (Continuum, 2010). She is also co-editor with Esther Breitenbach of *Women and Citizenship in Britain and Ireland in the Twentieth Century* (Continuum, 2010).

Annie Tindley is a lecturer in history at Glasgow Caledonian University. Her books include *The Sutherland Estate, 1850–1920: Aristocratic Decline, Estate*

Management and Land Reform (Scottish Historical Review Monographs, 2010).

Frank Trentmann is professor of history at Birkbeck College, University of London. His books include *Free Trade Nation: Consumption, Civil Society and Commerce in Modern Britain* (OUP, 2008).

James Walvin is emeritus professor of history at the University of York. His books include *The Trader, the Owner, the Slave* (Jonathan Cape, 2007).

Chris Whatley is professor of Scottish history at the University of Dundee. His books include *History of Everyday Life in Scotland, 1600–1800* (Edinburgh University Press, 2009).

Anna Whitelock is a lecturer in early modern history at Royal Holloway, University of London. She is the author of *Mary Tudor: England's First Queen* (Bloomsbury, 2009).

Glyn Williams is professor emeritus of history at Queen Mary, University of London. His books include *The Death of Captain Cook: A Hero Made and Unmade* (Profile Books, 2008) and *Arctic Labyrinth: The Quest for the Northwest Passage* (Allen Lane, 2009).

Phil Withington is a lecturer in history at Christ's College, University of Cambridge. His books include *The Politics of Commonwealth: Citizens and Freemen in Early Modern England* (Cambridge University Press, 2005) and *Society in Early Modern England. The Vernacular Origins of Some Powerful Ideas* (Polity Press, 2010)

Lucy Wooding is a lecturer in early modern history at King's College London. Her books include *Henry VIII* (Routledge, 2008) and *Rethinking Catholicism in Reformation England* (Oxford University Press, 2000).

Michael Worboys is a professor specialising in medical history at the University of Manchester. His books include *Spreading Germs: Disease Theories and Medical Practice in Britain, 1865–1900* (Cambridge University Press, 2000), *Fractured States: Smallpox, Public Health and Vaccination Policy in British India, 1800–1947*, with Sanjoy Bhattacharya and Mark Harrison (Sangam Books, 2005); and *Mad Dogs and Englishmen: Rabies in Britain, 1830–2000*, with Neil Pemberton (Palgrave Macmillan, 2007).

Barbara Yorke is professor of early medieval history at the University of Winchester. Her books include *The Conversion of Britain: Religion, Society and Politics 600–800* (Pearson, 2006).

Deborah Youngs is a lecturer in medieval history at Swansea University. Her books include *The Life Cycle in Western Europe, c.1300–c.1500* (Manchester University Press, 2006) and *Humphrey Newton (1466–1536): An Early Tudor Gentleman* (Boydell Press, 2008).

A–Z OF HISTORIC SITES

Albert Dock
Albert Dock, Liverpool L3 4AA
0151 708 7334
www.albertdock.com

Apsley House
London W1J 7NT
020 7499 5676
www.english-heritage.org.uk/daysout

Arbroath Abbey
Abbey Street, Arbroath,
Angus DD11 1EG
01241 878756
www.historic-scotland.gov.uk

Athelney Island
Lay-by on the A361 between East Lyng
and Burrowbridge, Somerset
Grid reference ST 3456 2924
(ST 32 NW)
www.visitsomerset.co.uk

Badbea Clearance Village
Badbea, Highland
Grid reference: ND084204

Bank of England
Threadneedle Street,
London EC2R 8AH
020 7601 4444
www.bankofengland.co.uk

Banqueting House
Whitehall, London SW1A 2ER
0844 482 7777
www.hrp.org.uk/banquetinghouse

**Bath – Queen Square, the Circus
and Royal Crescent**
Bath Preservation Trust
1 Royal Crescent,
Bath BA1 2LR
01225 338727
www.bath-preservation-trust.org.uk

**Battle Abbey and the Battlefield of
Hastings**
Battle, East Sussex TN33 0AD
01424 775705
www.english-heritage.org.uk/daysout

Battle of Britain Memorial
New Dover Road,
Capel-le-Ferne, Folkstone,
Kent CT18 7JJ
01303 249292 or 01732 870809
www.battleofbritainmemorial.org

Bevis Marks Synagogue
4 Heneage Lane,
London EC3A 5DQ
020 7626 1274
www.bevismarks.org.uk

Blackfriars' Hall
The Halls, St Andrews Plain, Norwich,
Norfolk NR3 1AU
01603 628477
www.standrewshall.co.uk
www.norwichblackfriars.co.uk

Blaenavon
World Heritage Centre, Church Road,
Pontypool, Torfaen NP4 9AS
01495 742333
www.world-heritage-blaenavon.org.uk

Blenheim Palace
Woodstock, Oxfordshire OX20 1PP
01993 810500
www.blenheimpalace.com

Bletchley Park
The Mansion, Bletchley Park, Milton
Keynes, Buckinghamshire MK3 6EB
01908 640404
www.bletchleypark.org.uk

Bosworth Battlefield
Sutton Cheney,
near Market Bosworth, Nuneaton,
Leicestershire CV13 0AD
01455 290429
www.bosworthbattlefield.com

**British Museum Round
Reading Room**
Great Russell Street,
London WC1B 3DG
020 7323 8299
www.britishmuseum.org

Brixham Harbour
Brixham, Devon TQ5
www.torbay.gov.uk

Canterbury Cathedral
11 The Precincts, Canterbury,
Kent CT1 2EH
01227 762862
www.canterbury-cathedral.org

Captain Cook Memorial Museum
Grape Lane, Whitby, North Yorkshire
YO22 4BA
01947 601900
www.cookmuseumwhitby.co.uk

Cartmel Priory Church
Priest Lane, Cartmel,
Grange-over-Sands,
Cumbria LA11 6PU
01539 536261
www.cartmelpriory.org.uk

Cavern Club
10 Mathew Street, Liverpool L2 6RE
0151 236 1965
www.cavernclub.org

The Cenotaph
Whitehall, London SW1

Conwy Castle
Conwy, North Wales LL32 8AY
01492 592358
www.cadw.wales.gov.uk

Covent Garden
London WC2E 8RF
0870 780 5001
www.coventgardenlondonuk.com

Derby Arboretum
Arboretum Square, Derby DE23 8FZ
01332 292612
www.derbyarboretum.co.uk

Derry/Londonderry City Walls
Derry/Londonderry
www.doeni.gov.uk/niea

Museum of Free Derry
Bloody Sunday Centre, 55 Glenfada
Park, Derry BT48 9DR
028 7136 0880
www.museumoffreederry.org

Dolbadarn Castle
500 metres (½ mile) southeast of
Llanberis on the A4086, Gwynedd
Grid reference: SH 5859
www.cadw.wales.gov.uk

Dr Johnson's House
17 Gough Square, London EC4A 3DE
020 7353 3745
www.drjohnsonshouse.org

Dover War Tunnels
Dover Castle, Harold's Road, Dover,
Kent CT16 1HU
01304 211067
www.english-heritage.org.uk/daysout

Down House
Luxted Road, Downe, Kent BR6 7JT
01689 859119
www.english-heritage.org.uk/daysout

Dunfermline Abbey
Dunfermline, Fife KY12 7PE
01383 724586
www.dunfermlineabbey.co.uk

Dunluce Castle
87 Dunluce Road, Bushmills,
County Antrim BT57 8UY
028 2073 1938
www.doeni.gov.uk/niea

Edward Jenner Museum
The Chantry, Church Lane,
Berkeley, Gloucestershire GL13 9BN
01453 810631
www.jennermuseum.com

Exeter Castle
Castle Street, Exeter,
Devon EX4 3PU
07968 797135
www.exetercastle.co.uk

Fishbourne Roman Palace
Salthill Road, Fishbourne,
Chichester, West Sussex PO19 3QR
01243789829
www.sussexpast.co.uk

Fort George
Inverness IV2 7TD
01667 460232
www.historic-scotland.gov.uk

Framlingham Castle
Church Street, Framlingham,
Suffolk IP13 9BP
01728 724189
www.english-heritage.org.uk/daysout

Free Trade Hall
Radisson Edwardian Hotel,
Peter Street, Manchester M2 5GP
http://peterloomassacre.org/

Hampton Court Palace
East Molesey
Surrey KT8 9AU
0844 482 7777
www.hrp.org.uk/hamptoncourtpalace

Hardwick Hall
Doe Lea, Chesterfield,
Derbyshire S44 5QJ
01246 850430 (New Hall);
01246 850431 (Old Hall)
www.nationaltrust.org.uk
www.english-heritage.org.uk/daysout

Harewood House
Harewood
Leeds LS17 9LG
0113 218 1010
www.harewood.org

Harlech Castle
Castle Square, Harlech,
Gwynedd LL46 2YH
01766 780552
www.cadw.wales.gov.uk

Hatfield House
Hatfield, Hertfordshire AL9 5NQ
01707 287010
www.hatfield-house.co.uk

Hever Castle
Hever, near Edenbridge, Kent TN8 7NG
01732 865224
www.hevercastle.co.uk

HMS *Warrior*
Portsmouth Historic Dockyard, Victory
Gate, HM Naval Base, Portsmouth,
Hampshire PO1 3QX
023 9277 8604
www.hmswarrior.org

Houses of Parliament
London SW1A 0AA
www.parliament.uk

Iona Abbey
Isle of Iona, Argyll PA76 6SQ
01681 700512
www.historic-scotland.gov.uk

Ironbridge Gorge
Coalbrookdale Museum of Iron,
Coalbrookdale, Telford,
Shropshire TF8 7DQ
01952 884391
www.ironbridge.org.uk

Kingston Coronation Stone
Outside the Guildhall, High Street,
Kingston upon Thames, Surrey KT1 1EU
www.kingston.gov.uk

Lincoln Castle
Castle Hill, Lincoln LN1 3AA
01522 511068
www.lincolnshire.gov.uk

Lincoln's Inn
The Treasury Office, Lincoln's Inn,
London WC2A 3TL
020 7405 1393
www.lincolnsinn.org.uk

Lindisfarne Priory
Holy Island, Berwick-upon-Tweed,
Northumberland TD15 2RX
01289 389200
www.english-heritage.org.uk/daysout

Longthorpe Tower
Thorpe Road, Peterborough,
Cambridgeshire PE3 6XP
01536 203230
www.english-heritage.org.uk/daysout

Ludlow Castle
Castle Square, Ludlow,
Shropshire SY8 1AY
01584 873355
www.ludlowcastle.com

Old Course
Bruce Embankment, St Andrews,
Fife KY16 9XL
01334 466666 (head office)
www.standrews.org.uk

Old Parliament Hall
Parliament Square,
Edinburgh EH1 1EW
0131 348 5200
www.scottish.parliament.uk

Old Royal Naval College
2 Cutty Sark Gardens, Greenwich,
London SE10 9LW
020 8269 4747
www.oldroyalnavalcollege.org

Pankhurst Centre
60–62 Nelson Street, Chorlton on
Medlock, Manchester M13 9WP
0161 273 5673
www.thepankhurstcentre.org.uk

Penydarren Tramway
Tourist Information Centre,
14a Glebeland Street,
Merthyr Tydfil CF47 2AB
01685 727474
www.trevithicktrail.co.uk
www.visitmerthyr.co.uk

People's Palace
Glasgow Green, Glasgow G40 1AT
0141 276 0788
www.glasgowlife.org.uk/museums

Piece Hall
Halifax, West Yorkshire HX1 1RE
01422 321002
www.thepiecehall.co.uk

Plymouth Hoe
Plymouth, Devon PL1 2RH
www.plymouthbarbican.com

Porthcurno Telegraph Station
Porthcurno Telegraph Museum,
Eastern House, Porthcurno,
Penzance, Cornwall TR19 6JX
01736 810966
www.porthcurno.org.uk

Rochdale Pioneers Museum
31 Toad Lane,
Rochdale OL12 0NU
01706 524 920
http://www.co-op.ac.uk/our-
heritage/rochdale-pioneers-museum

Royal Festival Hall
Southbank Centre, Belvedere Road,
London SE1 8XX
020 7960 4200
www.southbankcentre.co.uk

Runnymede
Near Old Windsor, Surrey
01784 432891
www.nationaltrust.org.uk

Rushton Triangular Lodge
Rushton, near Kettering,
Northamptonshire NN14 1RP
01536 710761
www.english-heritage.org.uk/daysout

**St Davids Cathedral and Bishops'
Palace**
The Close, St Davids,
Pembrokeshire SA62 6RH
01437 720202
www.stdavidscathedral.org.uk

St George's Hall
St George's Place, Liverpool L1 1JJ
0151 225 6909
www.stgeorgesliverpool.co.uk

St Giles' Cathedral
Parliament Square, Edinburgh EH1 1RE
0131 225 9442
www.stgilescathedral.org.uk

St John's College
Cambridge CB2 1TP
01223 338600
www.joh.cam.ac.uk

St Mary's Church
Putney High Street, London SW15 1SN
020 8788 4414
www.putneydebates.com
www.parishofputney.co.uk

Saltaire
Near Shipley, West Yorkshire BD18 3LA
01274 531163
www.saltairevillage.info

Scutchamer Knob
3 km (2 miles) south of East Hendred,
off the A417 east of Wantage,
Oxfordshire, Grid reference: SU 458851
www.nationaltrail.co.uk/ridgeway

Soho House
Soho Avenue (off Soho Road),
Handsworth, Birmingham B18 5LB
0121 554 9122
www.bmag.org.uk/soho-house

Spean Bridge Commando Memorial
Beside the A82, 3 km (2 miles) north of
Spean Bridge, Kilmonivaig,
Highland PH34
Grid reference: NN 224818
www.undiscoveredscotland.co.uk/
speanbridge

SS *Great Britain*
Great Western Dock, Gas Ferry Road,
Bristol BS1 6TY
01179 260680
www.ssgreatbritain.org

Stirling Castle
Castle Wynd, Stirling FK8 1EJ
01786 450000
www.stirlingcastle.gov.uk

Stockton and Darlington Railway
Head of Steam Museum – Darlington
Railway Museum, North Road Station,
Darlington, North Yorkshire DL3 6ST
01325 460532
www.darlington.gov.uk/Culture

Sutton Hoo
Tranmer House, Sutton Hoo,
Woodbridge, Suffolk IP12 3DJ
01394 389700
www.snationaltrust.org.uk

Tintagel Castle
Bossiney Road, Tintagel,
Cornwall PL34 0HE
01840 770328
www.english-heritage.org.uk/daysout

***Titanic*'s Dock and Pump-house**
Queens Road, Belfast BT3 9DT
02890 737813
www.titanicsdock.com

Tolpuddle
Tolpuddle Martyrs' Museum and
Memorial Cottages, Tolpuddle,
Dorset DT2 7EH
01305 848237
www.tolpuddlemartyrs.org.uk

Tower of London
Tower Hill, London EC3N 4AB
0844 482 7777
www.hrp.co.uk/toweroflondon

University Church
High Street, Oxford OX1 4BJ
01865 279111
www.university-church.ox.ac.uk

Verdant Works
West Henderson's Wynd, Dundee,
Angus DD1 5BT
01382 225282
www.rrsdiscovery.com

Verulamium
Verulamium Museum,
St Michael's Street, St Albans,
Hertfordshire AL3 4SW
01727 751810
www.stalbansmuseums.org.uk

Vindolanda
Chesterholm Museum, Bardon Mill,
Hexham, Northumberland NE47 7JN
01434 344277
www.vindolanda.com

Westminster Abbey
20 Dean's Yard, London SW1P 3PA
020 7222 5152
www.westminster-abbey.org

West Stow
Anglo-Saxon Village and Country Park,
Icklingham Road, West Stow,
Bury St Edmunds, Suffolk IP28 6HG
01284 728718
www.stedmundsbury.gov.uk

Wharram Percy
Wharram, North Yorkshire YO17 9TW
www.english-heritage.org.uk/daysout

Whitby Abbey
Abbey Lane, Whitby,
North Yorkshire YO22 4JT
01947 603568
www.english-heritage.org.uk/daysout

White Rocks Copper Works
National Waterfront Museum,
Oystermouth Road, Maritime Quarter,
Swansea SA1 3RD
01792 638950
www.museumwales.ac.uk

Wilberforce House
23–25 High Street, Hull, East
Yorkshire HU1 1NQ
01482 300300
www.hullcc.gov.uk

Winchester Cathedral
9 The Close, Winchester, Hampshire
SO23 9LS
01962 857200
www.winchester-cathedral.org.uk

Windsor Castle
Windsor, Berkshire SL4 1NJ
020 7766 7304
www.windsor.gov.uk

York Minster
Church House, Ogleforth
York YO1 7JN
0844 9390011
www.yorkminster.org

York Watergate
Embankment Gardens,
London WC2N 6NS

ACKNOWLEDGEMENTS

There are many people who have contributed to this book, most important of course being the historians who have been so generous with their time and knowledge in nominating the sites and outlining their reasons why. Clearly this idea wouldn't have worked at all without their support, so I thank them all for that.

I wouldn't have been able to research and write this book without my colleagues on *BBC History Magazine* picking up the slack of my frequent absences from the office, so I'm very grateful to Robert Attar, Susanne Frank, Spencer Mizen, Charlotte Hodgman, Sue Wingrove, Joe Eden, Sarah Lambert and Samantha Nott for that. Thanks also to Mark Blackmore and Rebecca Hoskins for the first read-through and fact check of the script, and to *BBC History Magazine*'s publisher Andy Healy for allowing me time to work on this project.

Albert DePetrillo and Caroline McArthur at BBC Books were excellent editors, while Trish Burgess went through the copy with a sharp and useful eye.

I'm grateful to the public relations professionals of the historic sites in the book for facilitating my visits. Thanks also to my parents and parents-in-law for hospitality and childcare in a demanding year, and to Stuart and Jo for providing a welcome refuge on the Scottish leg of the research.

Finally, I wouldn't have been able to spend a year visiting historic sites across the length and breadth of Britain without the understanding of my wife and daughters. So thanks Caroline, Eva, Caitlin and Rosie for putting up with too many long car journeys, too many difficult nights in uninspiring hotels, and too many days puttering around castles, abbeys and museums that really weren't designed for toddlers.

![BBC] **HiSTOry** *magazine*

5 issues for £5 *

If you enjoy history, you'll find *BBC History Magazine* a great read. We explore all aspects of Britain's past, with leading historians imparting their expert knowledge in an approachable but authoritative fashion.

Do you love getting out and visiting historical sites? Then our regular *Where History Happened* feature will give you inspiration.

The magazine is published every four weeks and is on sale in all good newsagents. You'll save money and have the magazine delivered to your door if you take up our subscription offer below.

Call us on
0844 844 0260†

† Calls to this number from a BT landline will cost no more than 5p per minute. Calls from mobiles and other providers may vary. Lines are open 8am-8pm weekdays & 9am-1pm Saturday.

Or go online
www.bbcsubscriptions.com/
historymagazine

PLEASE QUOTE CODE **HIBK11**